ICONS OF STYLE

Lady Gaga

Published in 2025 by Welbeck
An Imprint of HEADLINE PUBLISHING GROUP LIMITED

1

Cataloguing in Publication Data is available from the British Library

ISBN 9781035425167

Printed in China

MIX
Paper | Supporting responsible forestry
FSC® C104740

Headline's policy is to use papers that are natural, renewable and recyclable products and made from wood grown in well-managed forests and other controlled sources. The logging and manufacturing processes are expected to conform to the environmental regulations of the country of origin.

HEADLINE PUBLISHING GROUP LIMITED
An Hachette UK Company
Carmelite House
50 Victoria Embankment
London EC4Y 0DZ

The authorised representative in the EEA is Hachette Ireland, 8 Castlecourt Centre, Dublin 15, D15 XTP3, Ireland (email: info@hbgi.ie)

www.headline.co.uk
www.hachette.co.uk

ICONS OF STYLE

Lady Gaga

The story of a fashion legend

Kristen Bateman

WELBECK

"I don't think I could live **without hair, makeup** *and* **styling**, *let alone be the performer I am.*

I am a glamor girl through and through. I believe in the glamorous life and I live one."

LADY GAGA

Introduction

Few celebrities have crossed into fashion history territory the way that Lady Gaga has. The musician, actress, cultural icon and provocateur continually challenges the rules of fashion and turns everything conventional related to red carpet and celebrity fashion into something brand new and exciting, whether that means wearing runway-ready Gucci, studded denim hotpants or even her famously iconic, albeit controversial, dress constructed entirely out of raw meat.

To put it simply, many of Lady Gaga's looks are instantly recognizable and so many of them could ***only*** be executed by her. Who else could emerge from a Hussein Chalayan-designed egg-shaped vessel in a full latex look during the 2011 Grammys?

Like a colourful fashion chameleon, Lady Gaga changes and adapts her personal style and professional look to fit into characters. Her work in music, film and elsewhere has informed her fashion choices. And her unique vision has been seen everywhere from when she walks the streets of New York to out and about at the Met Gala, or on screen in major Hollywood blockbusters.

For Gaga, the idea of reinvention is a constant lived experience that she reinterprets over and over and over again through clothing, accessories, hair and make-up. Anything is on the table and nothing is off limits, and she's really done it all – from traditional ball gowns to grunge punk and back again. "I don't think I could live without hair, makeup and styling, let alone be the performer I am," she told *T Magazine* in 2010. "I am a glamor girl through and through. I believe in the glamorous life and I live one. I don't want anyone to separate who I am with my makeup on from who I am without it. I'm the same person."

But what really sets Gaga apart from your everyday celebrity is her commitment to the art of fashion. For her, it's not just about dressing the part, but rather about becoming it and pushing boundaries to a unique kind of extreme that shocks, inspires and rewrites the narrative of style history as we know it. "I'm not interested in fashion being functional for everyday life," Gaga told *Vogue* in 2021. "It's about being functional for art. I love becoming art." There is method acting, but what she does could potentially be considered method dressing! She brings her characters alive with the art of dress, no matter what project she's involved in.

This book charts the art of Lady Gaga's style history and evolution, from start to finish. Beginning with the early years when she was experimenting with her own personal style and making a name for herself through expressive dressing, to all the moments, designers, iconic stylists and jaw-dropping looks she's worn through the ages. It just so proves that Gaga's fashion evolution is never-ending and a definite point of inspiration for anyone who loves the idea of adornment, fashion and art.

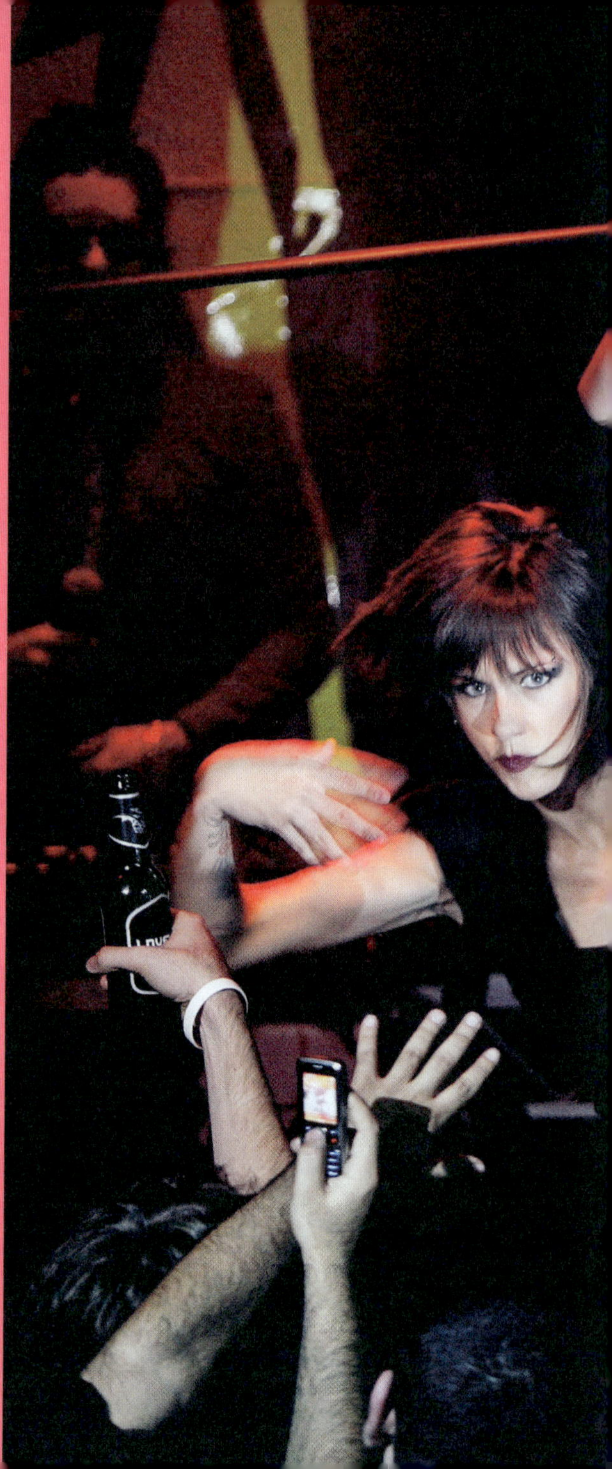

Lady Gaga early in her career, wearing her signature oversized sunglasses, leotard and fishnet tights.

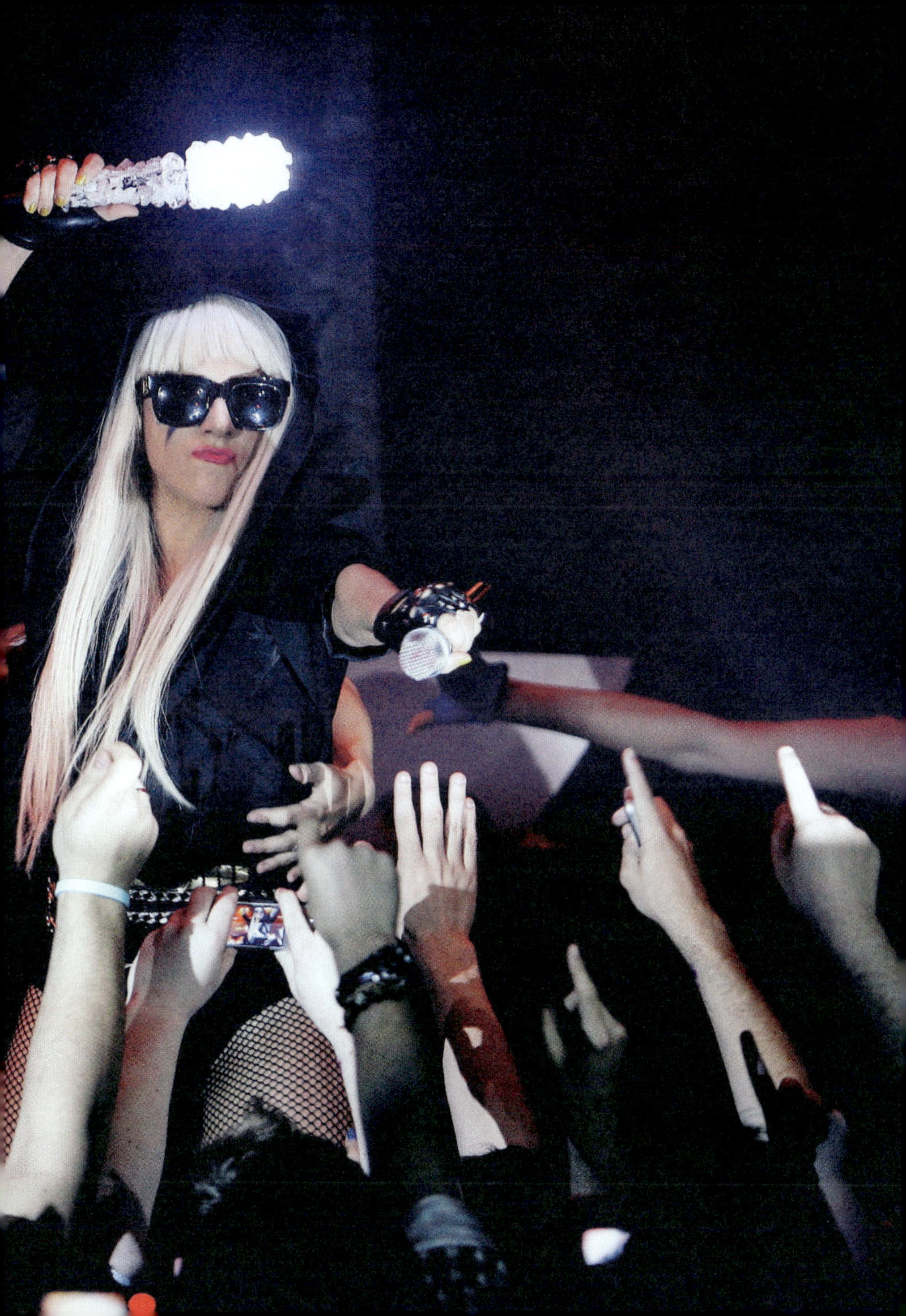

The Making

CHAPTER 1

of an Icon

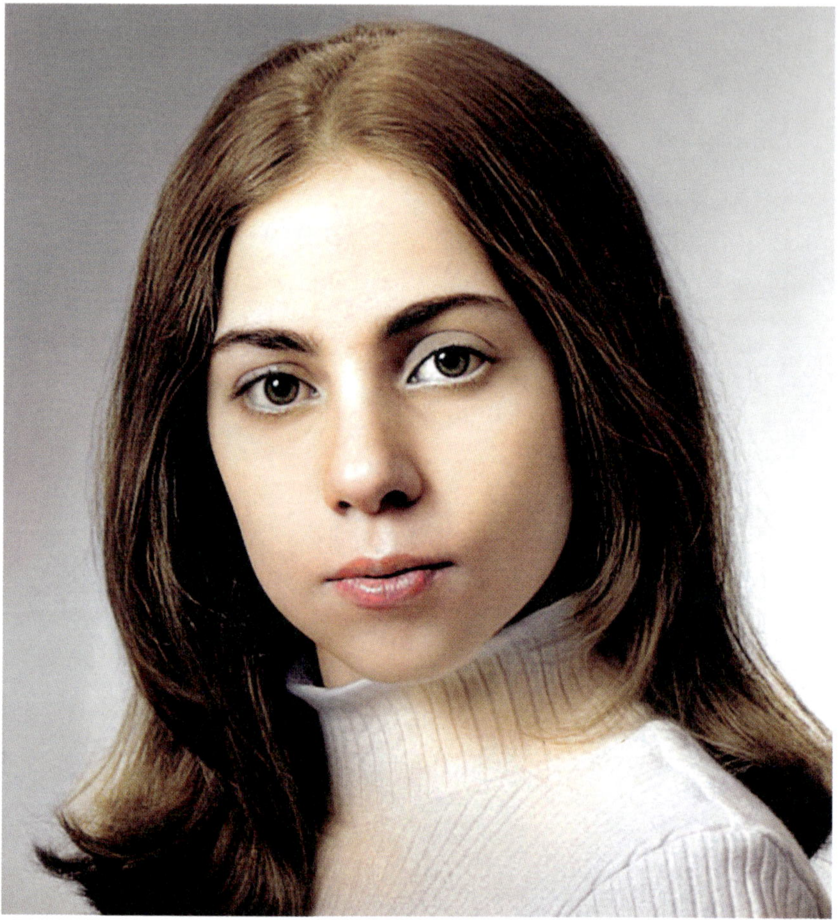

Gaga for Fashion

From the very start, Lady Gaga knew she was born to stand out. Born Stefani Joanne Angelina Germanotta in New York City in 1986 and raised on the Upper East Side, her parents encouraged her from a young age to get involved in music. At the age of four, she began playing piano. Once she was in high school at the Convent of the Sacred Heart, in Manhattan, she starred in various plays and also began auditioning for bigger productions in New York City. She studied method acting at the Lee Strasberg Theatre & Film Institute for 10 years.

Lady Gaga doesn't speak much about her sense of fashion or personal style growing up, but she has spoken about being different. For her prom, she wore a black carwash tube dress made out of chiffon, with fringe that faded to grey. And in terms of her inspiration? "I admired the women I grew up watching, the pop stars – Britney [Spears], Christina [Aguilera], Madonna, Blondie and Patti Smith, and Linda Perry and 4 Non Blondes," she once said. "I could go on and on. When I was around 13, I started to listen to older music, like Zeppelin, Queen, Pink Floyd. I was much more obsessed with male rock stars – Bowie in particular." Gaga has also mentioned the style icon Daphne Guinness and the late magazine editor and muse Isabella Blow as being inspirations to her visually. Both women are eccentric fashion lovers, often associated with the early

Young Lady Gaga before she found her iconic personal style.

days of Alexander McQueen. And it goes without saying, her own mother also inspired Gaga's larger-than-life style: "I'm so fascinated with my mother as a style icon," she told *Vanity Fair* in 2017. "She handled our life, and my father's life, with so much dignity and grace. She carries whatever she wears like a queen. My mother has this undeniable ability to lead with kindness – it's her strength, stealth, and power."

In 2003, Lady Gaga earned early admission to Collaborative Arts Project 21, a music school at New York University (NYU)'s Tisch School of the Arts. She studied there and lived in a dorm until 2005, when she dropped out to pursue her music career. "I used to get made fun of for being either too provocative or too eccentric, so I started to tone it down. I didn't fit in and I felt like a freak," she once said of her time growing up.

In 2005, Gaga's career started taking off and likewise, she instantly became known for her boundary-breaking style that set the tone for her big debut. That year, she started playing at clubs in New York and became a fixture of the downtown cool scene on the Lower East Side. By 2006, she debuted with the performance artist Lady Starlight, who she credits with helping her shape her early persona. They performed together at well-known downtown clubs including Mercury Lounge and the Rockwood Music Hall, and in 2007, Chicago's Lollapalooza music festival. Titled "Lady Gaga and the Starlight Revue", the duo called their act "The Ultimate Pop Burlesque Rockshow". She became known as Lady Gaga almost by accident. According to legend, her producer Rob Fusari began calling her "Radio Ga Ga" based on Queen's song of the same name, and accidentally coined her "Lady Gaga" when his phone automatically corrected the name.

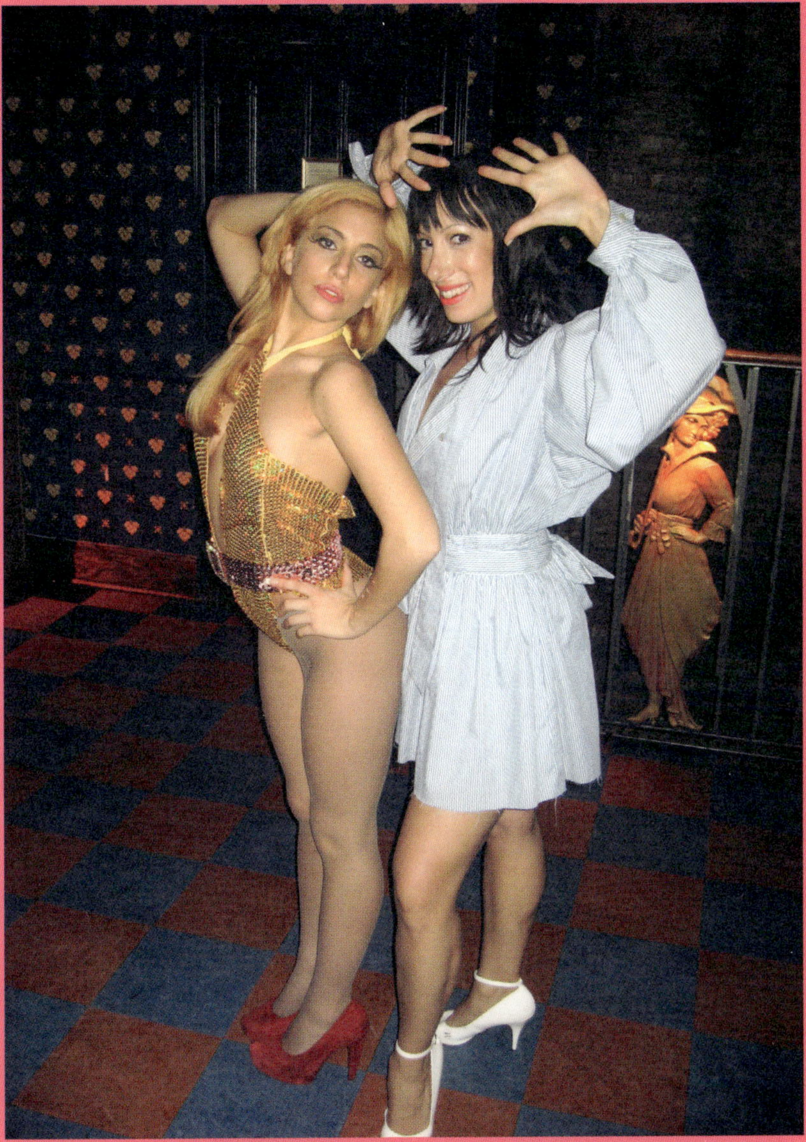

Gaga with Lady Starlight, with whom
she performed early on in her career.

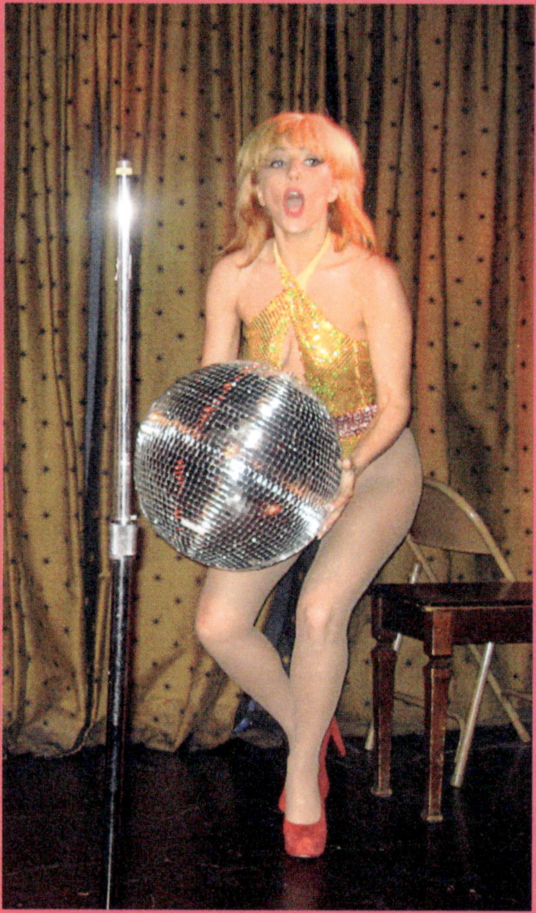

ABOVE In her early days, Gaga solidified her style with glittery leotards and high heels.

OPPOSITE Gaga cycled through blonde and brunette hair colours before landing on her iconic platinum look.

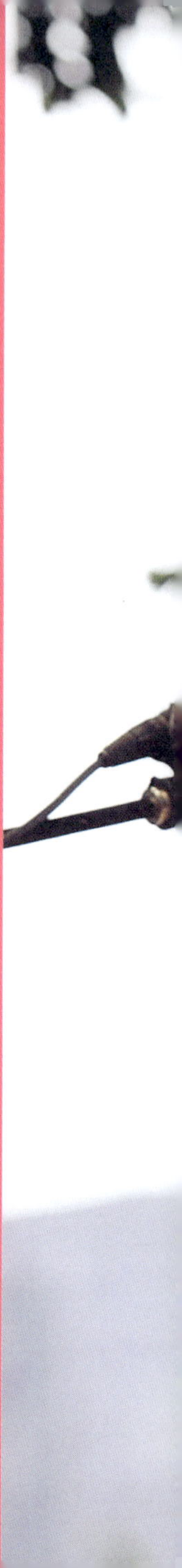

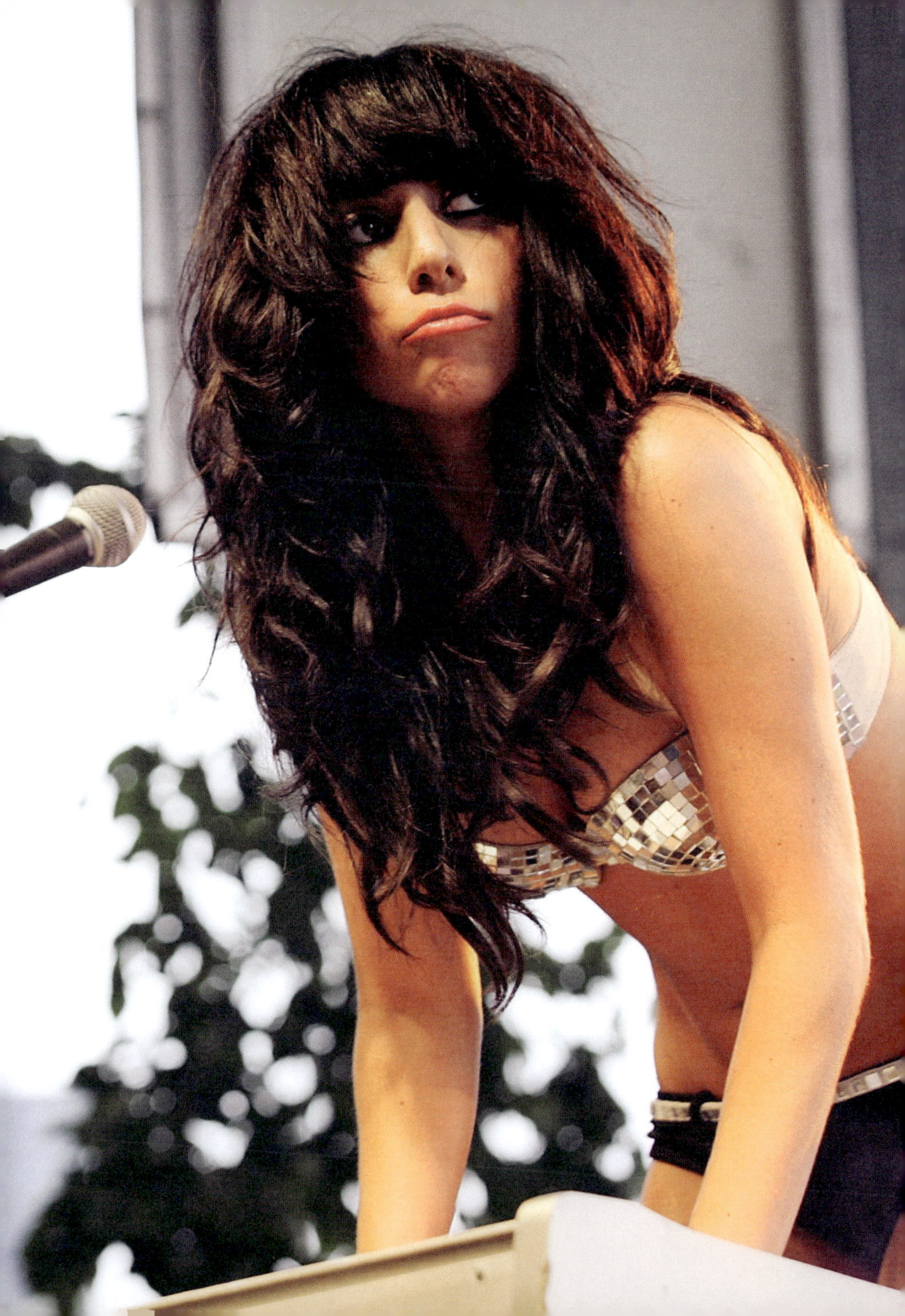

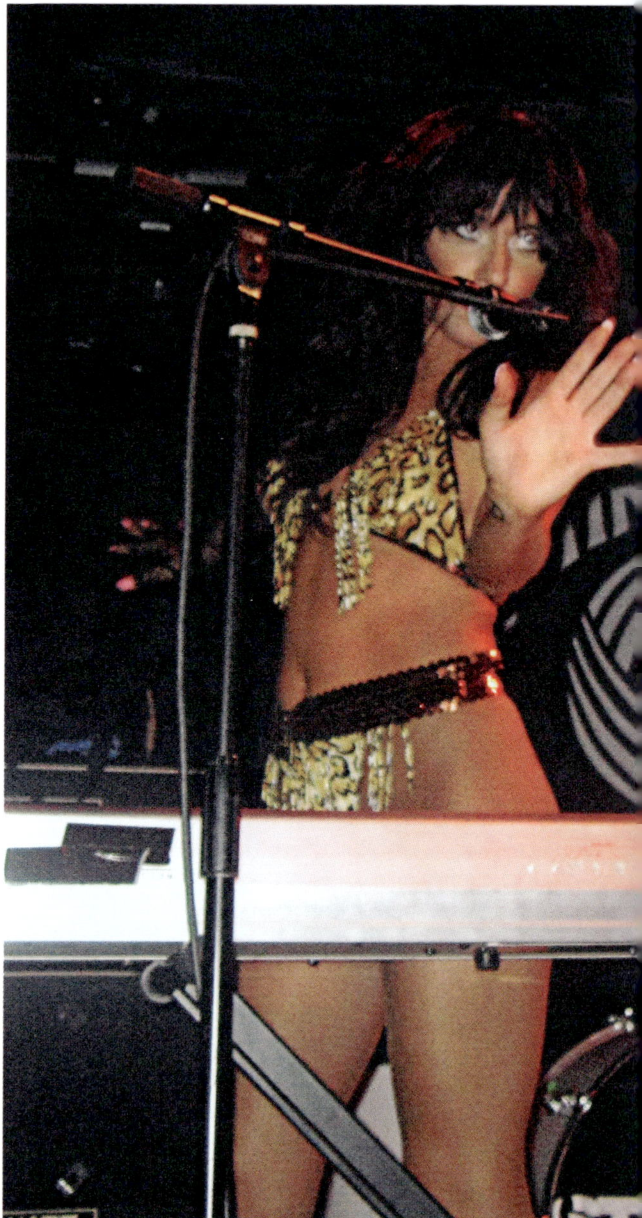

Lady Gaga's early style was synonymous with the aesthetic favoured on mid-2010s Tumblr at the time.

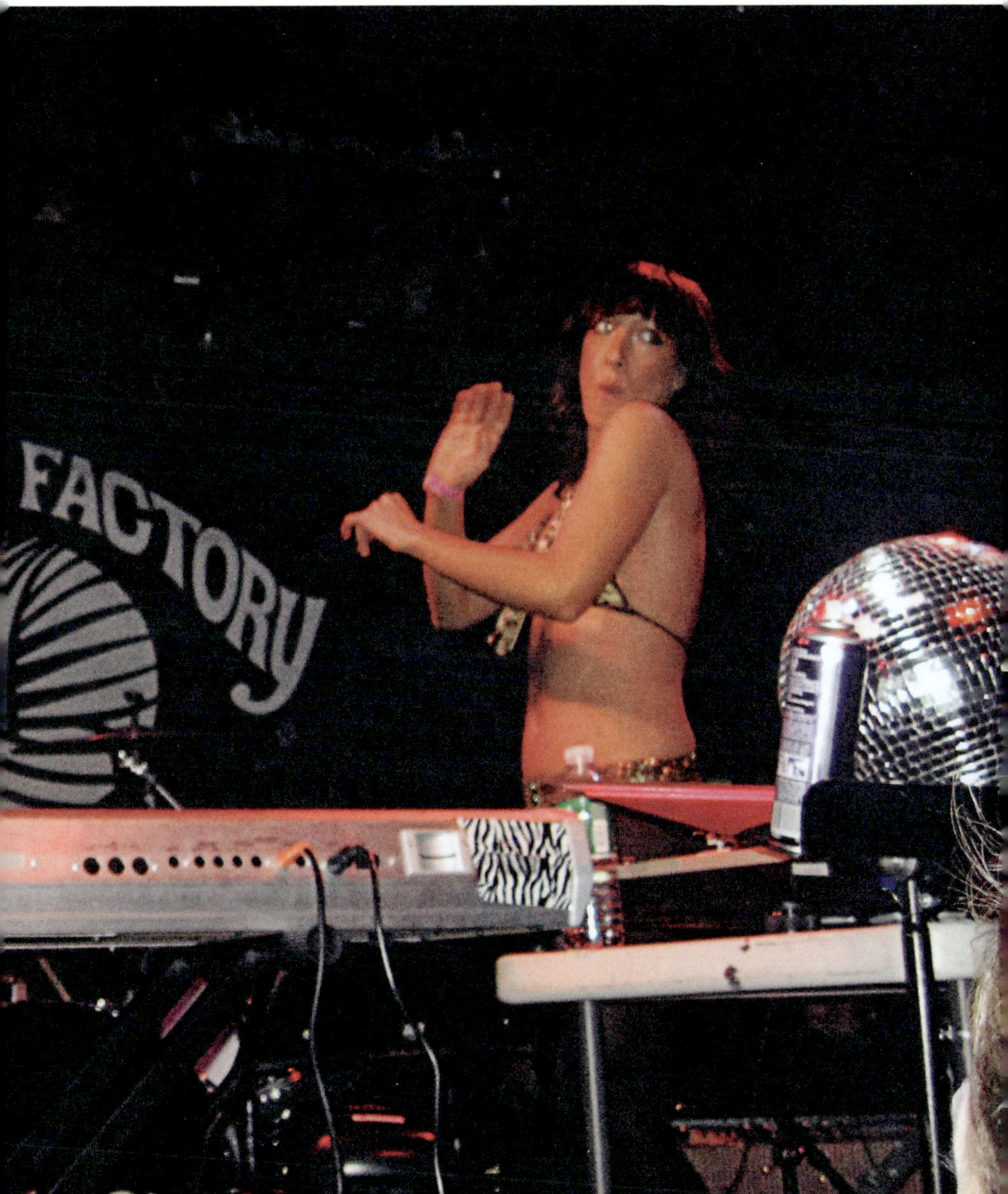
FACTORY

The "Lady Gaga and the Starlight Revue" show was ultimately inspired by 1970s burlesque and variety shows and that fact clearly impacted Lady Gaga's early sense of fashion and style persona. For example, Gaga mostly wore stylized underwear for the show. She had brunette hair at the time, which was her natural hair colour. There were bras and matching bottoms decked out in disco ball material, thigh-high fishnets and stark black heels, shiny sequin one-piece halter bodysuits that were belted and leopard G-strings. She and Lady Starlight set cans of hairspray on fire and did other quirky bold acts to captivate their audiences. The lingerie-inspired get-ups from Gaga's early days would quickly become one of the most signature pieces of her fashion lexicon.

Later, she wore hotpants and just underwear in place of pants when performing or walking around the streets of New York while getting photographed. Celebrities have always loved underwear as outerwear, but with Gaga, there has always been an edge that subverts the idea that it's done to be sexy, in favour of being weird in a good way. "I feel freer in underwear, and I hate fucking pants," she told *Rolling Stone* in 2009. "Plus, it's easier to dance."

Another one of Gaga's early style signatures: the hair bow and a supersized bag.

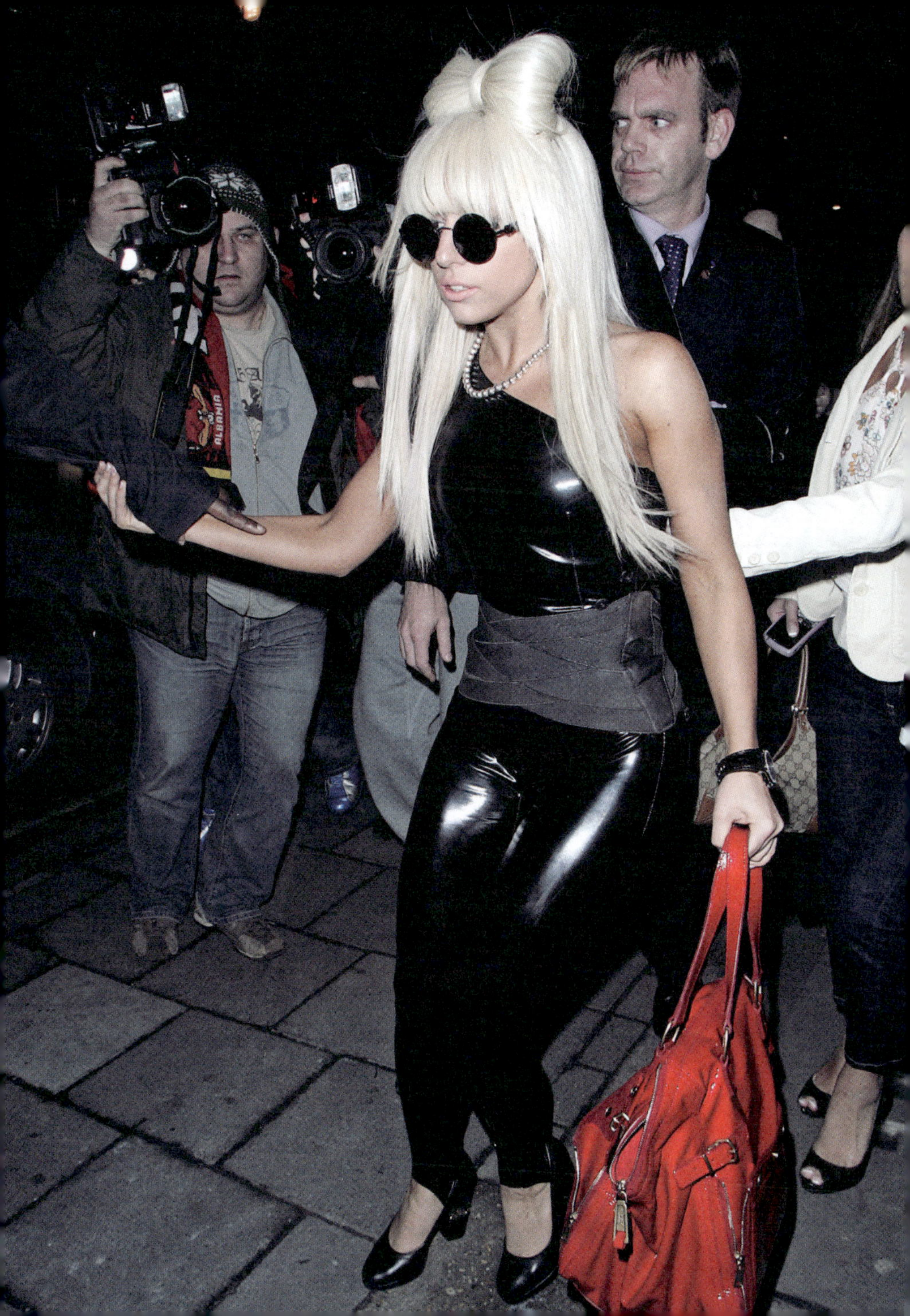
ALBANIA

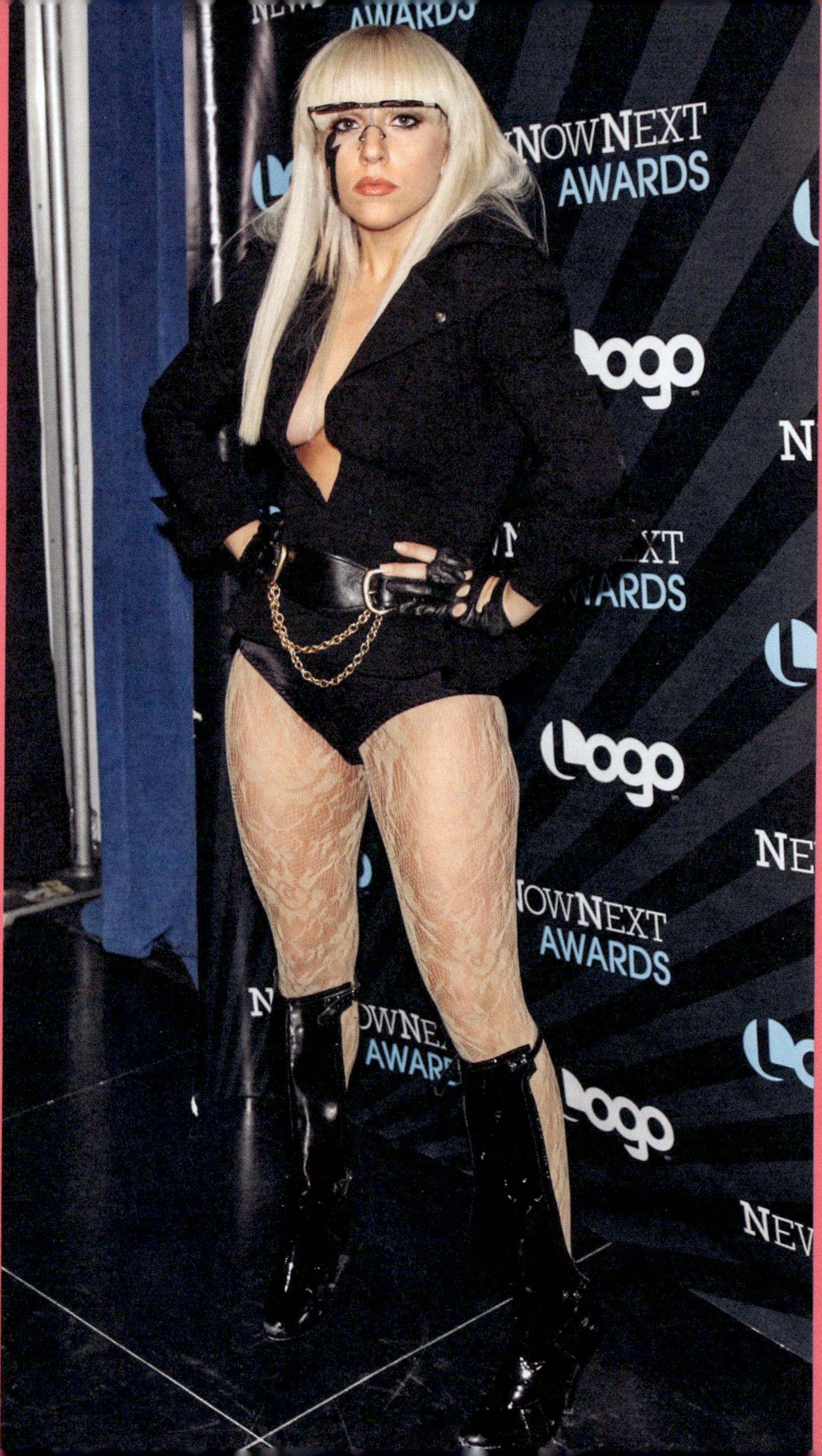
NOWNEXT
AWARDS

"I think music and fashion have always mirrored each other as part of a creative context. They cannot be separate. I need fashion for my music, and I need music for my fashion."

LADY GAGA

Lady Gaga often makes a bold statement in a leotard with oversized glasses.

Gaga started getting out of her comfort zone and trying more extreme looks that didn't revolve around underwear as outerwear in 2008. Take, for example, the ensemble she wore to the 2008 Jingle Ball in New York. She performed in a voluminous white minidress exploding with three-dimensional natural crystal shapes. The dress, which was actually a bodysuit with a detachable skirt, was made by Haus of Gaga and recalled Thierry Mugler's Spring/Summer 2008 collection. This was the year she released her debut album, *The Fame*, on 19 August 2008. "I think music and fashion have always mirrored each other as part of a creative context," she told *SHOWStudio* in 2010. "They cannot be separate. I need fashion for my music, and I need music for my fashion."

By 2009, Gaga achieved more widespread fame and with it, her signature look developed into something incredibly recognizable. She often wore leotards and underwear as pants with stockings, accompanied by extreme accessories. There were massive shield-like sunglasses, belts with chains, colourful gloves, big gold chains and huge designer handbags. Distinctly 2010s, the style was heavily popular on internet culture sites like Tumblr. Gaga would often wear big scarves as hoods, which recalled the Alaïa outfits iconic performer Grace Jones used to wear in the 1980s. "I am a feminist," she told *SHOWStudio* during this time. "I reject wholeheartedly the way we are taught to perceive women. The beauty of women, how a woman should act or behave. It's exciting because all avant-garde clothing and music and lyrics that at one time were considered shocking or unacceptable are now trendy."

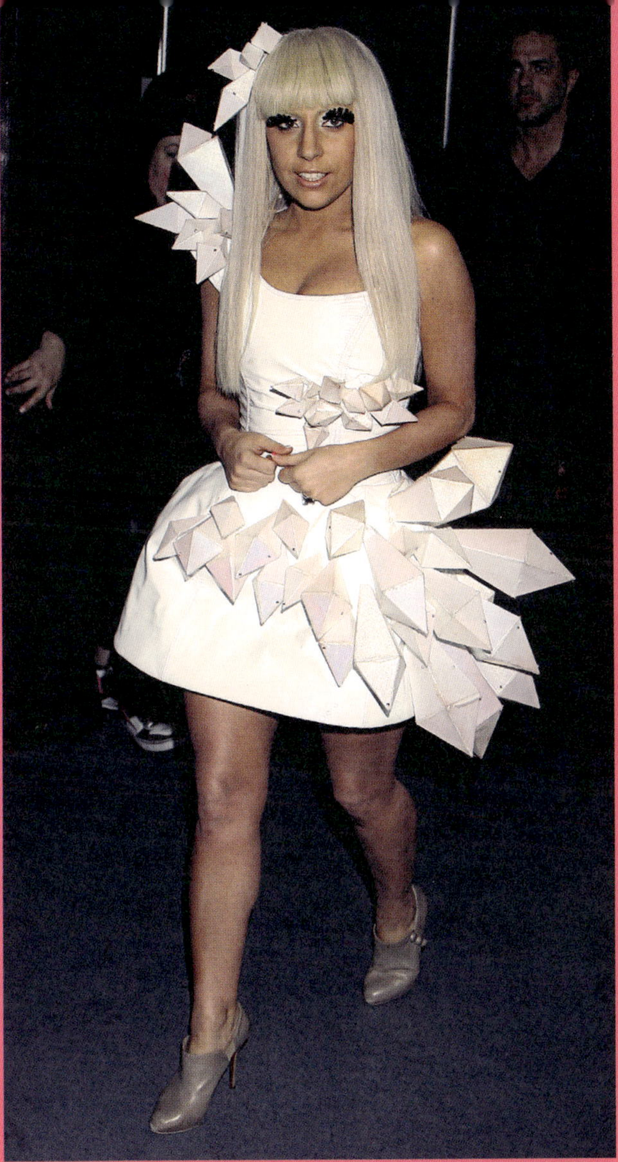

ABOVE Gaga has worn this dress in three different colours – all designed by the Haus of Gaga and inspired by Mugler's Spring/Summer 2008 collection.

OVERLEAF Lady Gaga follows the rules of major icons such as Jacqueline Kennedy Onassis and Audrey Hepburn, who both had a love of huge sunglasses.

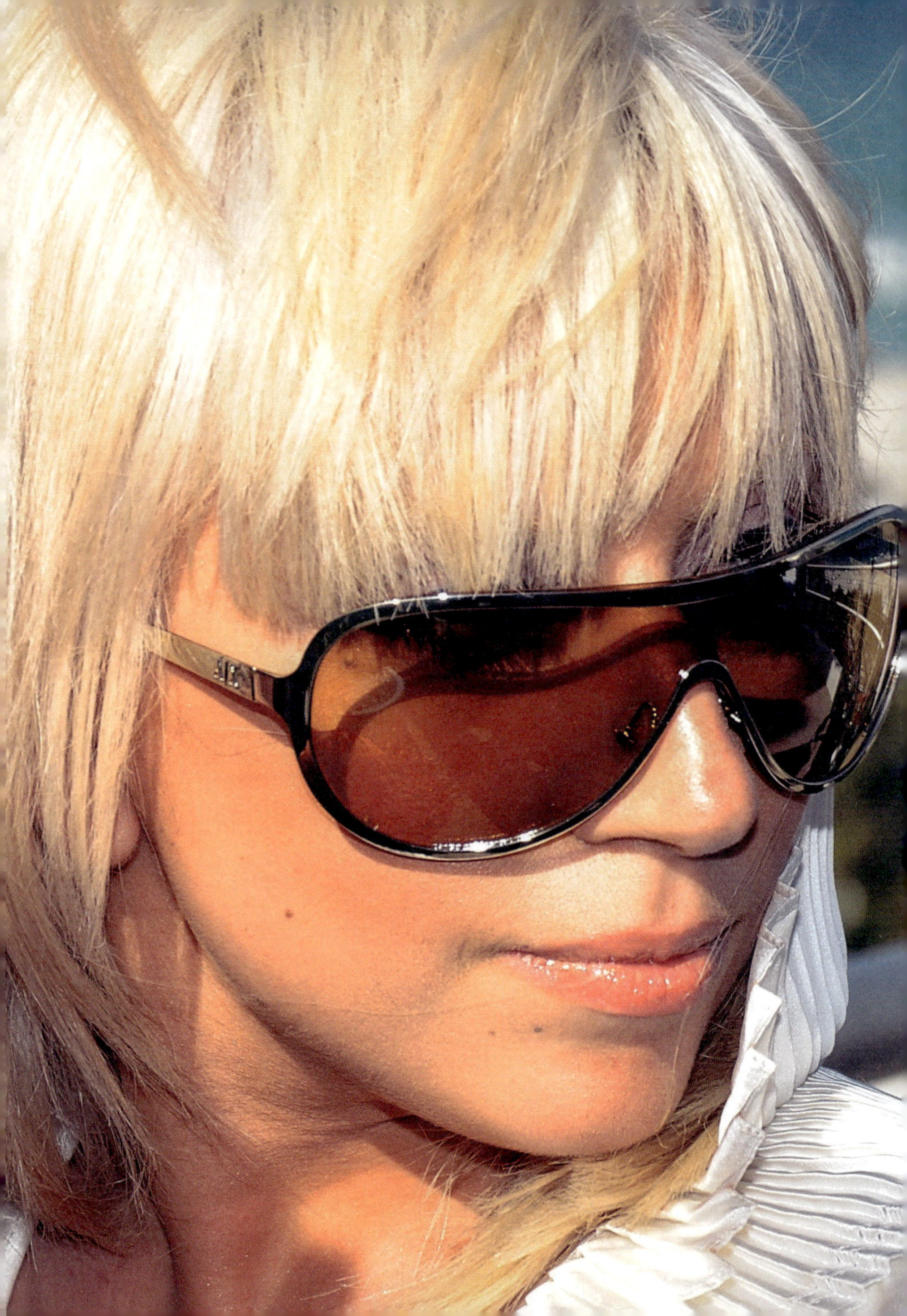

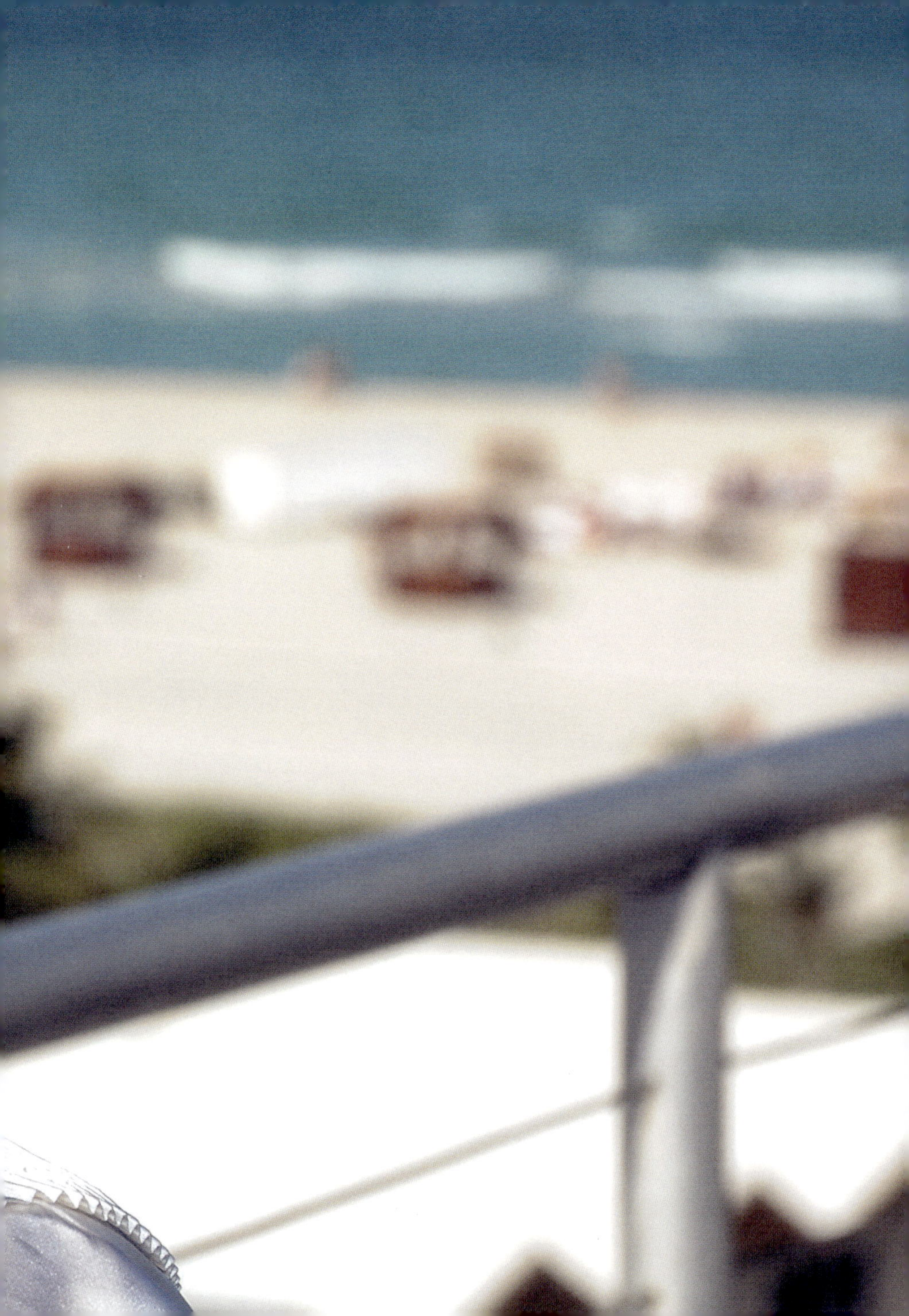

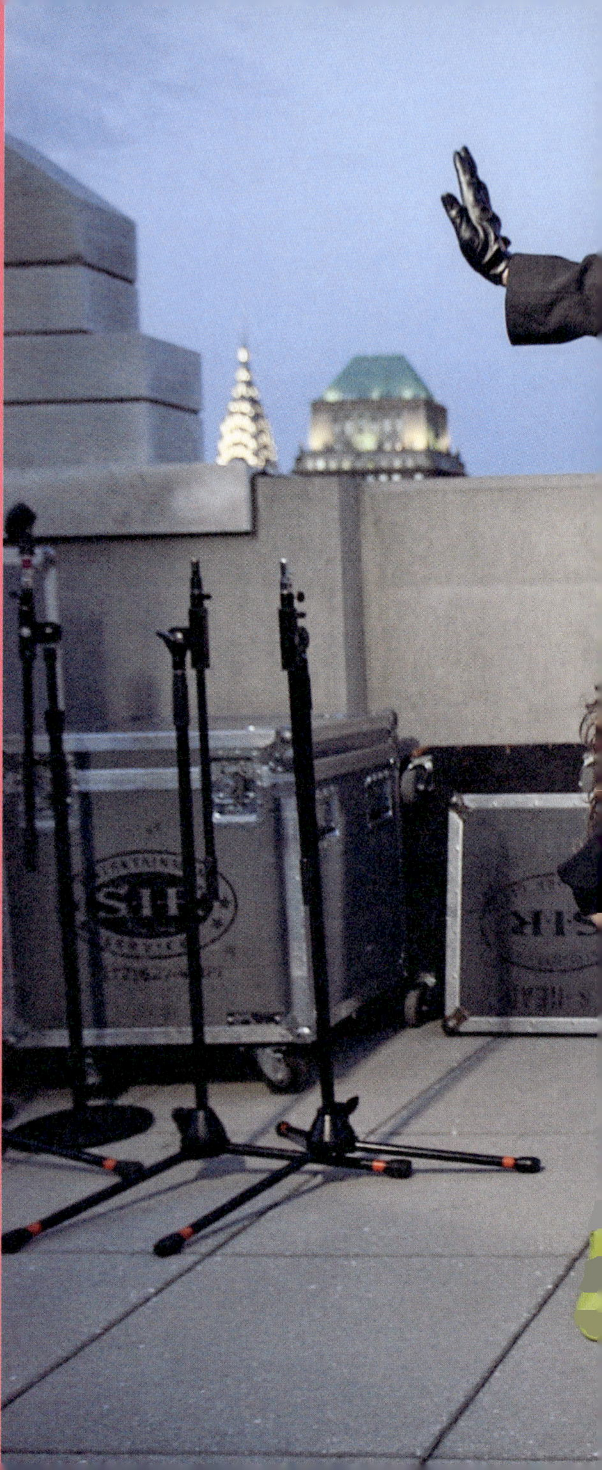

When Lady Gaga was wearing her signature leotards and tights early on in her career, she was pulling from various eras, including the 1980s.

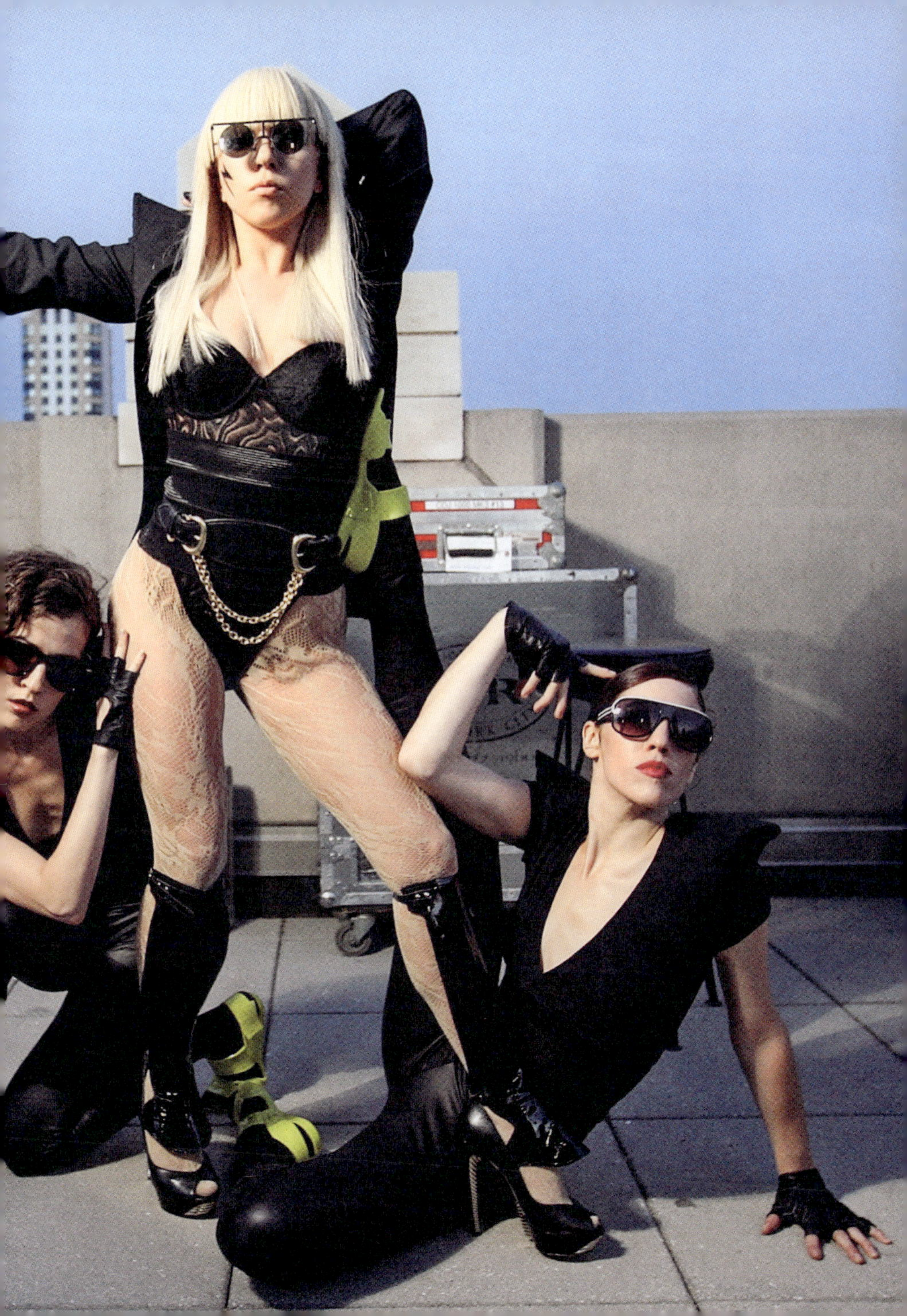

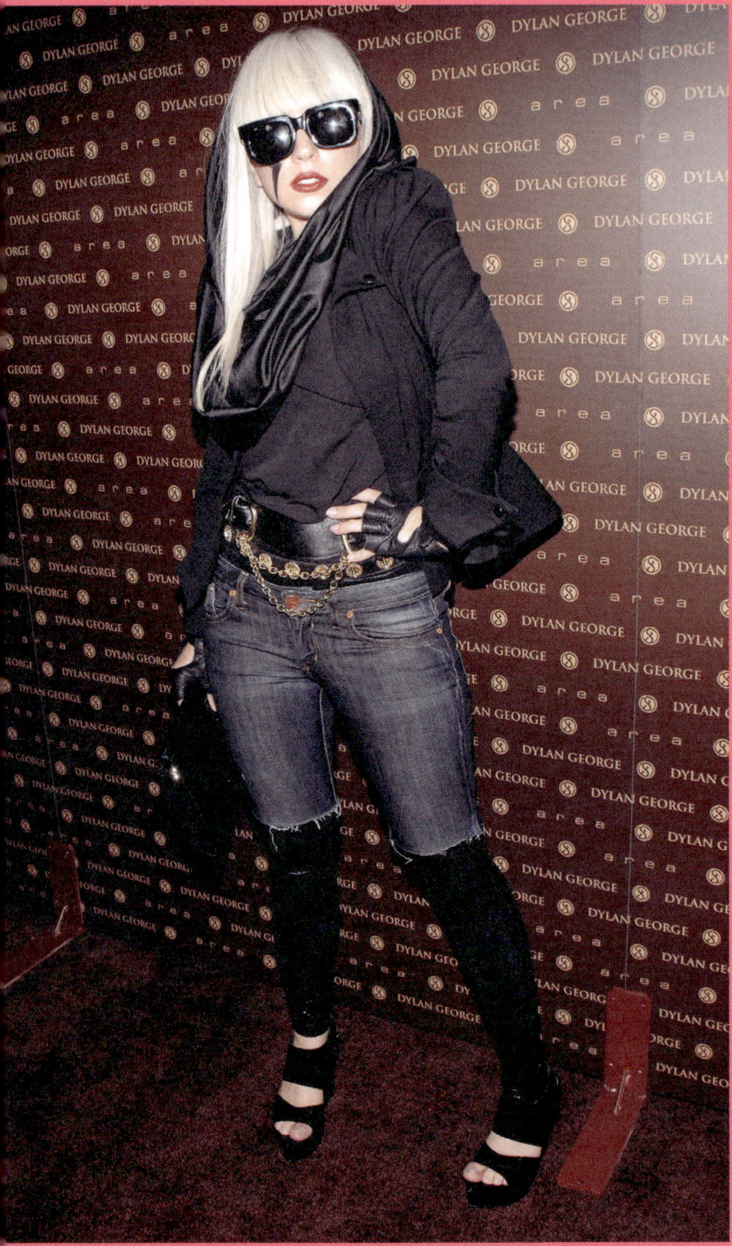
DYLAN GEORGE
area

"I wore probably one of three different outfits for about five years straight because that's what I could afford at the time and I wanted people to always recognize me."

LADY GAGA

Gaga creates a distinctive style through repetition, shaking things up with statement glasses or new twists – like layered belts.

This was around the same time that Gaga changed her hair colour to the now signature platinum blonde that's become so associated with her character. In 2008, stylist Patricia Morales created one of the most iconic and often-worn looks by Gaga at the time: the giant blonde bow made out of hair which she wore on the top of her head.

Los Angeles-based costume designer Muto-Little designed many of Lady Gaga's iconic leotards throughout the ages and she often accessorized them with vintage Versace sunglasses. Her hair was styled long, straight and very blonde and during this time, it was a wig that she wore almost everywhere. "I wore probably one of three different outfits for about five years straight because that's what I could afford at the time and I wanted people to always recognize me," Gaga told *Vogue* in 2022.

The leotard and sunglasses that became so synonymous with Lady Gaga's look went along with the music she was releasing during this time. For example, her 2008 debut album, *The Fame*, spoke of her fascination with other iconic celebrities and the idea of fame. Her aforementioned leotards with hoods referenced iconic performer Grace Jones, while the Versace sunglasses she wore, for her, were a reference to Biggie Smalls (aka The Notorious B.I.G.).

Here, Gaga mixed in pieces such as shoulder pads and fingerless gloves to add to her statement style.

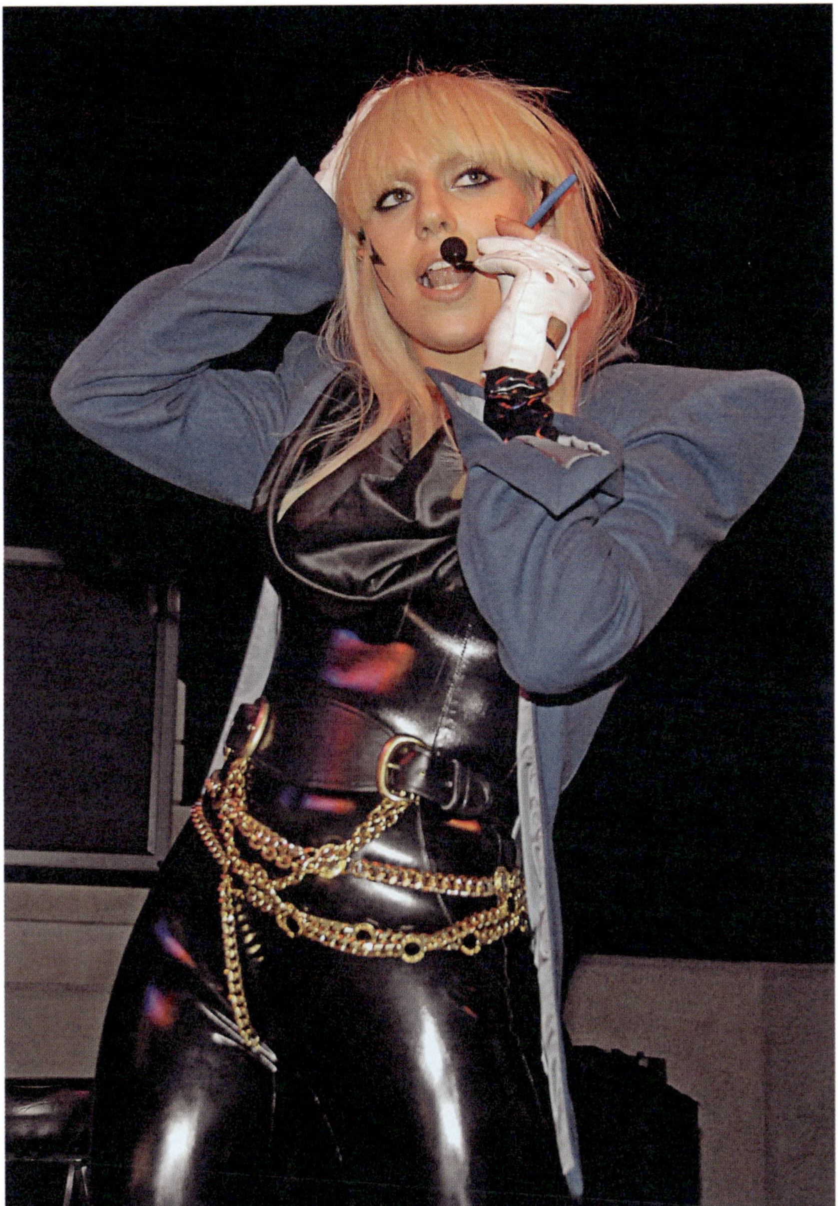

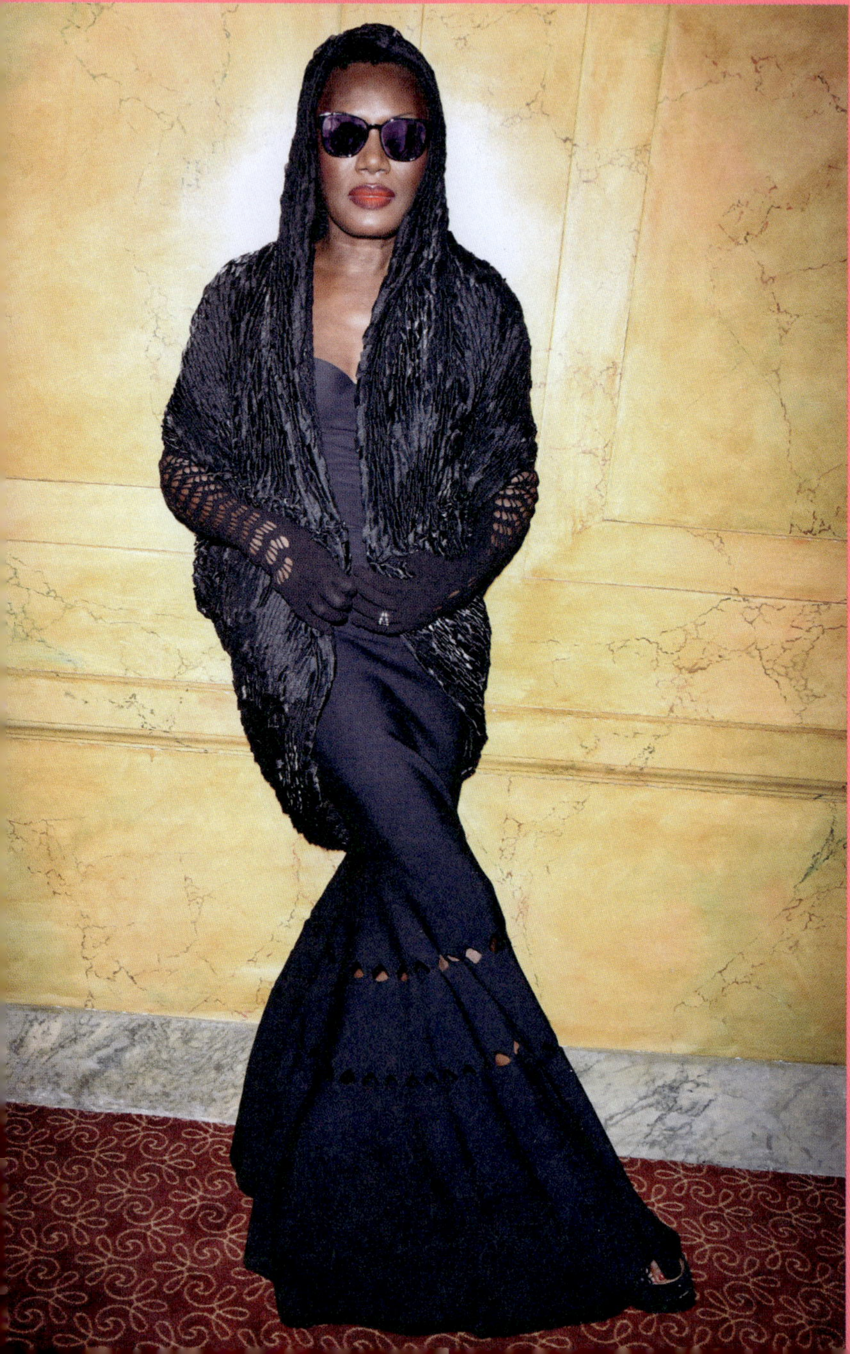

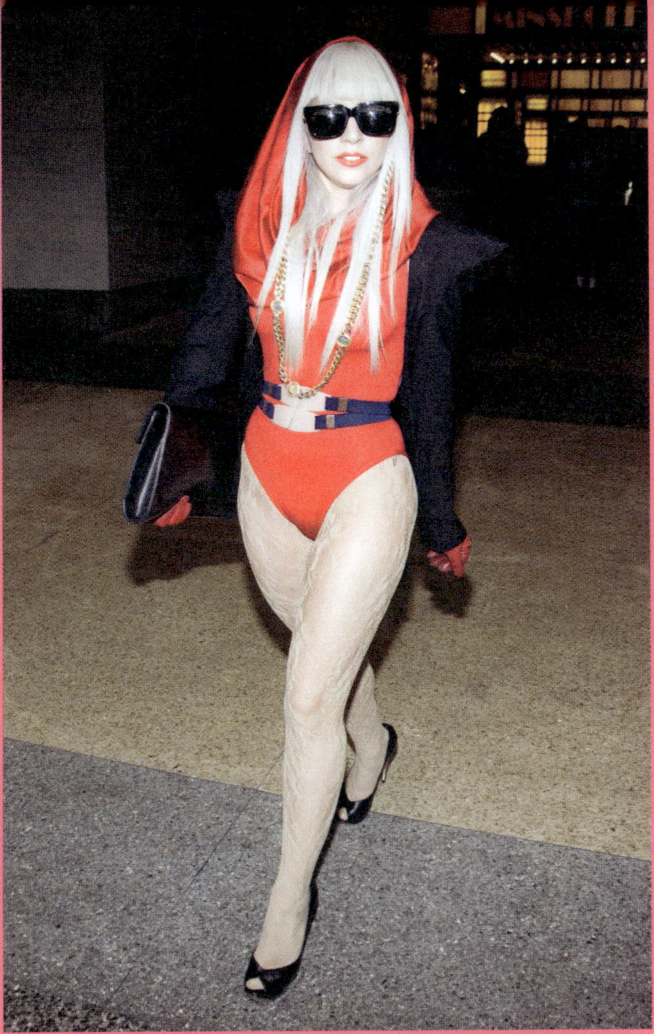

ABOVE Gaga also pulls style inspiration from Madonna, Michael Jackson and more.

OPPOSITE It's impossible not to notice the influence of certain artistic personalities on Lady Gaga. Like singer-songwriter Grace Jones, who often wore hooded leotards and dresses accompanied by big sunglasses.

OVERLEAF For Gaga, the beauty look is just as important as the clothing and accessories – she has always had an iconic hairstyle and experimented with make-up.

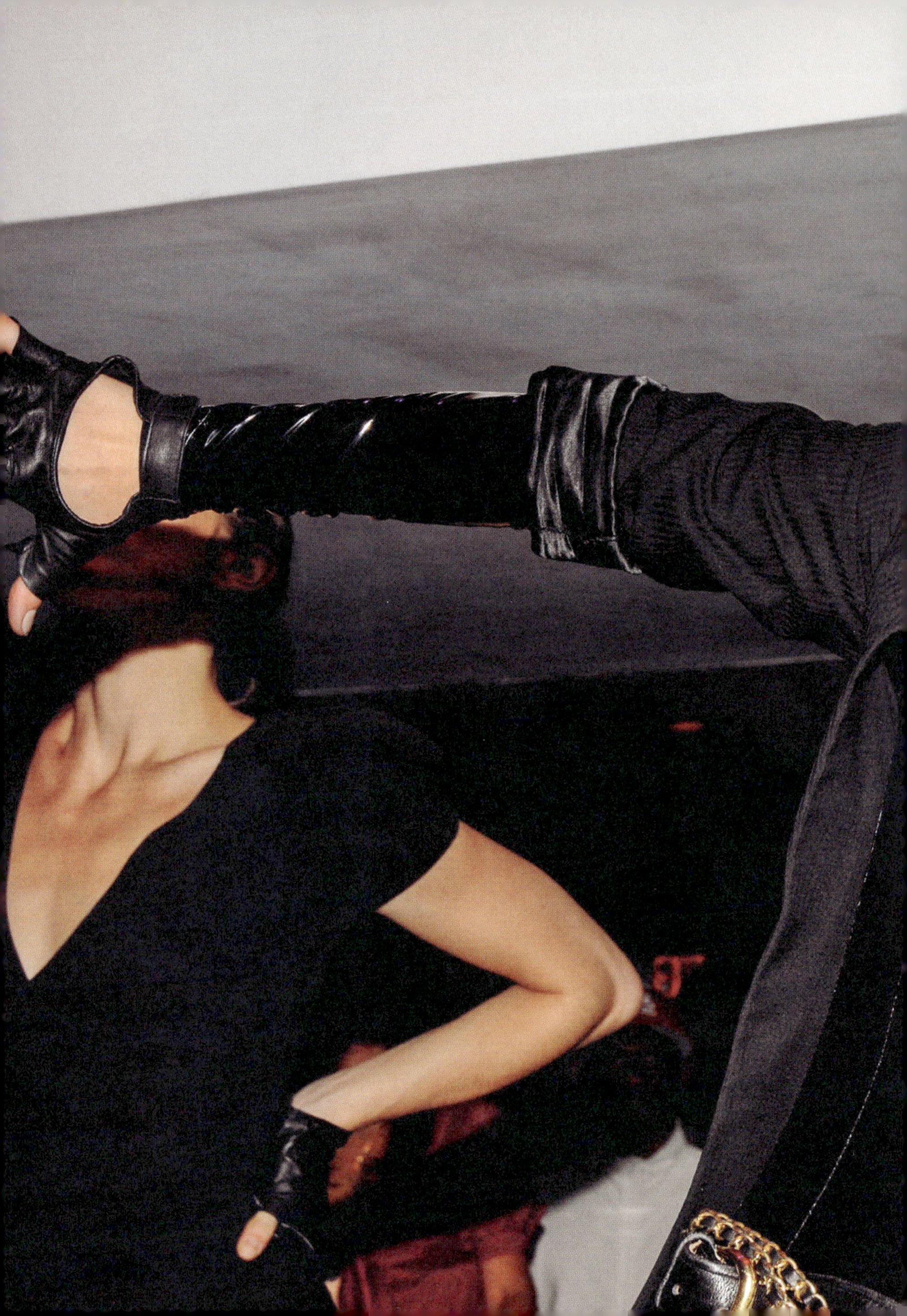

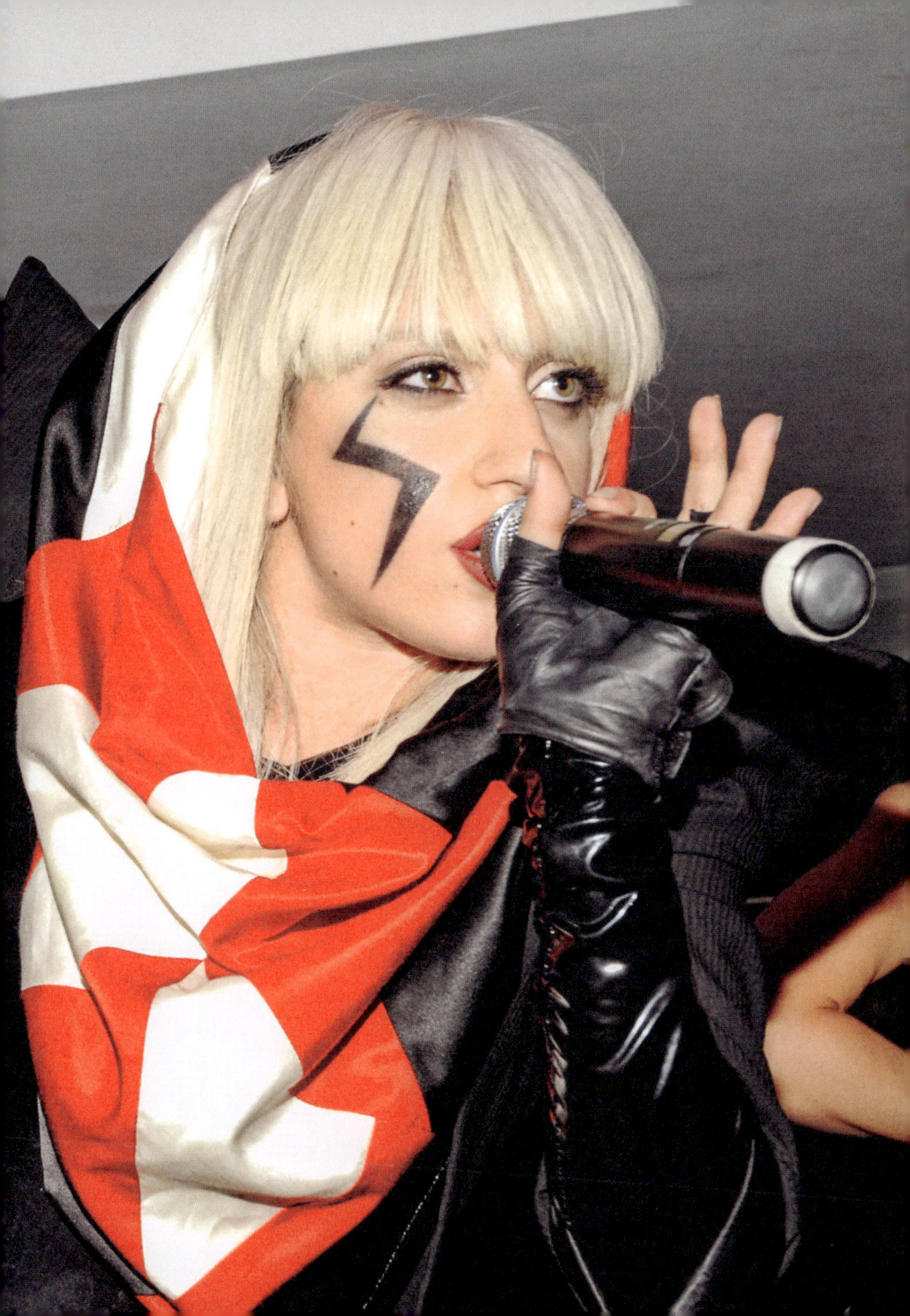

"I reject wholeheartedly the way we are taught to perceive women. The beauty of women, how a woman should act or behave.

It's exciting *because all* avant-garde clothing and music and lyrics *that at* one *time were* considered shocking or *unacceptable are* *now* trendy."

LADY GAGA

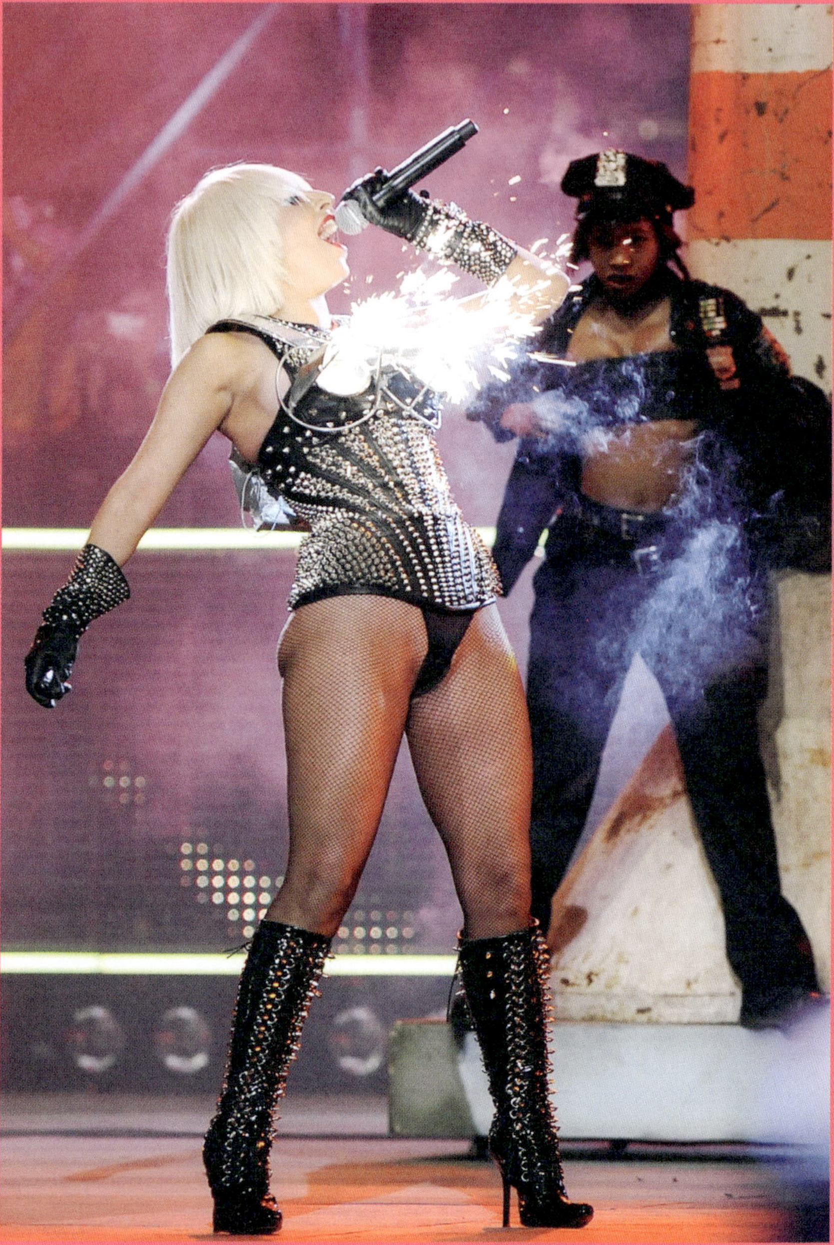

Working with stylists

In 2009, Lady Gaga met her stylist Nicola Formichetti, who would go on to have a major influence on her personal style and identity. The two met during a shoot for *V Magazine*. The first major appearance he styled her for was the 2009 MuchMusic Video Awards (MMVAs) in Toronto, Canada. She was nominated for "International Video of the Year (Artist)" and "People's Choice: Favorite International Video" for her video, *Poker Face*.

This was one of the biggest fashion moments from her early career. She wore several different outfits, each one more extreme than the next. Like a dress made of blonde hair, braided into a bustier corset with a flowing skirt and a matching bag shaped like a bow made out of hair. The dress was created by Haus of Gaga, which was what she called her creative team, including Formichetti. To perform onstage, she wore one of her signatures but with a very extreme twist: a studded black leather leotard with a hood and a "fire bra" with explosive pyrotechnics which deployed during the performance. The studded open hood was designed by Atsuko Kudo and the pyro-bra was made by Tom Talmon Studio for Haus of Gaga, while the studded bodysuit was created by Muto-Little Costumes for Haus of Gaga. During the performance, she used a remote control to activate the bra, throwing flames of fire from it. She also wore knee-high stiletto black pleather Pleaser boots that were hand-studded.

Lady Gaga's first big fashion moment took place at the 2009 MuchMusic Video Awards (MMVAs) in Toronto, where she wore a pyrotechnic bra.

"I've worn the same stripper heels my entire career," she told *Vogue*. "They're tried and true and they're worth it." Another time she said of her shoes: "There's this one pair of shoes I've had for years, and they cost like $25," she told *Harper's Bazaar*. "I have such an emotional attachment to the shoes that every time I see them, I can hear the fans and feel the bass coming through the bottom of the stage."

Formichetti helped Gaga take her style to the next level when it came to awards shows and performances. The looks she wore were often shocking and extreme, and went along with her persona of being completely avant-garde and someone who was setting out to blur the lines between pop culture, art, music and fashion. To go along with her newfound fame and her solid execution, she started wearing some of the world's most high-end, big name designers that felt seamlessly on brand for her identity as a performer. Think Alexander McQueen and Jean Paul Gaultier, both considered avant-gardists themselves, who played in the space between art and fashion. "She totally embraced that fashion culture, and she, in a way, made fashion alive," Formichetti told *Paper* in 2019. "She kind of bridged pop culture and fashion and music. She opened the door for other artists to do that today, because today you have to work with fashion. It's all together. It has to be 360 [degrees]. But at that time, it wasn't like that."

In the hands of her stylist Nicola Formichetti, nothing is off limits, even clothing made out of hair.

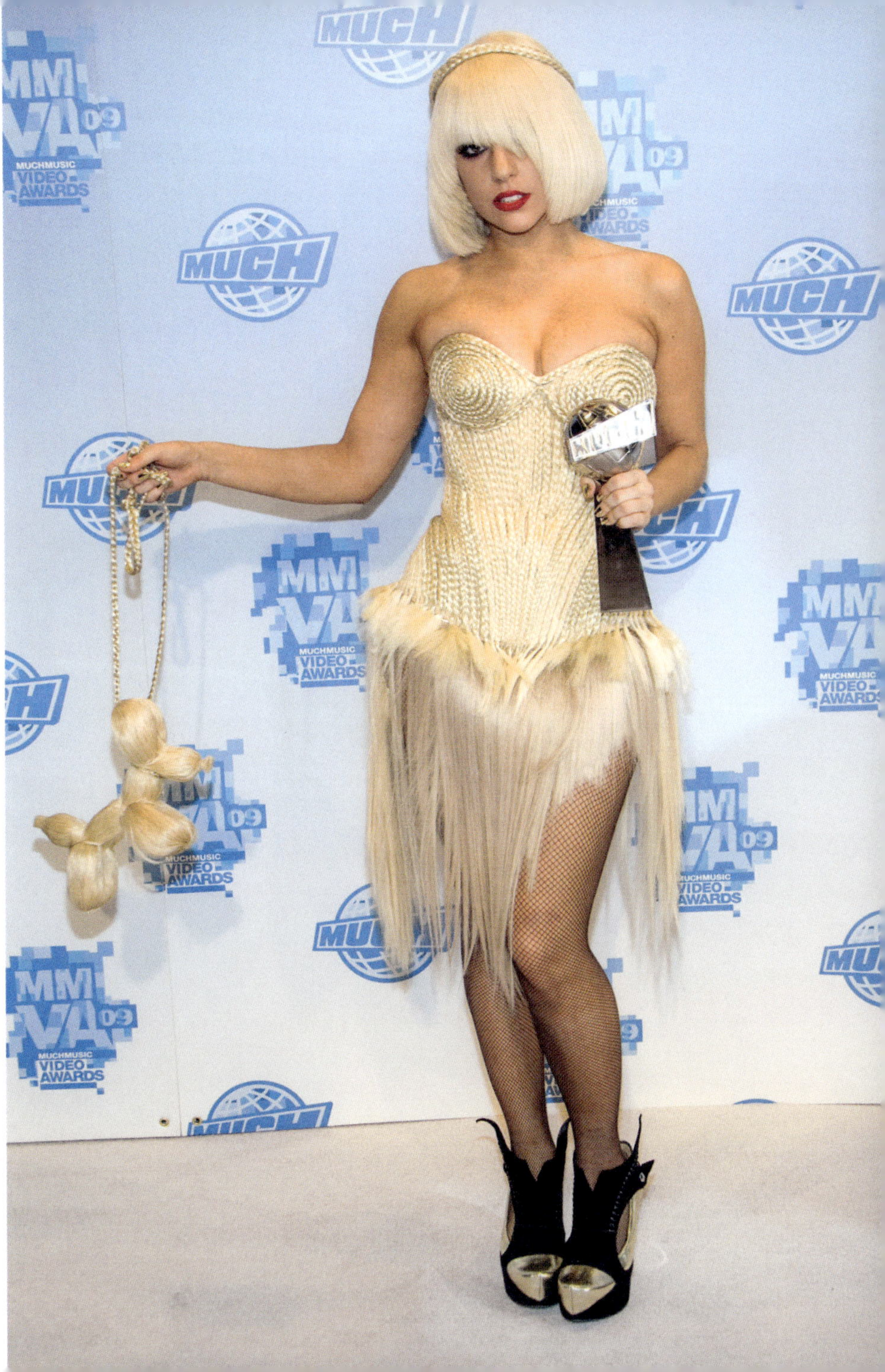
MUCH
MMVA 09
MUCHMUSIC
VIDEO
AWARDS

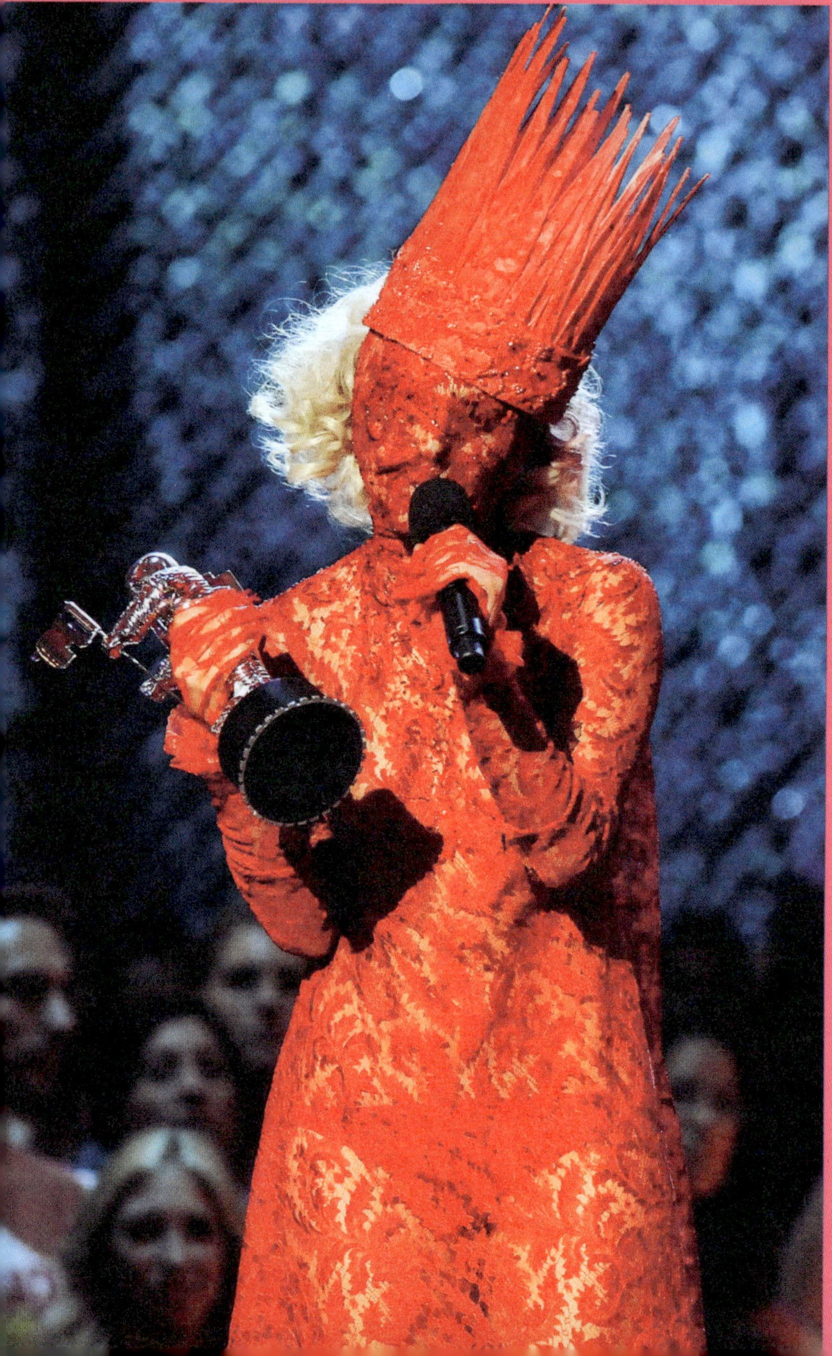

Dressed in a red lace Alexander McQueen look straight from the brand's runway archives, Lady Gaga wore a matching lace crown and face covering to accept the award for Best New Artist at the 2009 MTV Video Music Awards (VMAs). During the same evening, she wore a puffy, three-dimensional, futuristic, grey Jean Paul Gaultier leotard with black glittery boots – a high fashion take on her usual look.

Still, part of Gaga will always identify with her roots, or her very first iconic look, which is the leotard. During her 'Paparazzi' performance at the 2009 VMAS, she wore white underwear and a matching crystal-covered crop top spattered with drippy fake blood. The look was designed by Haus of Gaga. Alluding to her total commitment to the concept and fascination of fame, it was reportedly a nod to Princess Diana. She began the performance by stating, "Amidst all of these flashing lights, I pray the fame won't take my life." As she played piano live, Gaga moved her head back and forth dramatically and toward the end, was raised up on the stage by the chandelier, with fake blood dripping and cameras flashing. To say this performance shocked the audience and viewers at home would be an understatement. "When they wanted me to be sexy, when they wanted me to be pop, I always put some absurd spin on it to make me feel like I was in control," she recalled in her 2017 Netflix documentary, *Gaga: Five Foot Two*. "If I'm gonna be sexy on the VMAs singing about the paparazzi, I'm gonna do it while bleeding to death, reminding you of what fame did to Marilyn Monroe."

In 2009, Gaga stepped out her high-fashion credibility and started wearing top-tier designers, like Alexander McQueen, as seen here at the 2009 MTV Video Music Awards (VMAs).

"If I'm gonna be sexy *on the VMAs* singing *about the* paparazzi, *I'm gonna do it while* bleeding to death, *reminding you of what fame did to Marilyn Monroe."*

LADY GAGA

At the 2009 VMAs, Lady Gaga wore a Haus of Gaga white bra and underwear set dripping with fake blood in a nod to the late Princess Diana – one of her most memorable and controversial outfits ever.

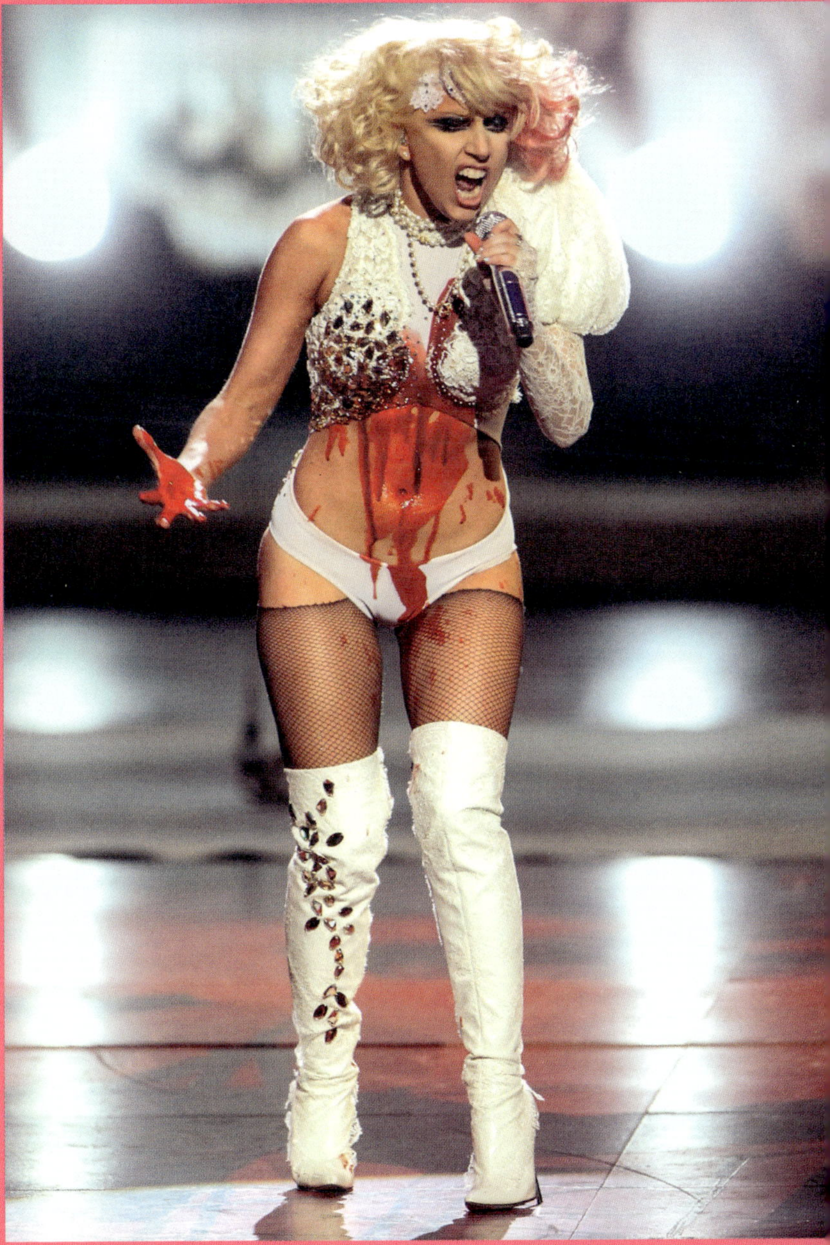

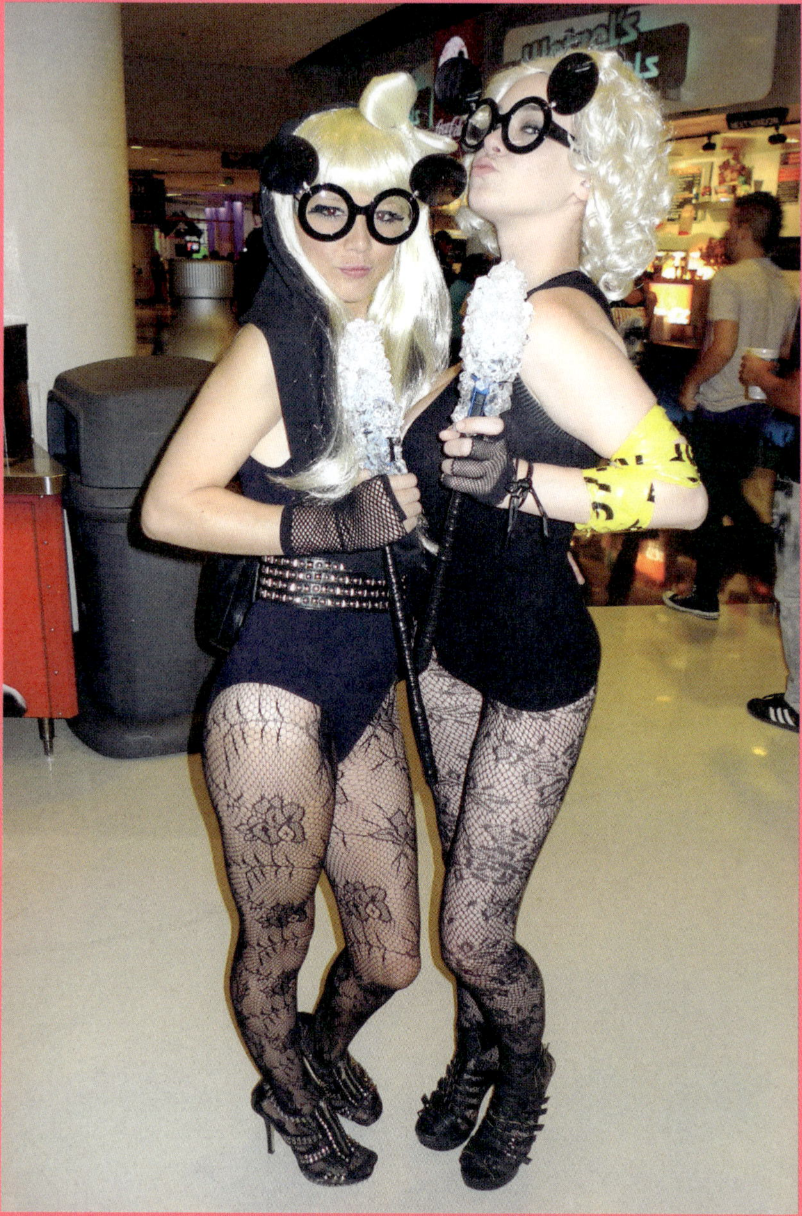

Gaga's foray into high fashion was fast and it suited her personality and character. Her music sought to push boundaries and her visuals even more so – who better to represent this than some of fashion's most visionary, controversial and well-respected designers? With an eye for accessorizing and going all out, she often wore either an experimental hairstyle or hat. Take, for example, when she wore a dramatic feathered Philip Treacy wreath headpiece with a white sequined Jean Paul Gaultier dress.

What set the star apart in terms of fashion too was her approach to wearing emerging designers or talented brands that are underrepresented by celebrities. In 2009, Gaga met Queen Elizabeth II in England and wore a bright cherry red dress by the London-based, Japanese latex designer Atsuko Kudo. "I wanted to dress like a queen in a British fashion and I also wanted to do it my way. We thought that we would give this look of a queen a modern spin by making it in latex," she told British *Vogue*. Gaga would go on to collaborate with the designer numerous times throughout her career.

Above all else, Lady Gaga created a unique fan culture that surrounded her music and her fashion that paved the way for other artists to do the same. While working on her second album – *The Fame Monster* – in 2009, she began calling her fans "Little Monsters". The name stuck and has been used to describe Gaga fans globally. She has been credited as the first Western artist to give their fandom a nickname (a common occurrence in K-pop culture). The fan culture created more of a direct connection between artist and fan but it also inspired the fans to dress up for Lady Gaga concerts.

Gaga's fans are called "Little Monsters" and some of them dress up just like her to attend her concerts or other events.

"I wanted to **dress like a queen** *in a British fashion and I also wanted to do it my way. We thought that we would give this look of a queen a* **modern spin** *by making it in* **latex.***"*

LADY GAGA

When Gaga met Queen Elizabeth II in 2009, she opted for something different: a red latex puff-sleeve ball gown by Atsuko Kudo.

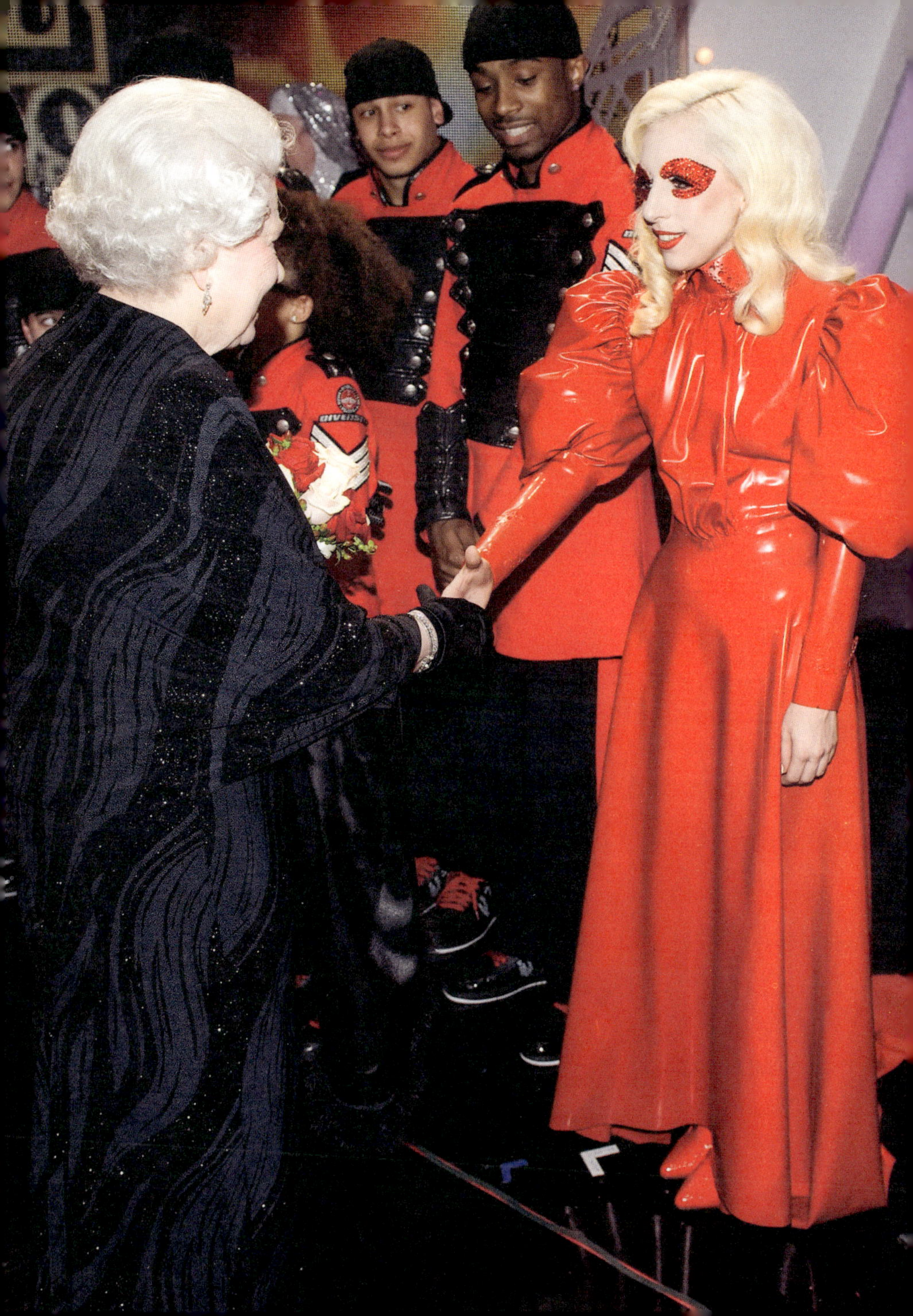

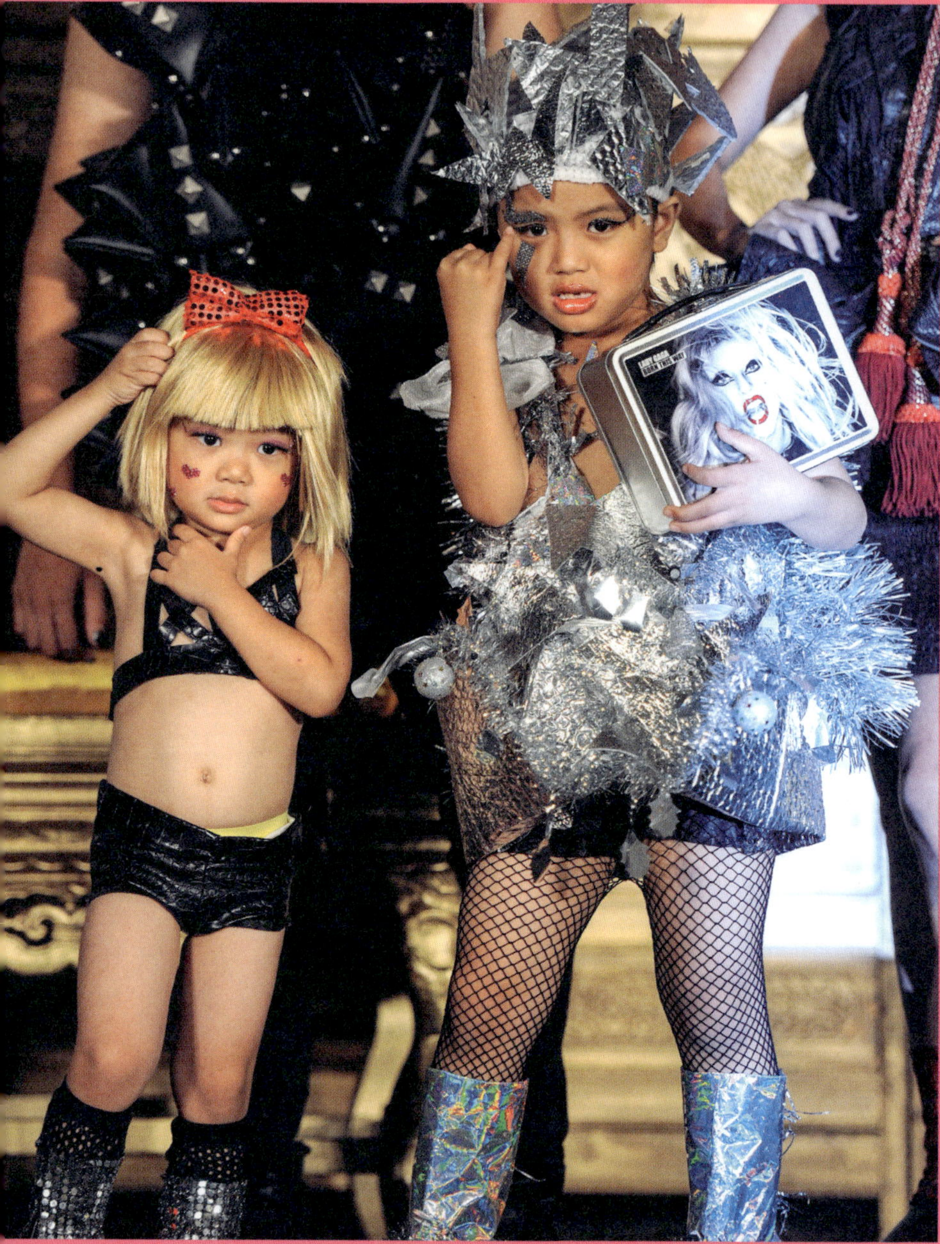
LADY GAGA
BORN THIS WAY

Often, they DIY some of Gaga's most iconic looks using found objects or what they have to hand, or they create entirely new looks that combine fantasy and surrealism, inspired by Lady Gaga's whimsically wild takes on fashion. In 2011, 121 "Little Monsters" dressed up in looks inspired by Gaga, earning the 2011 Guinness World Record for Largest Gathering of Lady Gaga Impersonators.

Gaga took her love of extreme, avant-garde fashion to new heights when she appeared on *Saturday Night Live* in 2009. This allowed her to reach a massive, broader audience and showcase her conceptual looks on live TV. In the episode, Gaga appears in several spellbinding looks that go beyond high fashion and into territory verging on art and costume. For one scene, she wears a clear dress that looks like it's constructed entirely out of clear bubbles. The piece was created by Muto-Little via Haus of Gaga and referenced Hussein Chalayan's Spring/Summer 2007 collection. Going a step further, for her performances of 'Love Game' and 'Bad Romance', Gaga wore a huge orbit sphere dress created by Haus of Gaga and London-based designer Nasir Mazhar. Then a very new, emerging designer, previously Mazhar mostly made hats. For her 'Paparazzi' performance, Gaga wore red latex underwear and a matching bra by Atsuko Kudo, and in another skit with Madonna, she wore a black version of the same outfit.

Little Monsters are all different ages. In 2011, 121 Little Monsters dressed up in looks inspired by Gaga, earning themselves a 2011 Guinness World Record for Largest Gathering of Lady Gaga Impersonators.

"When they wanted me to be sexy, *when they wanted me to be* pop,

I always put some
absurd spin on it
to make me feel like
I was in control."

LADY GAGA

Following in the footsteps of other performers like Madonna, Lady Gaga aligned herself with high fashion early on. For example, her song 'Bad Romance' from *The Fame Monster* (2009) – the reissue of her debut studio album, *The Fame* (2008) – premiered during the final walk of Alexander McQueen's spring 2010 runway show, in October 2009. The fact that the singer chose one of the most hotly anticipated fashion shows to debut her new single was groundbreaking enough. But the fact that this was the first fashion show in history to be livestreamed (now a common occurrence) and the fact that it was Alexander McQueen's final show with the designer himself as creative director, before he sadly passed away in 2010, made it all the more historically important in terms of fashion and music coming together. On Twitter, Gaga mentioned the fact that her new song would be debuting at the show on the livestream, which created even more buzz, causing the livestream to crash.

By now, the world was clearly listening to her music, but everyone was also very tuned in to what Gaga was wearing. She had solidified herself as a definite contemporary fashion icon who was doing things differently and making statements with her clothing. Lady Gaga didn't just dress. She sparked deep discourse, interesting conversations and even more importantly, she made the world rethink the very concept of fashion itself.

Gaga won three awards at the 2010 BRIT Awards, and did so in one of her art-inspired outfits.

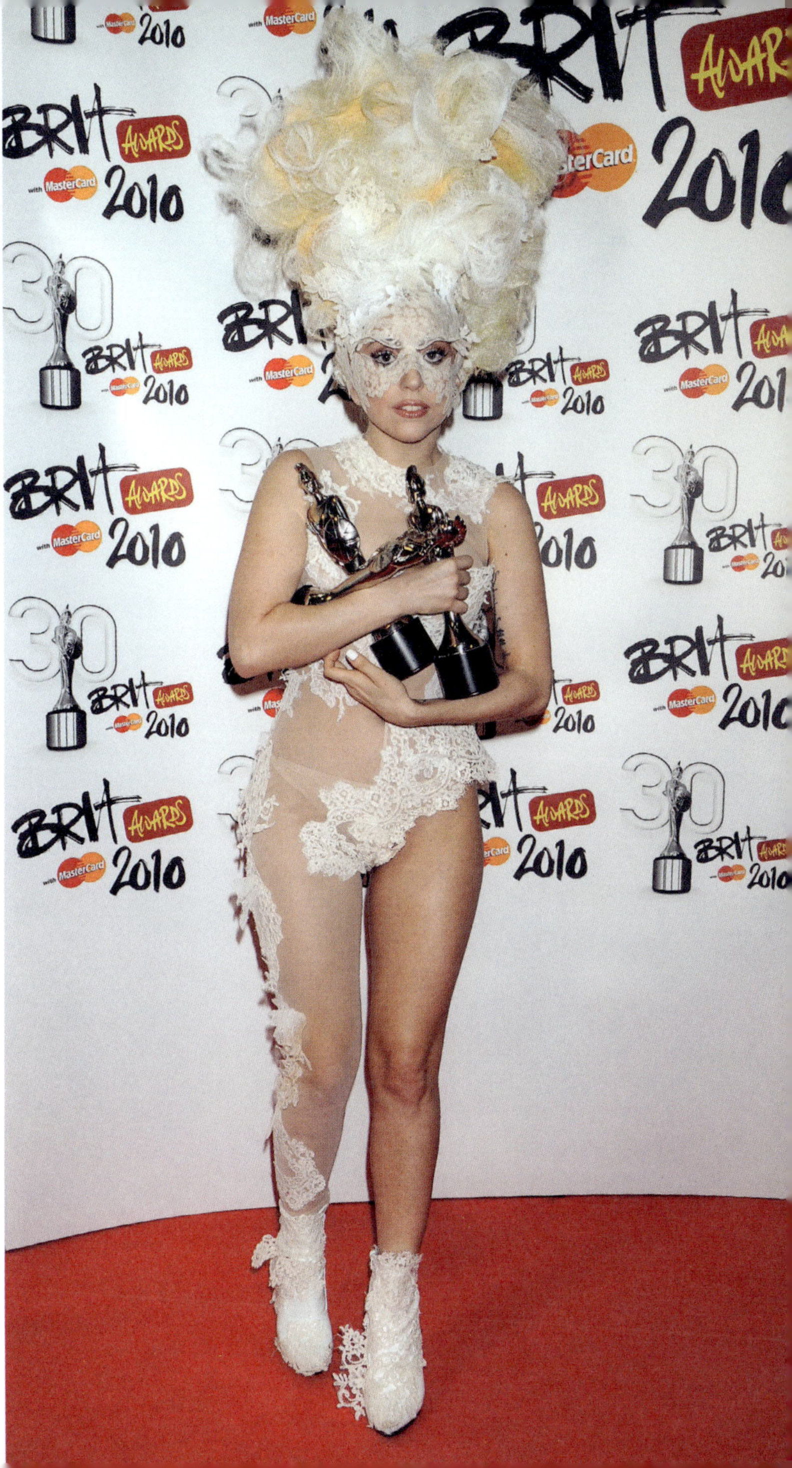
BRIT AWARDS
with MasterCard
2010
30

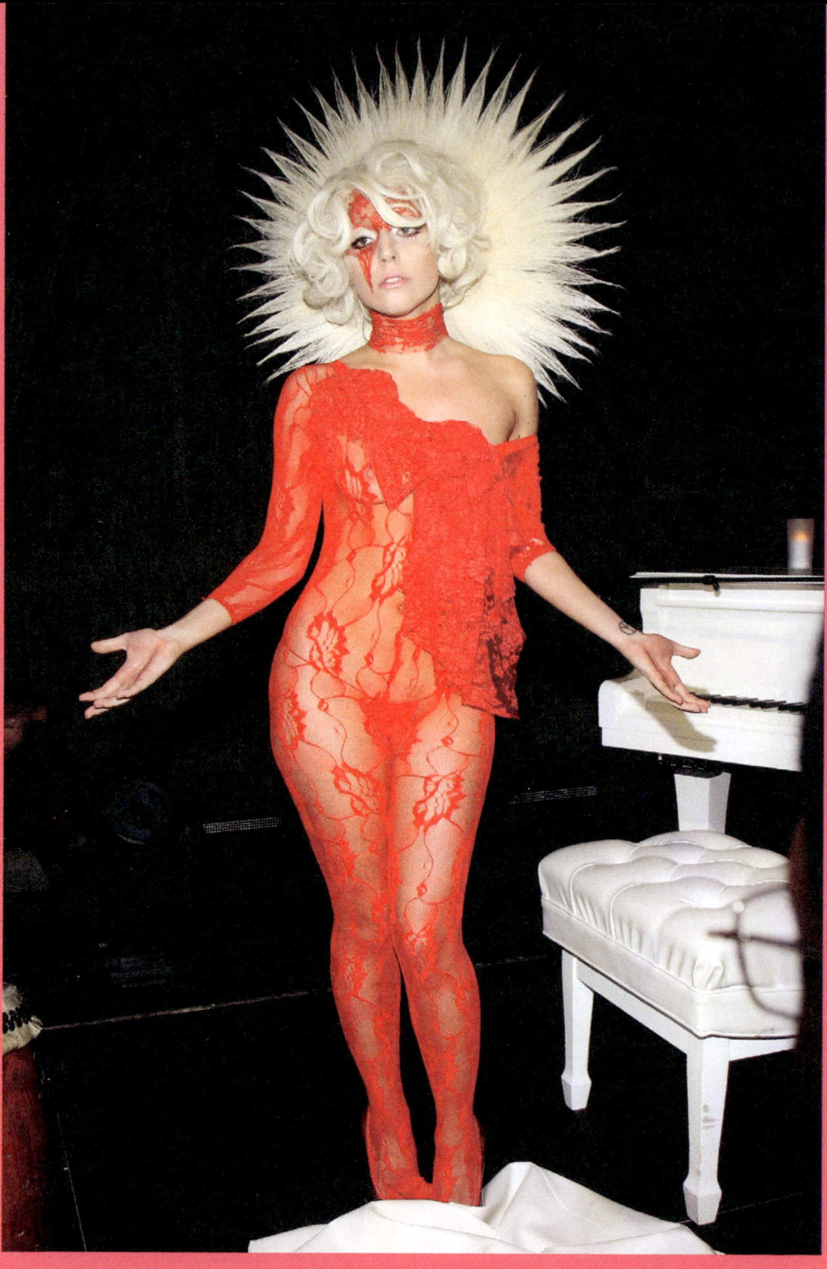

By the early 2010s Lady Gaga was taking huge fashion risks and breaking down stereotypes of what a female musician should – and could – wear.

"She totally embraced that fashion culture, *and she, in a way, made* fashion alive. *She kind of bridged* pop culture *and fashion and music. She opened the door for other artists to do that today."*

NICOLA FORMICHETTI

The Art

CHAPTER 2

# of Dressing

Total transformation

Wearing an Armani Privé lavender glittery Space Age gown complete with orb-like rings around the hips and shoulders, Lady Gaga's look at the 2010 Grammys proved that her next stage of fashion domination had everything to do with blending clothing into art and vice versa. Later on that night, she wore a scintillating white dress that revealed her behind covered in crystals.

Using awards shows and public appearances to her advantage, Gaga took every opportunity to turn fashion into an act of performance art. Perhaps one of the most iconic moments of celebrity fashion was when, for the 2010 VMAs, she wore the meat dress that so shocked viewers. It was a record moment for the star: she had 13 nominations, including 2 for Video of the Year. Gaga wasn't performing her music at this particular awards show, but she did perform in a very different way by making her statement with the meat dress. No other celebrity in fashion history had ever done anything so daring, but stars such as Bjork and Madonna paved the way with fashion that verged on performance.

Gaga went high fashion for the 2010 Grammys, wearing a Space Age-inspired Armani Privé gown.

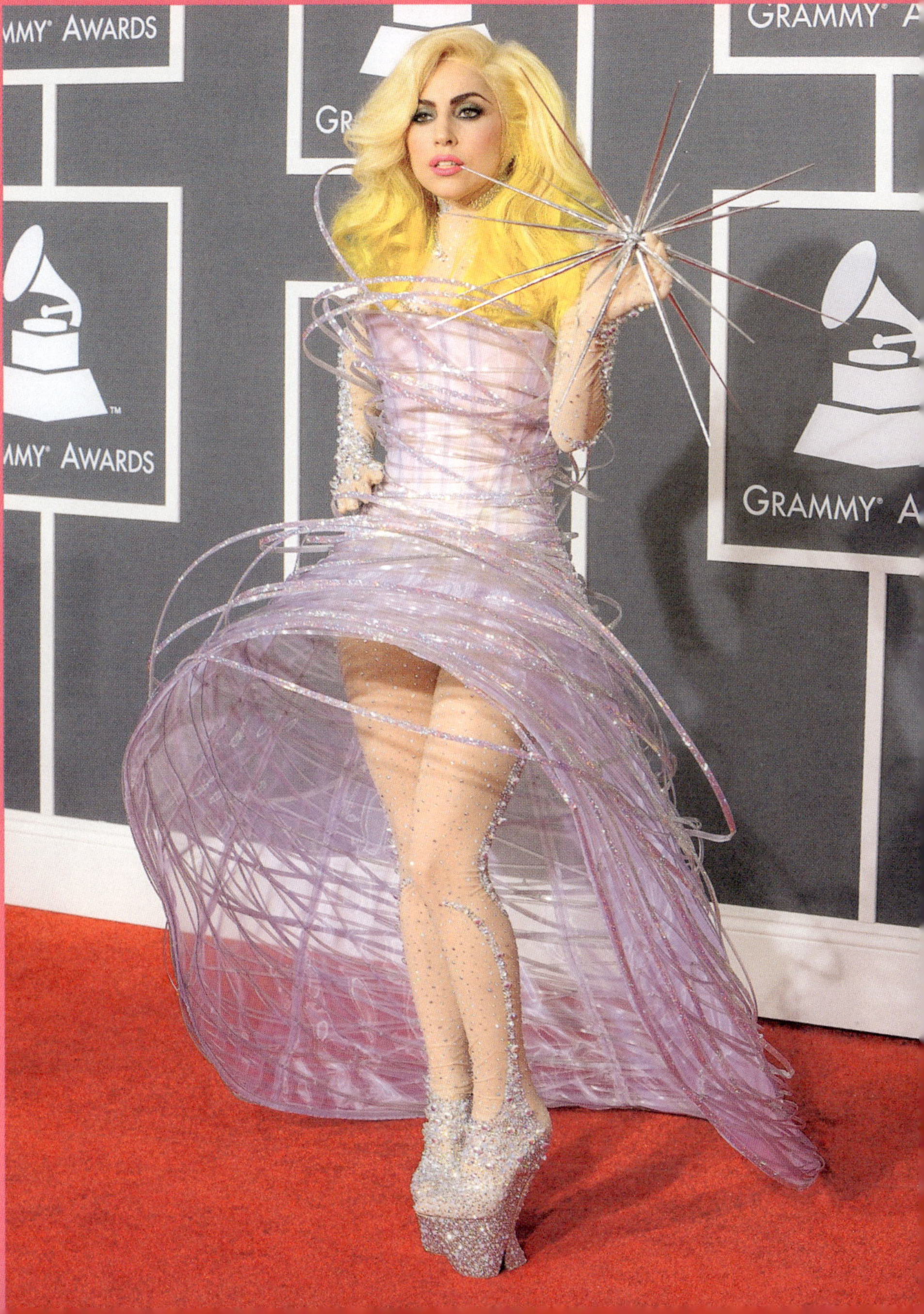
GRAMMY

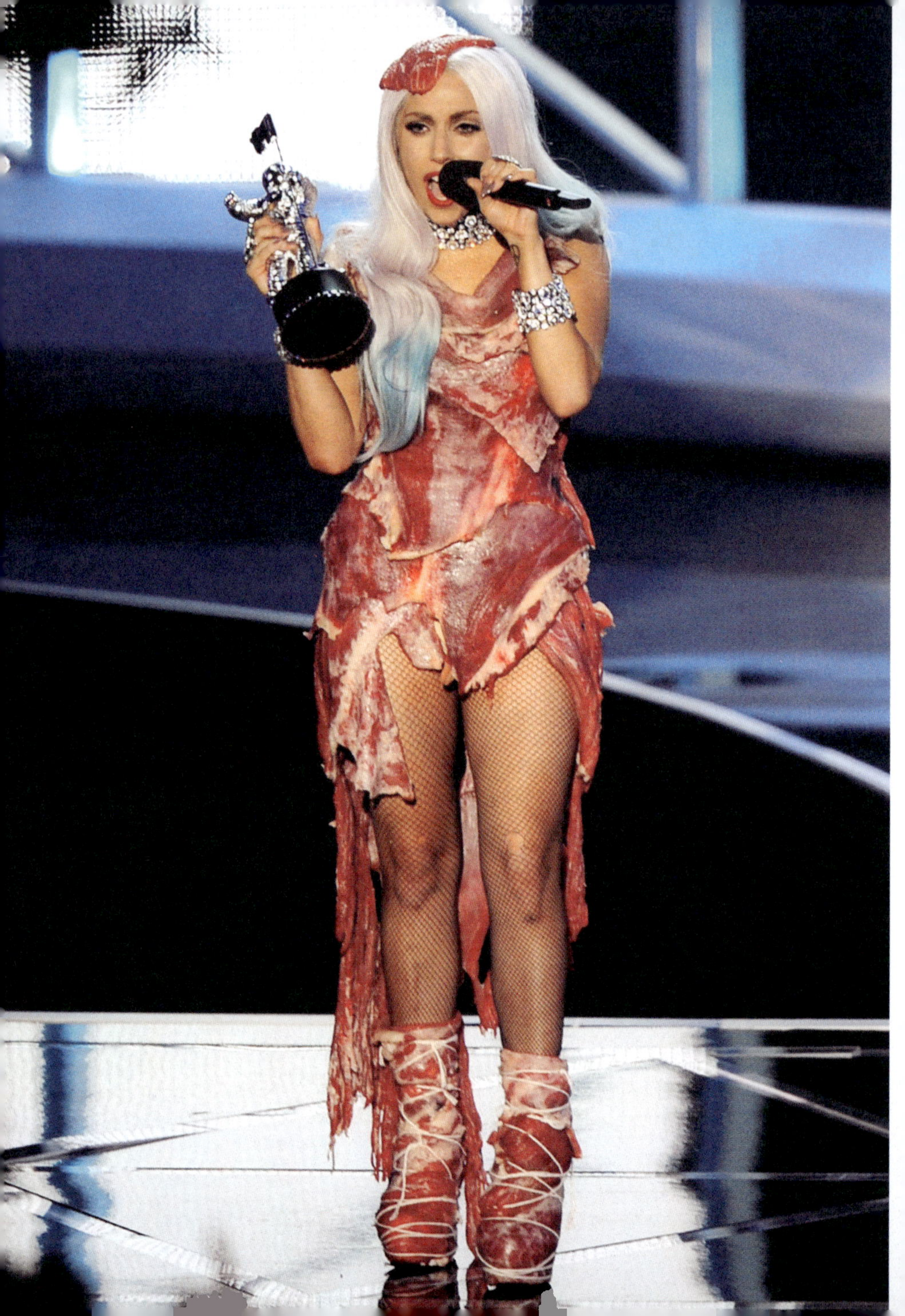

Previously, Lady Gaga wore a meat bikini shot by Terry Richardson for the Autumn/Winter 2010–11 Issue (Vol. 5) of *Vogue Hommes Japan*, but her look for the VMAs was all the more extreme. Gaga said she was inspired by the legendary make-up artist Val Garland, who has worked with fashion icons such as Alexander McQueen, John Galliano, and many more. "Her and I worked together for a long time, and she shared a story with me where she had gone to a party wearing sausages, and I thought this was quite funny. And I said, 'Well, that's a great way to make sure that everybody leaves you alone at a party,'" she told *Vogue* in 2011. Gaga also wanted to use the dress to make a political statement related to the US military's policy "don't ask, don't tell" – governmental restrictions placed on the rights of LGBTQ+ military members. "If you were willing to die for your country, what does it matter how you identify?" she explained of the concept.

Franc Fernandez, a designer who previously created some of the extraordinary hats worn by Lady Gaga, created the meat dress with a matching purse and shoes in collaboration with the Haus of Gaga team. With advice from his family butcher, he selected a thin cut of beef, similar to skirt (flank) steak. Fernandez bought roughly 18 kilograms (40 pounds) of meat and string at a butcher supply store and then got to work constructing the dress from scratch.

Possibly one of Lady Gaga's most iconic and memorable outfits of all time is the meat dress, designed by Franc Fernandez.

He used a light blue corset by Kiki de Montparnasse and applied clear-stitching over a two-day period while in constant refrigeration. Because of the delicate nature of the dress, on the day of the event, it had to be transported in a refrigerator and Gaga needed to be sewn into it. Fernandez also applied meat and twine to Gaga's Pleaser Delight-1020 patent white platform ankle boots and created a bag made of meat too. Naturally, the look shocked viewers and caused considerable controversy, but it also went down as one of the most iconic celebrity fashion moments of all time.

After the event, the dress was donated to the Rock & Roll Hall of Fame museum in downtown Ohio, Cleveland. Lady Gaga wanted the dress to be allowed to rot and decompose, but the museum convinced her and her team to preserve the look with salt. The result is a kind of cured beef jerky that stands as a dehydrated version of the dress. California taxidermist Sergio Vigilato helped preserve the dress using extensive restoration methods and dyes to make it look as close as possible to what it looked like when first worn by Gaga.

Although Lady Gaga made the intentions behind the dress crystal clear, the world speculated and used it as an example of cultural commentary. A leading woman artist wearing raw meat has obvious connotations related to perception of image, age and the world perceiving women as pieces of meat, devouring them metaphorically.

The meat dress was later preserved and donated to the Rock & Roll Hall of Fame in Cleveland, Ohio.

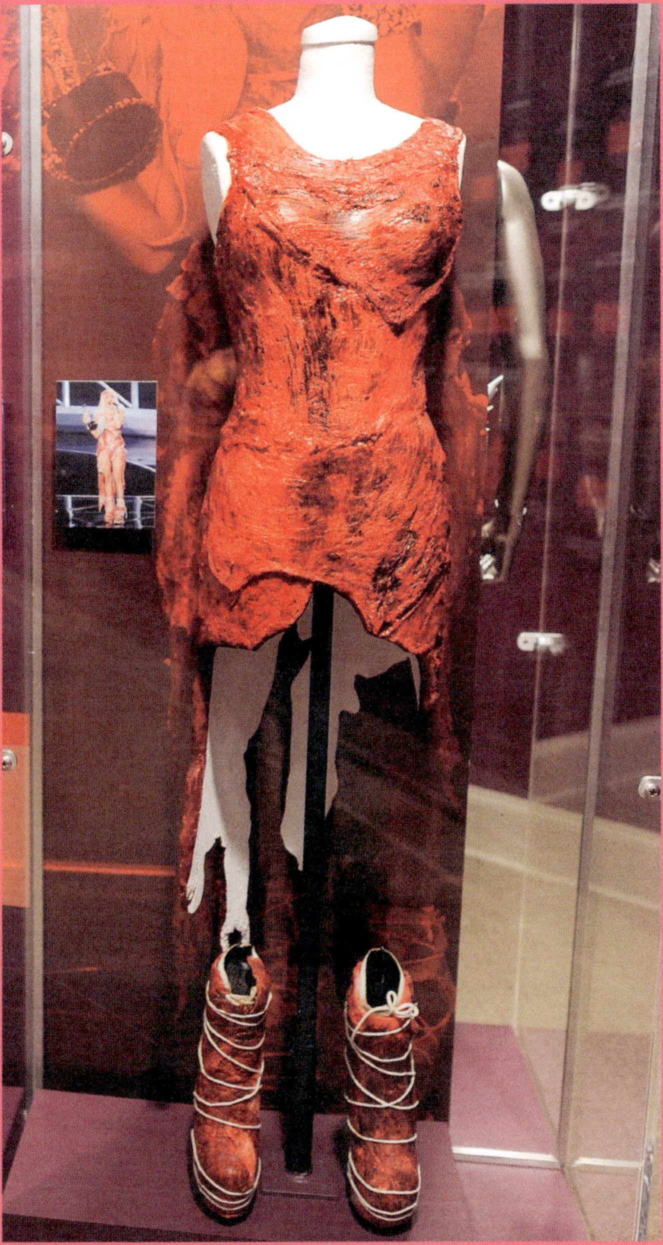

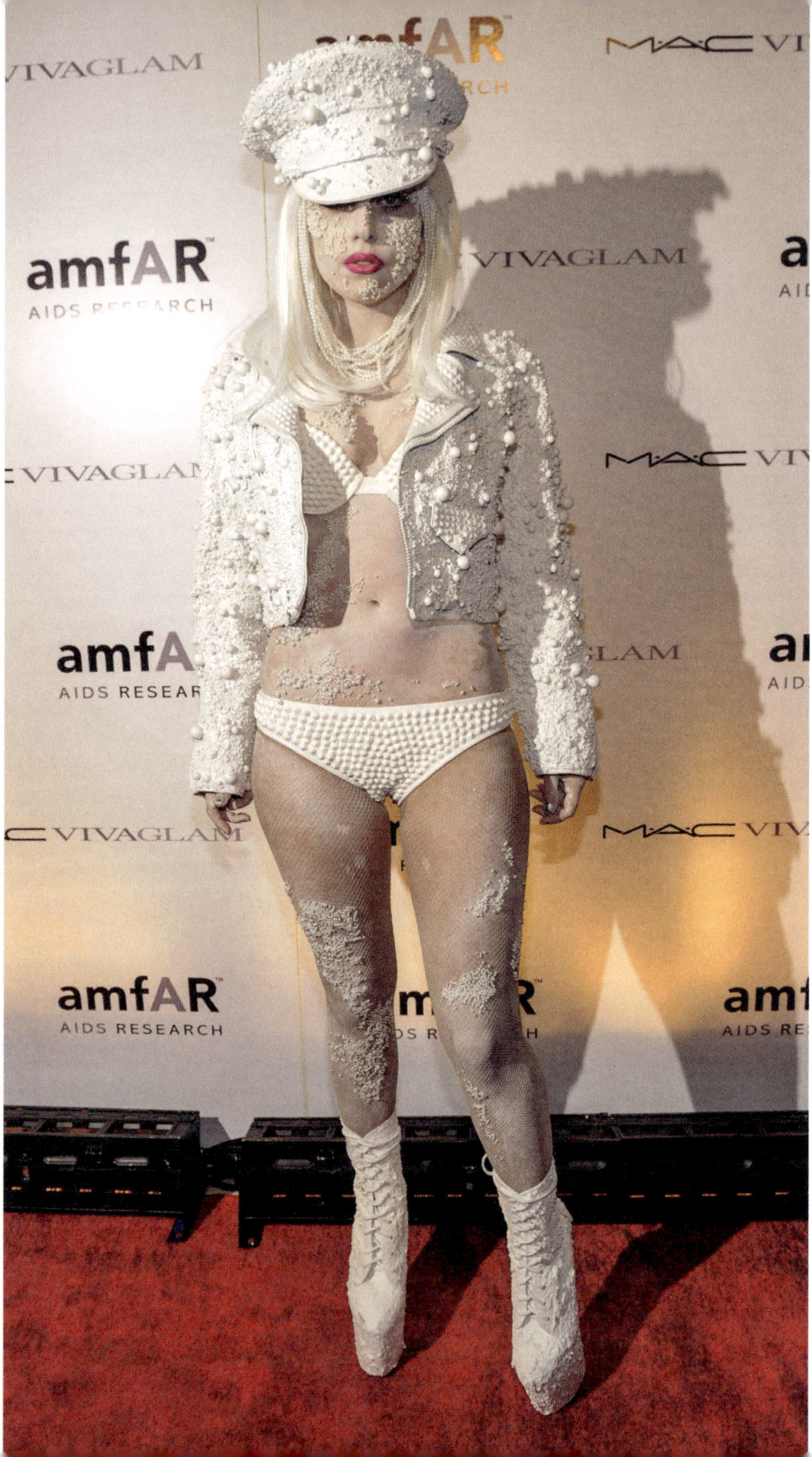
amfAR
AIDS RESEARCH
VIVAGLAM
M·A·C VIVAGLAM

Fashion as art

The early 2010s was Lady Gaga's most experimental fashion era. She was in a time of total expressiveness and she used her sense of style as an element of performance. In her everyday life, during performances and in music videos, she took her look to the next level. Coinciding with her albums *Born This Way* (2011) and *ARTPOP* (2013), during this time, Gaga transformed into one of the most experimental mainstream living pop artists in the world.

In 2010, Lady Gaga released the video for her song 'Telephone', which was created in collaboration with Beyoncé. For the occasion, Gaga wore a mix of looks that shocked and delighted, and would forever be burned into the collective cultural consciousness. For example, a retro striped dress by Jean-Charles de Castelbajac, a skimpy dress made out of custom-made crime scene tape by Brian Lichtenberg, a studded jacket by Search and Destroy, vintage archival Thierry Mugler and perhaps most memorable: a telephone hat by Fred Butler. Inspired by a play on Americana capitalism and camp, both Gaga and Beyoncé sported outfits inspired by the American stars and stripes flag too.

OPPOSITE Gaga transforms herself into living art with the help of her team, building upon her original signature leotard look.

OVERLEAF Merging high fashion, art and music, Lady Gaga was carried down the stairs inside a vessel shaped like an egg, designed by Hussein Chalayan for the 2011 Grammys.

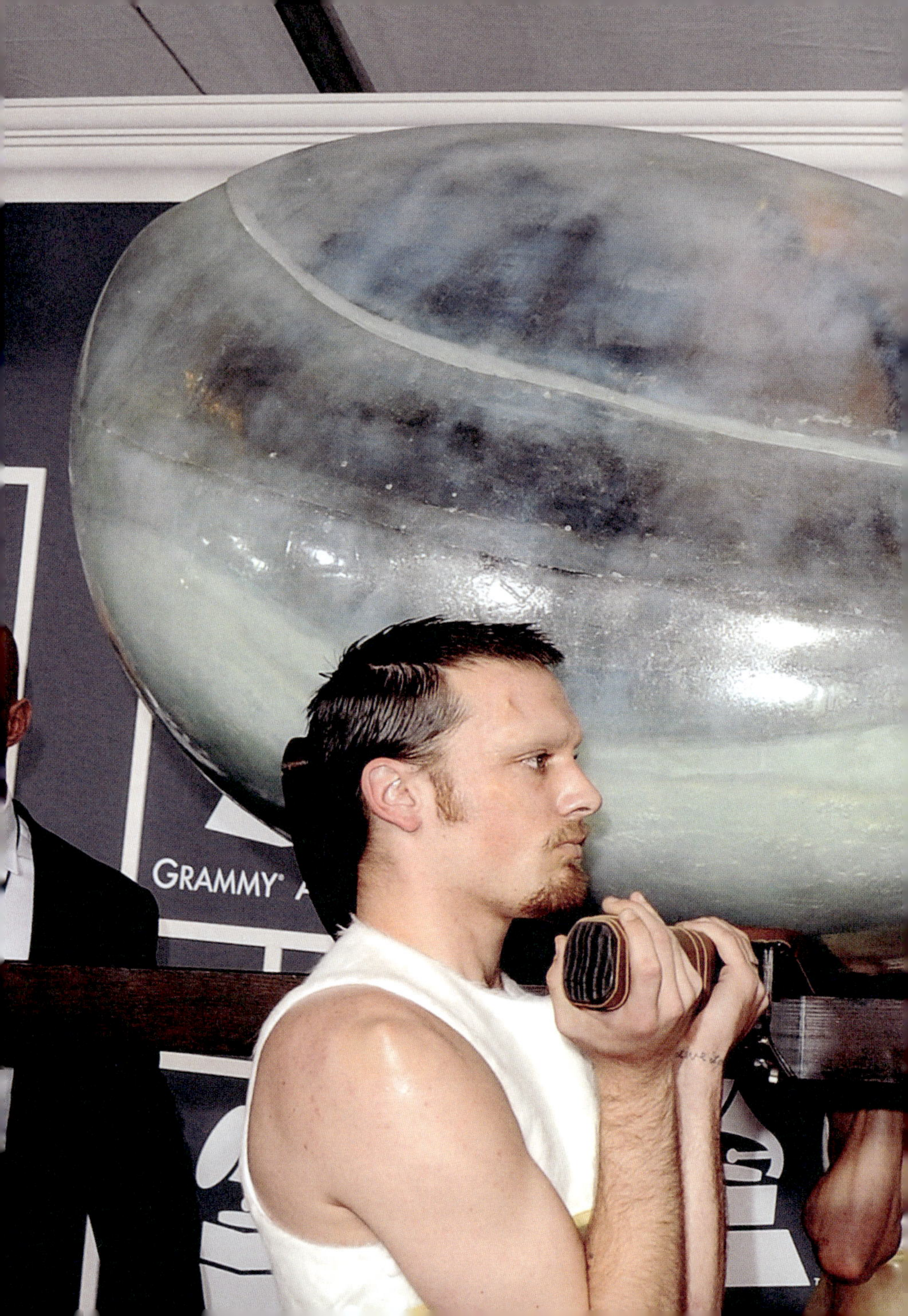
GRAMMY

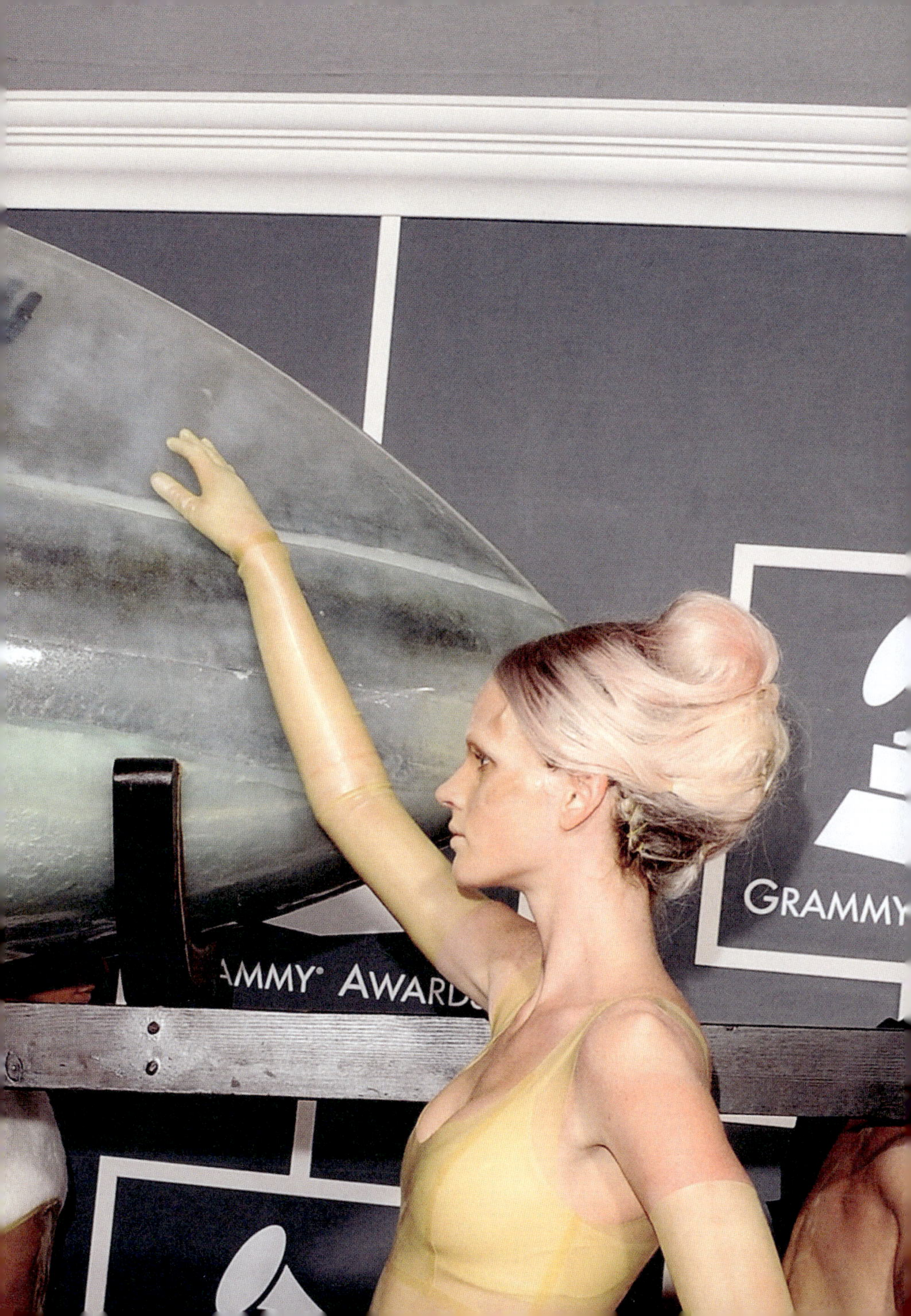
GRAMMY
AMMY® AWARDS

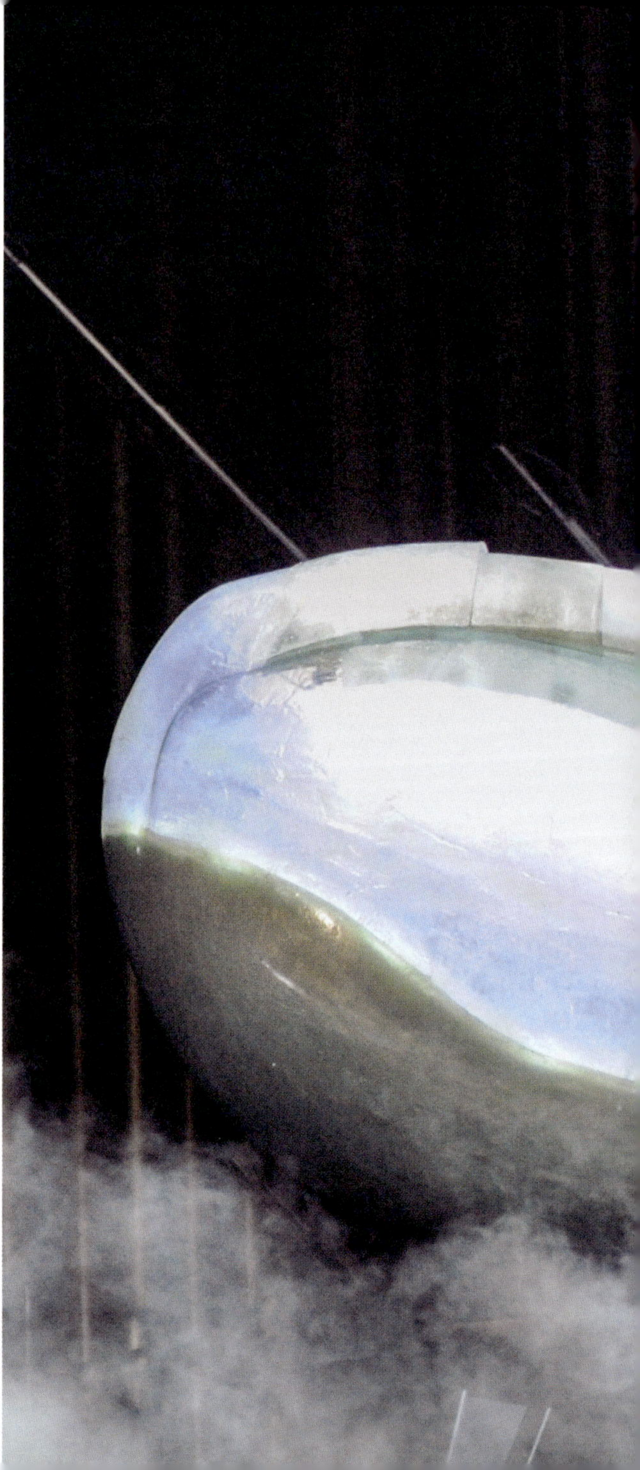

When Gaga emerged from the egg, she made fashion and music history and served an equally iconic look at the 2011 Grammys.

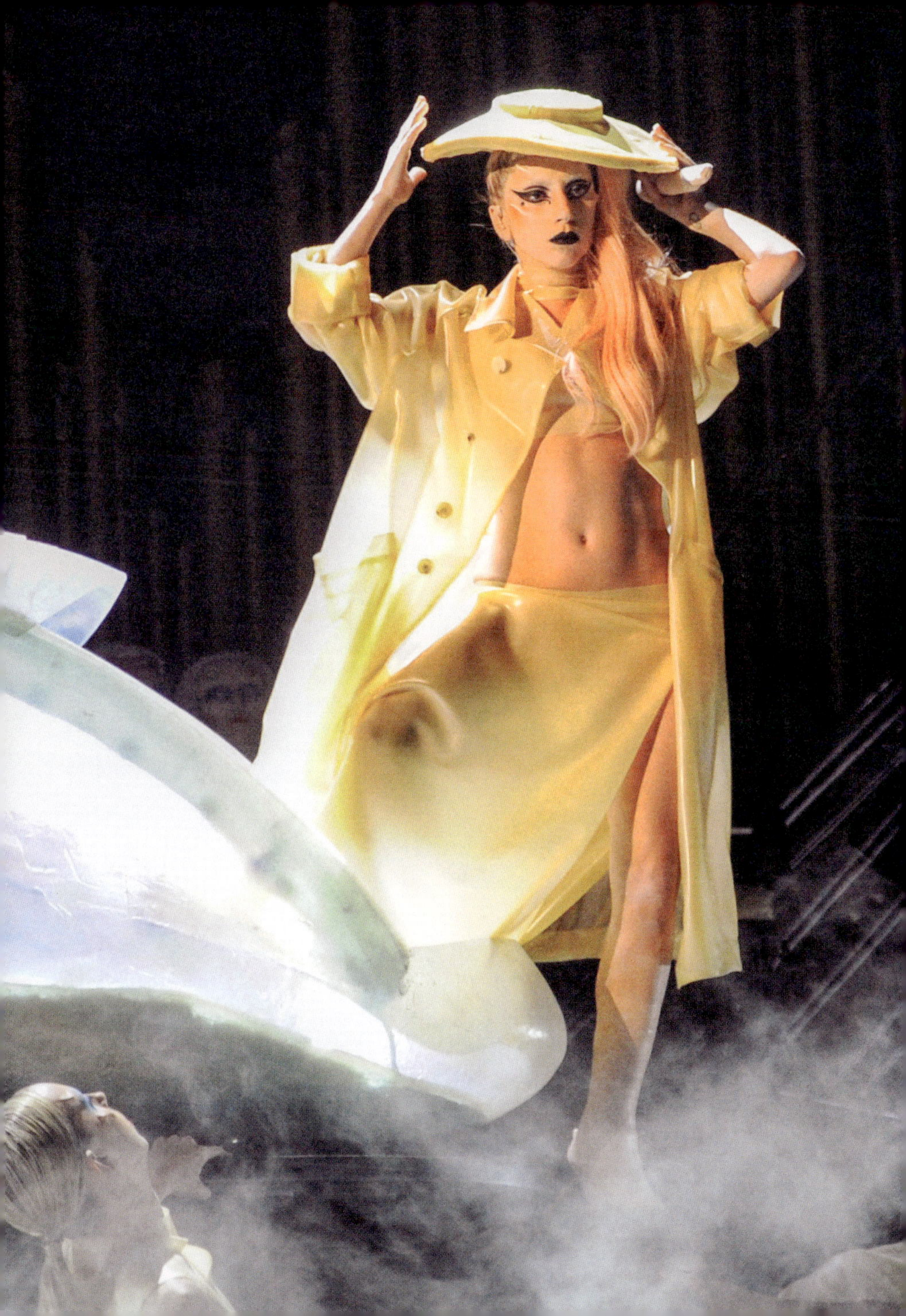

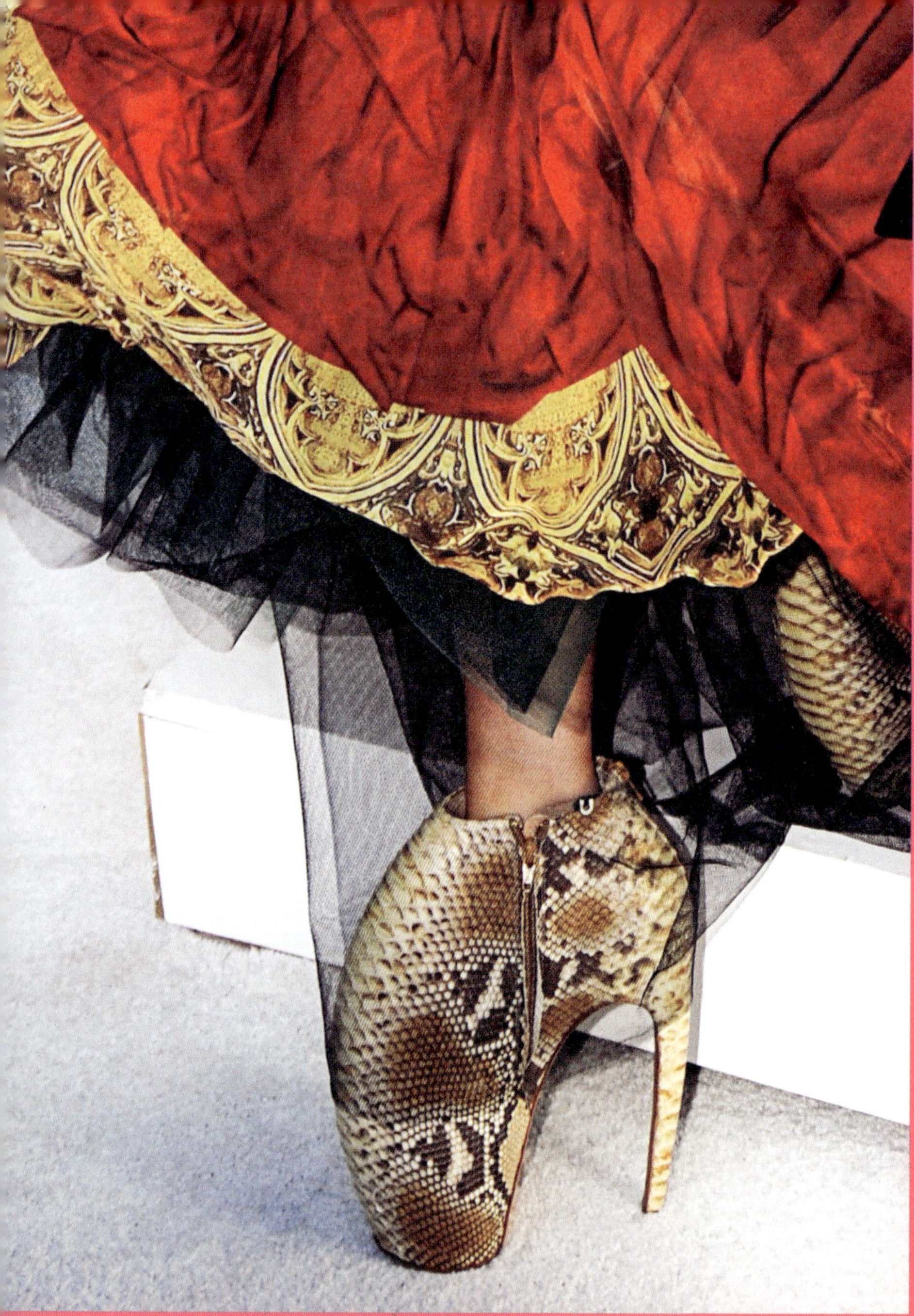

With all the outfit changes and evolutions in her music videos in the mid 2010s, Lady Gaga changed the public's perception of what a music video was through the lens of fashion. Take, for example, her nearly 14-minute-long 'Marry the Night' music video which debuted in 2011. She starts out in a hospital gown and is then shown nude, in a ballerina costume covered in embellished denim, in black leather and more. "We were looking at it as more of a fashion story in a magazine," Nicola Formichetti, her stylist, told *Paper* in 2019. "Every shot is a different outfit. We really went into the extreme of it. That time was very important – the fashion and the photographers and film directors, from Nick Knight to Steven Klein and Inez & Vinoodh. We really worked with them to elevate the whole thing. It was like an orgasm."

With all the extreme dressing in her videos, Lady Gaga kept up an equally dramatic approach in public. For the 2011 Grammys, for example, she was carried down the stairs inside a vessel shaped like an egg, designed by Hussein Chalayan. The team who carried her all wore beige latex, which was sourced by unusual means. "Where we found this latex was a bus company had latex that they were using to cover the seats of their buses and we found the latex and we asked if we could buy it from them," Gaga explained in a video interview. "So everybody's fashion that's made here was made from the fabric from seats for a bus." When Gaga emerged, she wore a skin-coloured latex crop top and matching bottoms, her hair tied back tightly in a high ponytail.

Lady Gaga wears pieces directly from the runway, like these famous Alexander McQueen shoes.

For her other public appearances in 2010 and 2011, Lady Gaga opted for some of the most avant-garde designers, spearheaded by her stylist at the time, Nicola Formichetti. During this period of her career she wore iconic items that would later be remembered as important pieces in the canon of fashion history. Like the Armadillo heels donned at the 2010 MTV VMAs, from Alexander McQueen's very last collection, "Plato's Atlantis". To match, she wore a dress from the same collection, complete with golden feathers on top of her hair.

She also continued to push the boundaries of the music and fashion world. For the 2011 MTV VMAs, Lady Gaga opened up the show as her male alter ego Jo Calderone. First seen in her music video for 'You and I', the character was an amalgamation of stereotypical male cultural figures, including James Dean, Elvis and the classic Italian-American male cliché. Wearing a dirty white T-shirt with oversized black trousers, a big suit jacket and thick black hair gelled back, Calderone was typically seen smoking and posing in hyper-masculine ways.

Before the late designer's death, Gaga frequently collaborated with Alexander McQueen, wearing his experimental, editorially leaning looks on the red carpet and at awards shows.

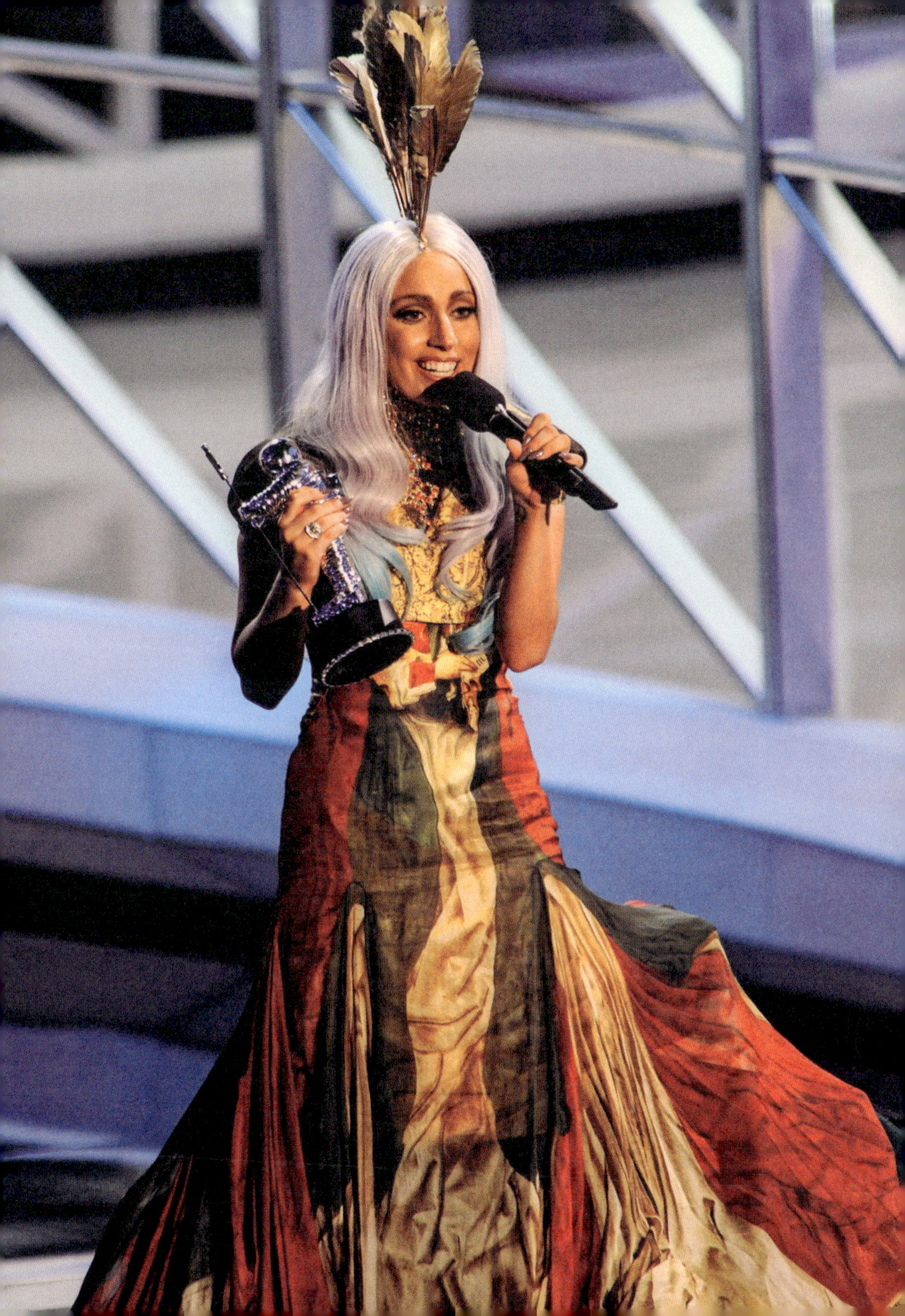

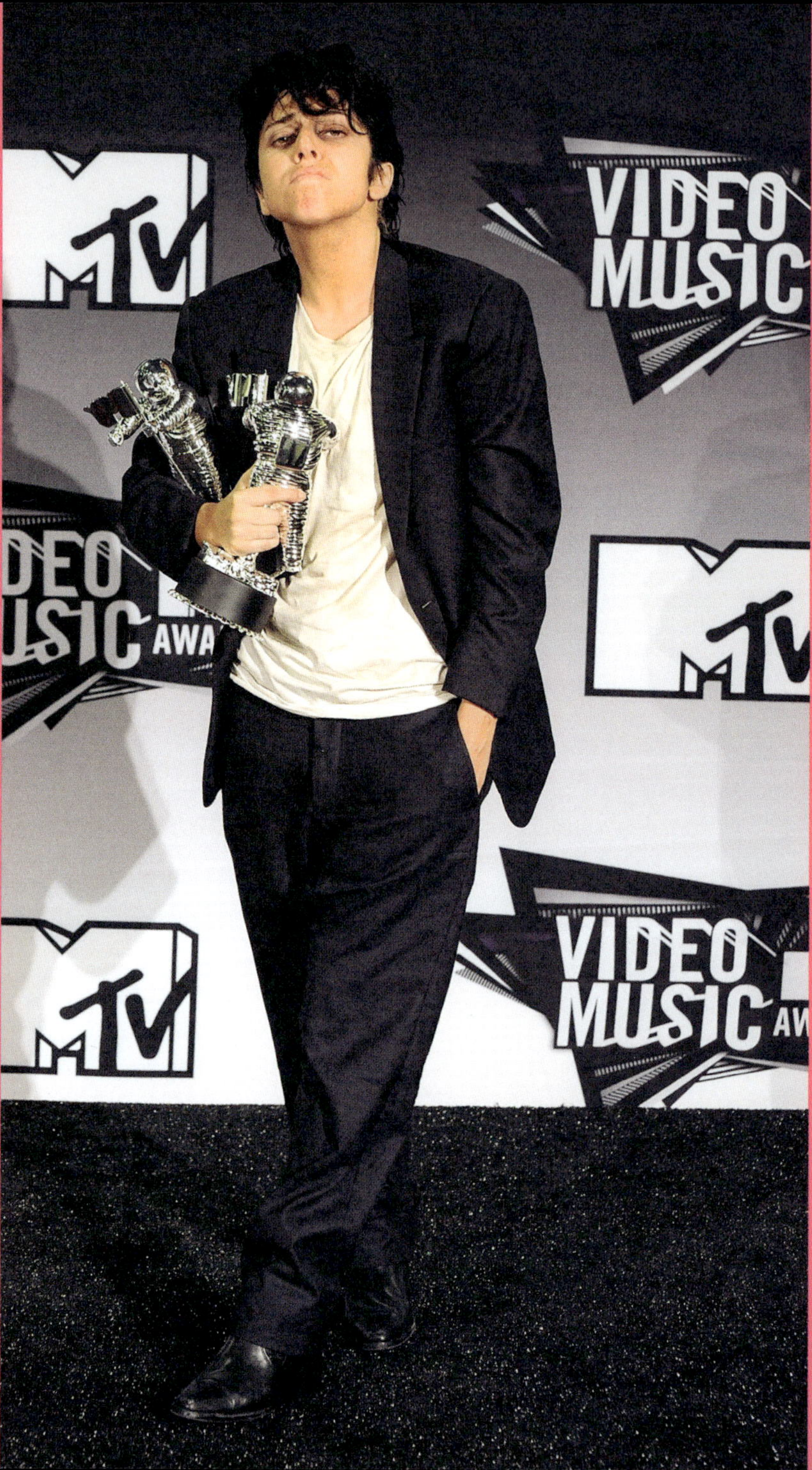
VIDEO
MUSIC
VIDEO
MUSIC
VIDEO
MUSIC

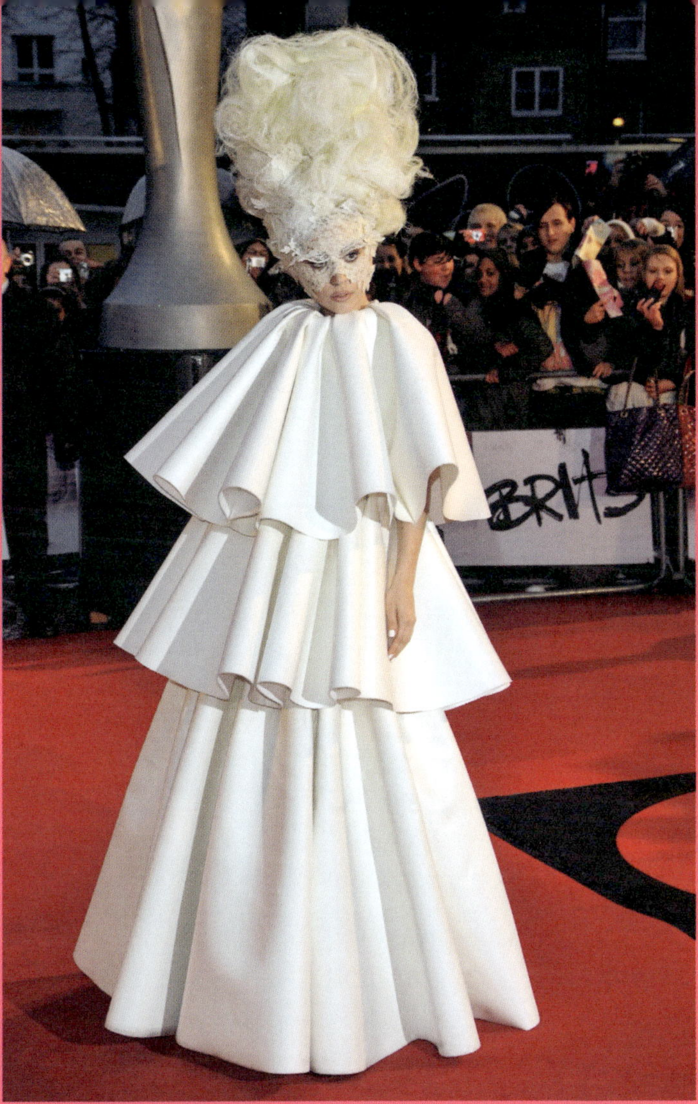

ABOVE Lady Gaga loves an outfit change. For most of her awards shows and concerts, she showcases many different looks, as seen here at the BRIT Awards in 2010.

OPPOSITE For the 2011 MTV VMAs, Lady Gaga posed as her male alter ego, Jo Calderone, wearing a low-key, casual look that was at the opposite end of the spectrum to her normal wardrobe.

The queen of pop (fashion)

Lady Gaga was so well-associated with fashion by this time that she was given her own column in *V Magazine* in 2011. "I myself can look at almost any hemline, silhouette, beadwork or heel architecture and tell you very precisely who designed it first, what French painter they stole it from, how many designers reinvented it after them and what cultural and musical movement parented the birth, death and resurrection of that particular trend," she wrote in her debut article. In the column, she wrote about her experiences with fashion, some of her most intense looks and she also addressed the idea of healthy reinterpretation of past ideas in fashion and culture, referencing examples from the art world.

Around this time, Gaga also solidified her presence as a music figure who was firmly connected to fashion. And the industry was firmly behind her, supporting her as an icon too. At the 2011 Council of Fashion Designers of America (CFDA) Awards, Lady Gaga was named the Fashion Icon of the Year, a huge honour given the CFDA is so deeply connected to the fashion industry. When she accepted the award, she made a joke about how *Vogue*'s Anna Wintour texted her to tell her that she had won the award and she mistakenly thought it was her stylist.

Gaga wearing another iconic Alexander McQueen runway look, at the 2011 Bambi Awards in Germany.

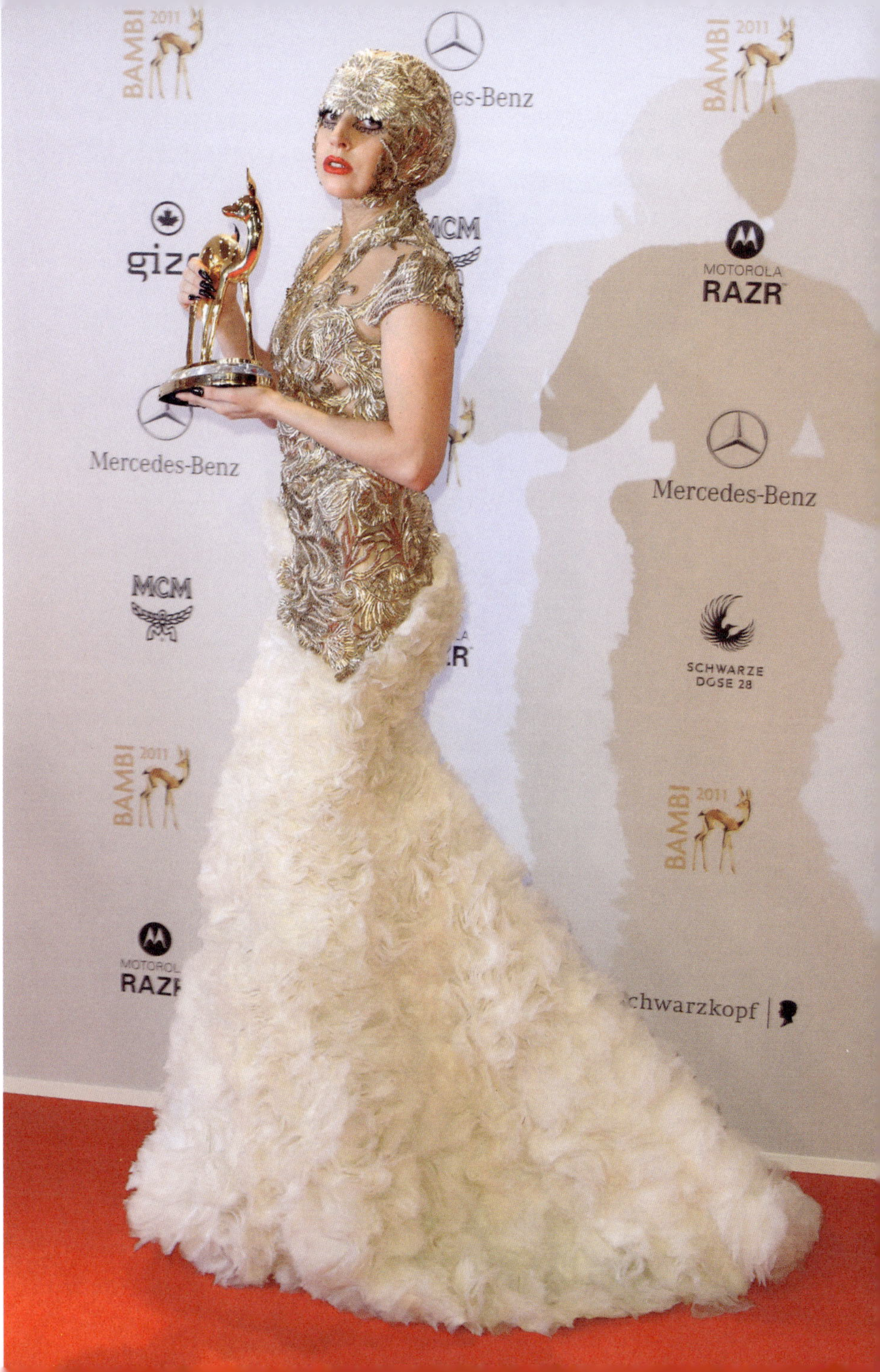
BAMBI 2011
Mercedes-Benz
MOTOROLA
RAZR
MCM
Mercedes-Benz
SCHWARZE
DOSE 28

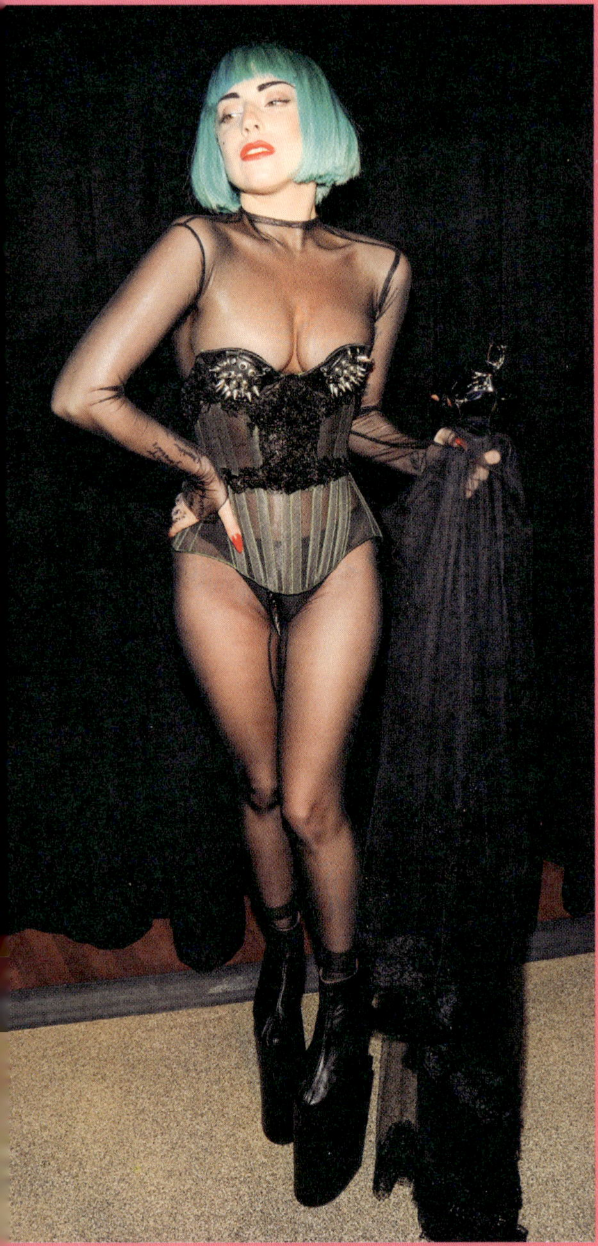

Of course, it wouldn't be a Lady Gaga public appearance without a dramatic look, and for the CFDA Awards, she firmly leaned into her title as fashion icon. She wore a sculptural black Mugler dress with a sheer layer underneath, which exposed lots of skin throughout the event. The dress was designed by her stylist Nicola Formichetti, who was also working at Mugler as the creative director at the time. Stylist Anna Trevelyan also styled her for the event. It was a full circle moment; in her acceptance speech Gaga reminisced on saving up to buy vintage Mugler when she was younger. She also mentioned fashion as it relates to her fans during her acceptance speech: "They wake up in the morning, and it's their leather jacket that makes them feel like they can be anyone. Or it's that YSL blazer that they saw in the window that makes them feel like they could be president one day," she added.

Lady Gaga also scored her first ever *Vogue* cover in 2011, which was a huge moment for her in terms of cementing her achievements in fashion. Previously, she appeared in the December 2009 issue alongside Andrew Garfield and Lily Cole, photographed by the legendary Annie Leibovitz for a whimsical Hansel and Gretel-inspired shoot. With her powdery pastel-pink, flapper-inspired bob, Gaga wore some of the most incredible runway looks from Alexander McQueen for her debut cover.

For the 2011 CFDA Awards, Lady Gaga switched it up with a green bob and a runway Mugler look.

"I want to be your cool older sister who you feel really connected with, who you feel understands you and refuses to judge anything about you because she's been there."

LADY GAGA

She was introduced to fans but also a whole new crop of fashion lovers. "I am not going to saunter around the stage doing pelvic thrusts and lip-synching," she told *Vogue*. "That's not at all why I am in this. I don't feel spiritually connected to anyone in Hollywood makeup and a gown with diamond earrings on. I am just a different breed. I want to be your cool older sister who you feel really connected with, who you feel understands you and refuses to judge anything about you because she's been there."

Just a year later, Gaga would return as the *Vogue* cover star for the September 2012 issue – *Vogue*'s 120th anniversary. In October 2018, she celebrated her first lead role in the film, *A Star Is Born*, and 10 years in the music industry by starring on the cover of *Vogue* once again, and she returned yet again in September 2024 as cover star.

In her *ARTPOP* era, Lady Gaga used every public opportunity as a way to transform into her eccentrically dressed characters. While on tour to promote the album, she would create incredibly dramatic looks for events as simple as leaving her hotel. Many of these outfits also involved extreme hair and make-up. Above all else, Gaga was inspired by the concept of interpreting art in your own way. She also pulled direct references from some of the prominent art figures throughout history and incorporated them into her looks. For example, at one time she had bright yellow hair, inspired by the sixties pop artist Roy Lichtenstein's depictions of blonde women with bright yellow hair. Patti Song was Lady Gaga's colourist and Frederic Aspiras was the wigmaker and hairstylist responsible for the look at the time.

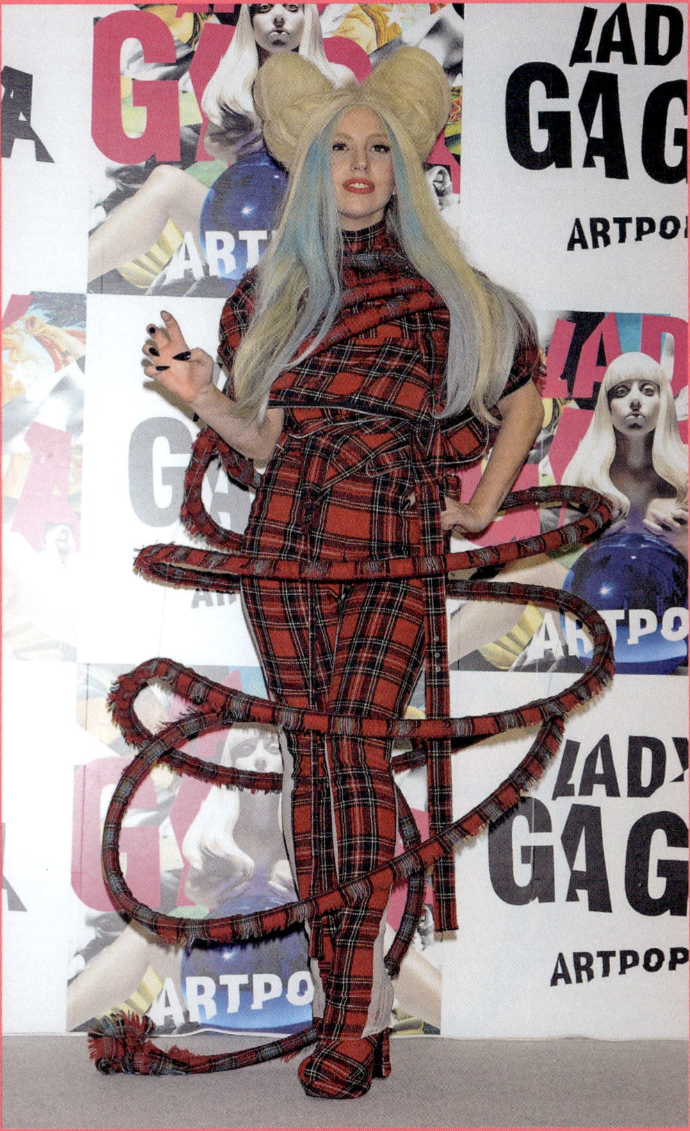

While promoting her 2013 *ARTPOP* album, Gaga's fashion became even more extreme, as seen here in Tokyo.

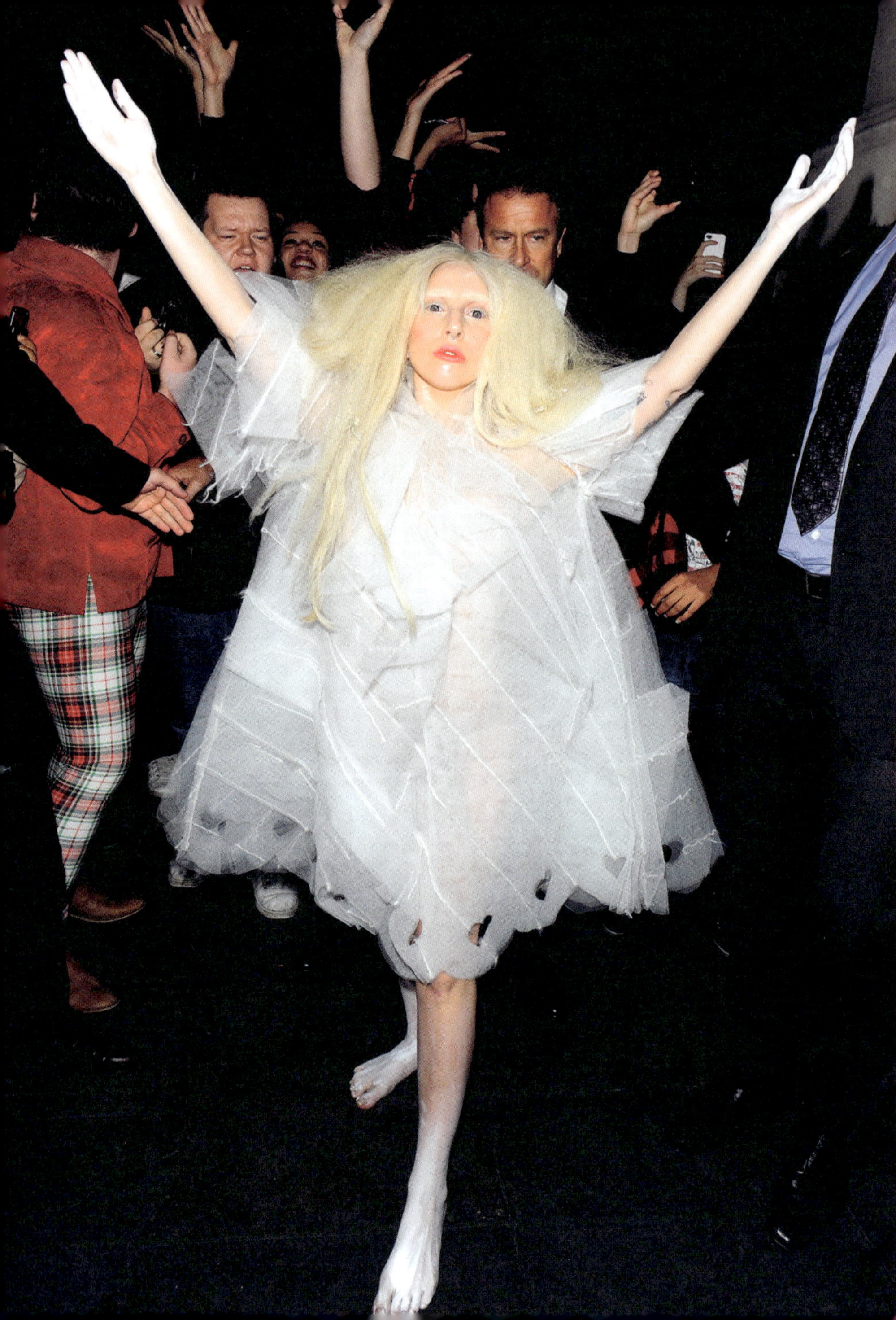

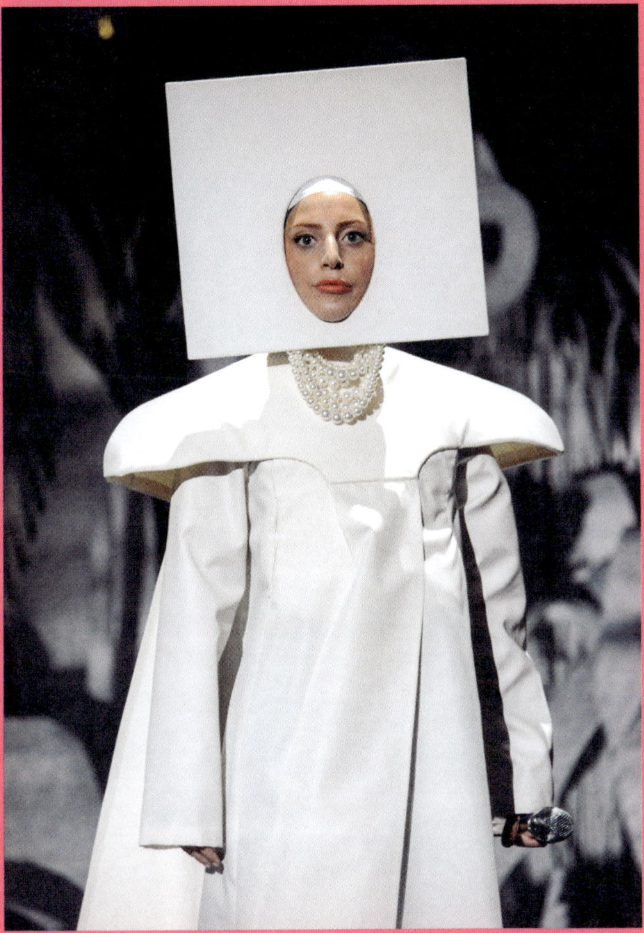

ABOVE At the 2013 VMAs, Gaga wore an art-inspired white outfit, with a headpiece to match.

OPPOSITE For a visit to Berlin in 2013, Lady Gaga wore a ghostly white gown, matching make-up and no shoes.

For one occasion in London, Gaga left her hotel wearing a full face of distorted make-up by make-up artist Tara Savelo, inspired by a Picasso painting. Accompanying this, she wore a painterly sweatshirt from the edgy streetwear shop Dog in Tokyo, a pink skirt and ruffled socks. While in Japan to promote her *ARTPOP* album in 2013, Gaga continued her tradition of bringing art to the forefront of fashion with outfits that were extremely over-the-top. In one instance, she surrounded herself with multiple lifelike dolls in various outfits and entered the stage wearing a sculptural plaid outfit, dimensional hair cones and her signature huge sunglasses. Her outfits during this promotional period in Japan were incredibly theatrical, each one becoming more and more expressive than the last.

In 2013, Gaga was working with Versace as a brand ambassador and took her role to the next level by bringing to life a look inspired by the advert she did for the brand's Spring/Summer 2014 campaign. For the 2013 American Music Awards, she arrived on a massive white mechanical horse. Wearing a long lilac gown with her lovely white-blonde hair flowing, she resembled a fairy tale come to life. At the time, the star was known for shocking to the extreme with her outfit choices, but she also showed she could make just as much as an impact with an exciting entrance. In a video interview, Gaga said that the horse itself was actually made out of Chanel bags.

Gaga's 2013 *ARTPOP* album was a tribute to living art and while promoting it, she wore a look inspired by Picasso, right down to the make-up.

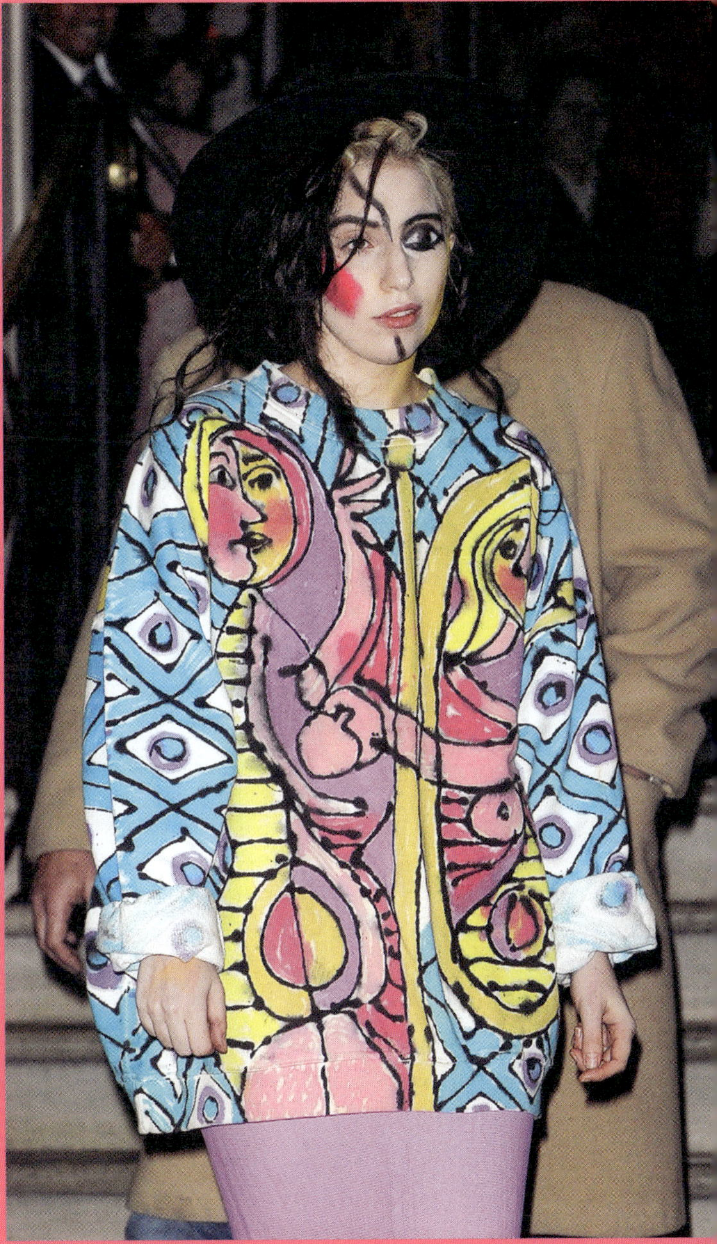

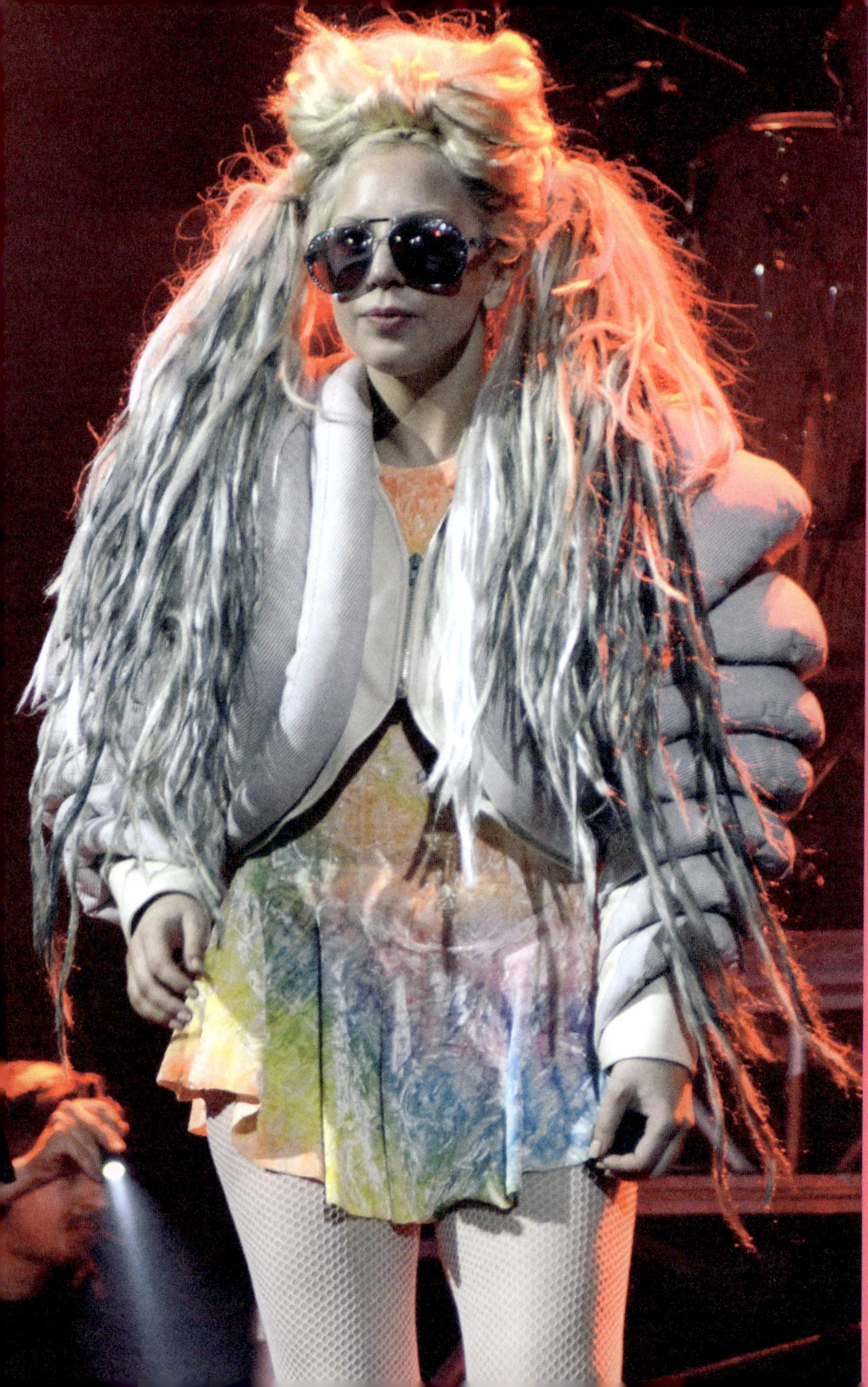

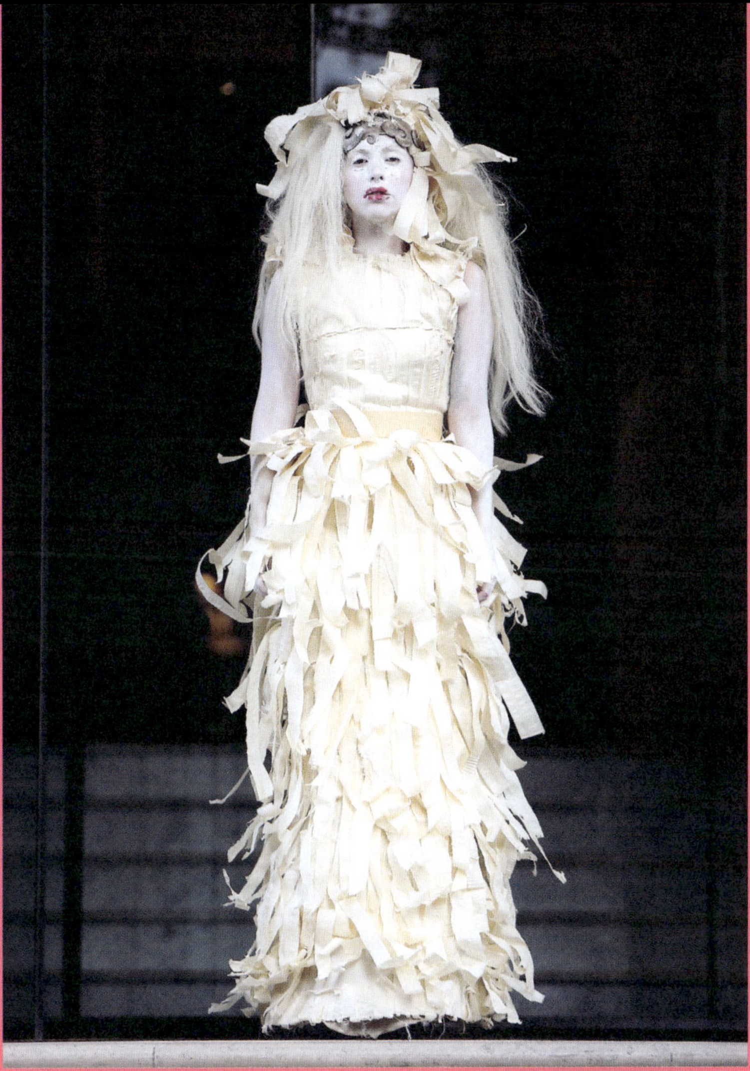

OPPOSITE In 2014, Lady Gaga performed at SXSW in Austin, Texas, and shocked the audience with her unconventional fashion choices.

ABOVE In 2013, while promoting her *ARTPOP* album, Lady Gaga would often leave her hotel in art-inspired looks, as seen here in London.

OVERLEAF Gaga took her role as an ambassador for Versace with enormous gravitas, wearing a purple gown by the brand while riding a massive fake horse at the American Music Awards (AMAs) in 2013.

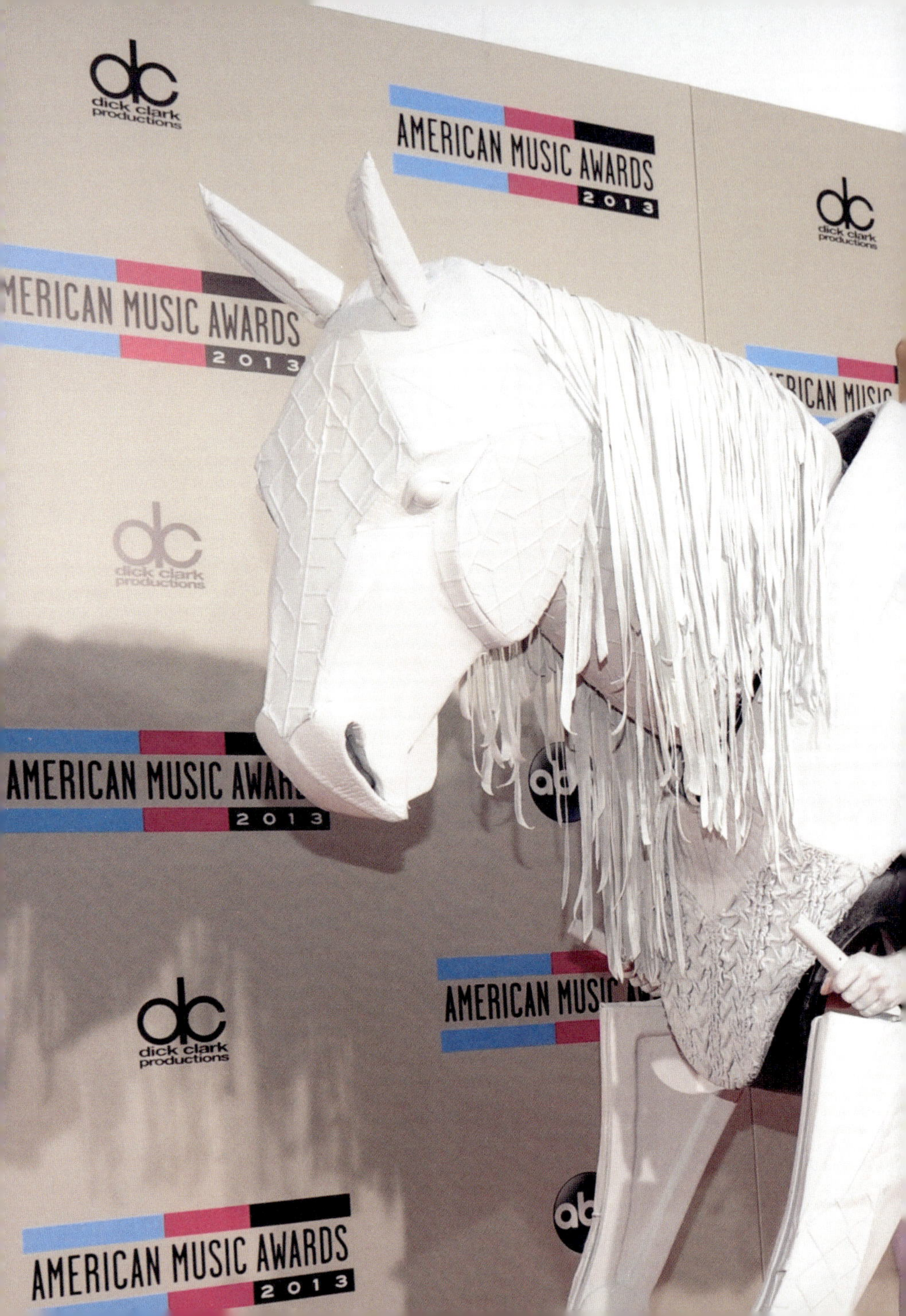
dick clark productions
AMERICAN MUSIC AWARDS 2013
dick clark productions
AMERICAN MUSIC AWARDS 2013
dick clark productions
AMERICAN MUSIC AWARDS 2013
dick clark productions
AMERICAN MUSIC AWARDS 2013

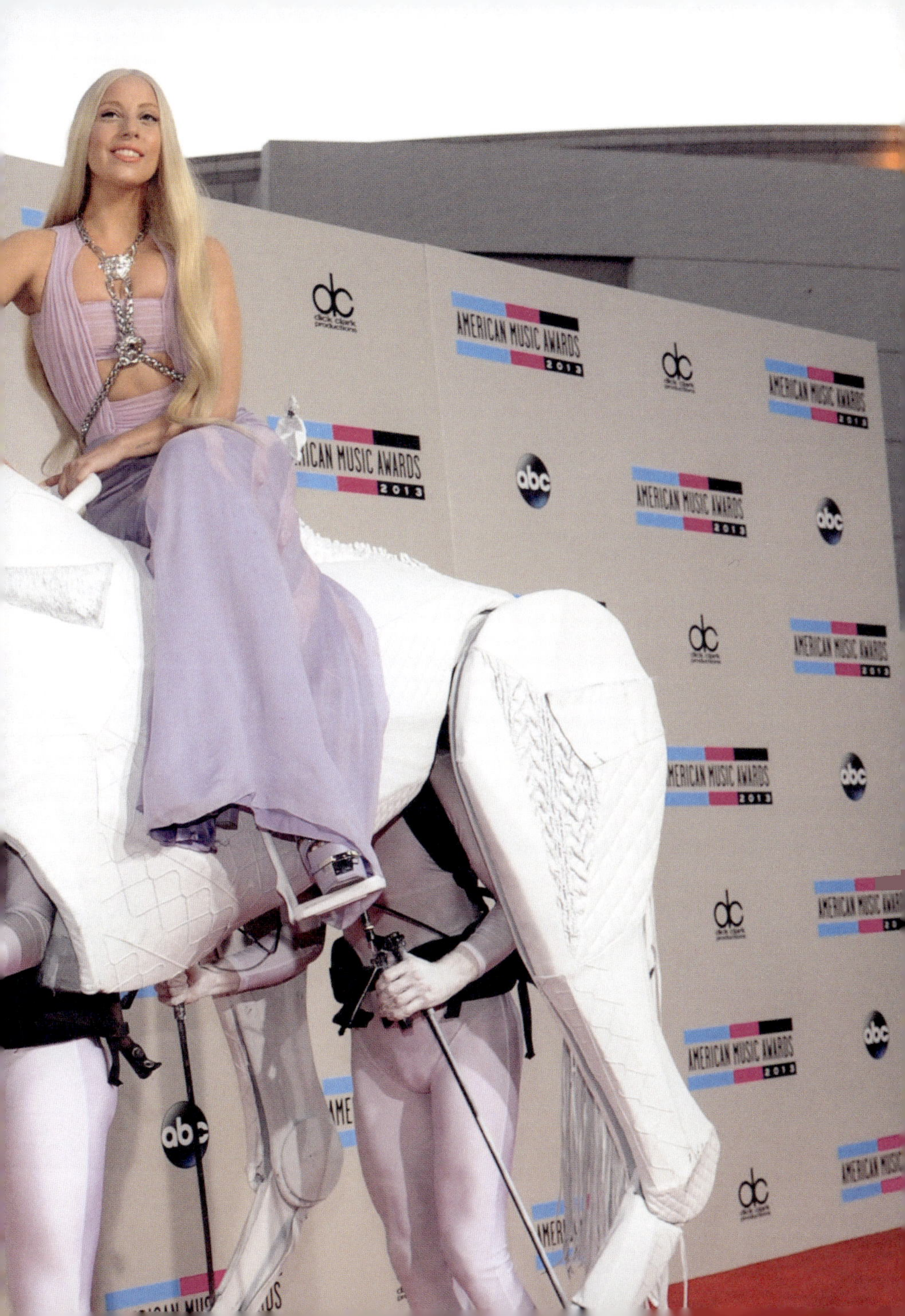
AMERICAN MUSIC AWARDS
2013
abc
dc

"I myself can look at almost [anything] and tell you very precisely who designed it first, what French painter they stole it from, how many designers reinvented it."

LADY GAGA

Gaga took her *ARTPOP* era literally at times, often wearing pieces inspired by real works of art, such as *The Mona Lisa*.

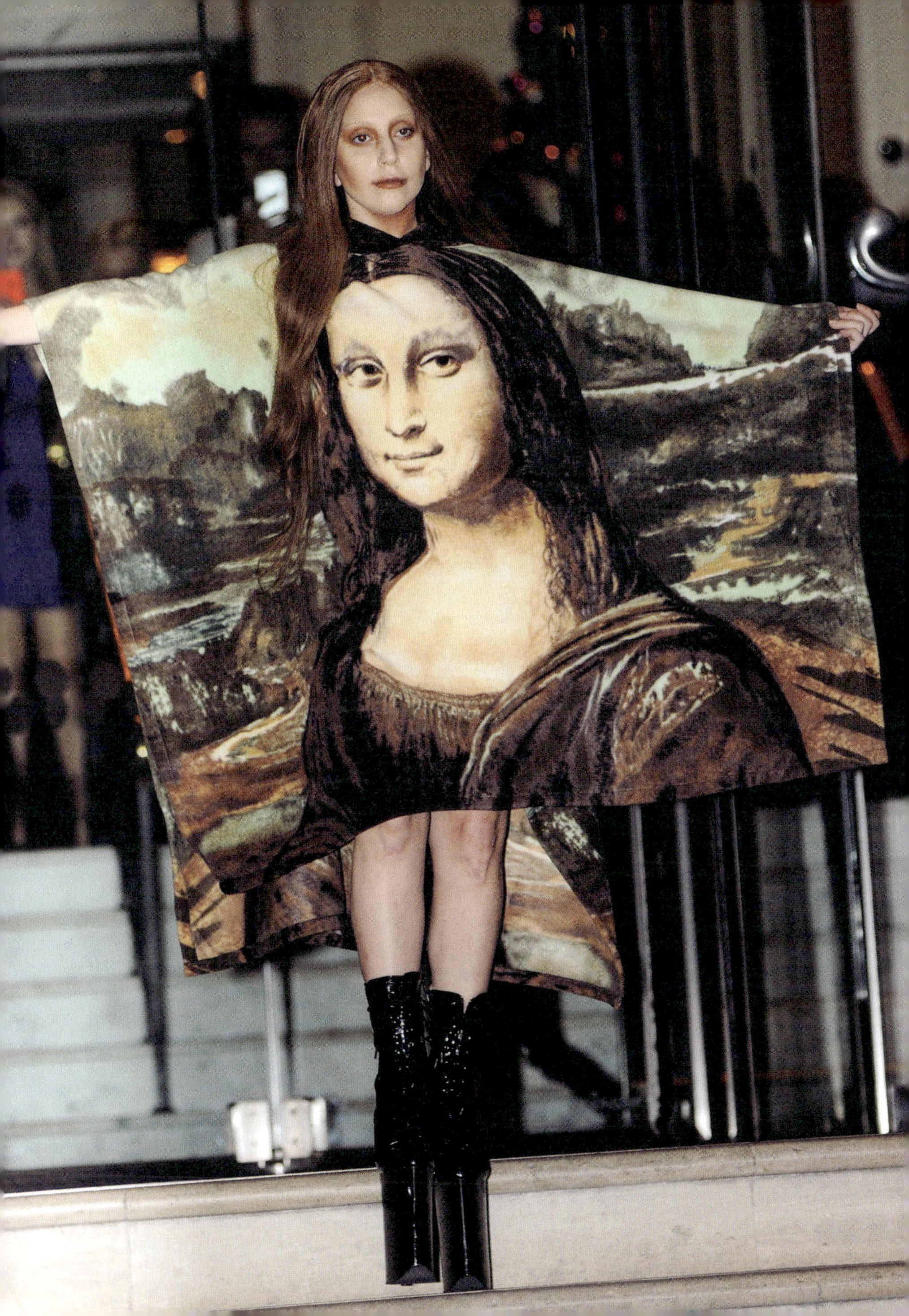

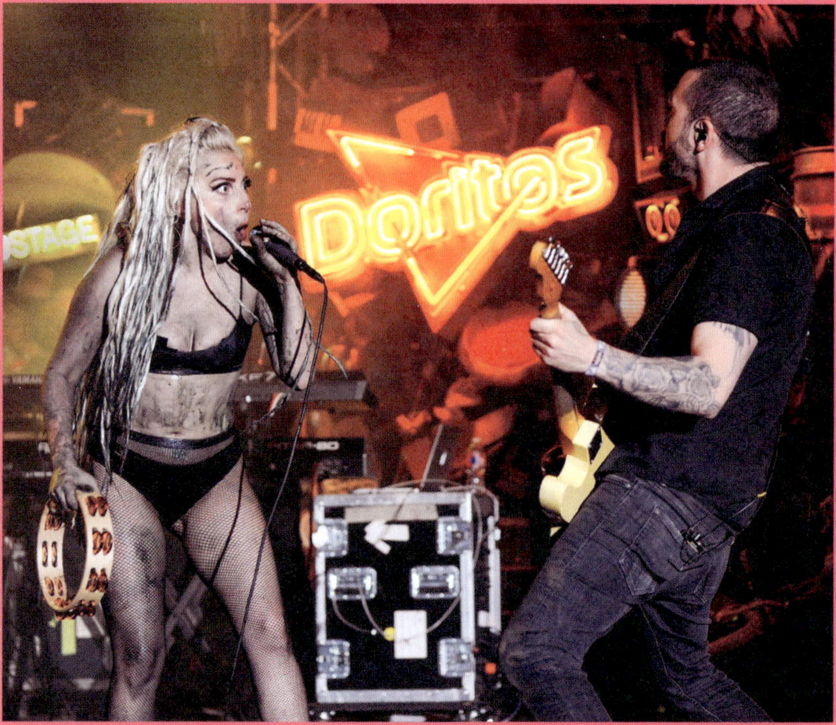

In 2014 while performing at SXSW in Austin, Texas, Lady Gaga merged fashion with performance art and looked back to her original underwear-as-outerwear outfits.

Fashion as performance art

In 2014, the *ARTPOP* era reached peak fashion-meets-art. Gaga staged a performance at the South by Southwest (SXSW) music festival for her song 'Swine' and it may have been one of her most controversial to date. She was carried onto the stage horizontally on a pole, wearing black underwear and fishnet stockings, as if to mimic a pig being roasted. During the performance, the "vomit artist" Millie Brown expelled green soy milk all over Gaga. The moment sparked criticism and shock from some people online.

In 2014, Gaga also introduced her tour, ArtRave: The Artpop Ball, which combined her eclectic sense of fashion with her totally over-the-top sensibilities at the time. Before the official tour, she hosted a two-day promotional event in Brooklyn Navy Yard in New York called ArtRave to celebrate the album and showcase fashion that bridged the worlds of art and style together. Prominent artist Jeff Koons designed a statue of Gaga for the occasion, which was stationed at the event. The fashion was at the centre of it all: Lady Gaga debuted "the world's first flying dress", dubbed the TechHaus Volantis. As the singer stood on the stage, she was strapped into a bustier-style corset and started levitating across the stage.

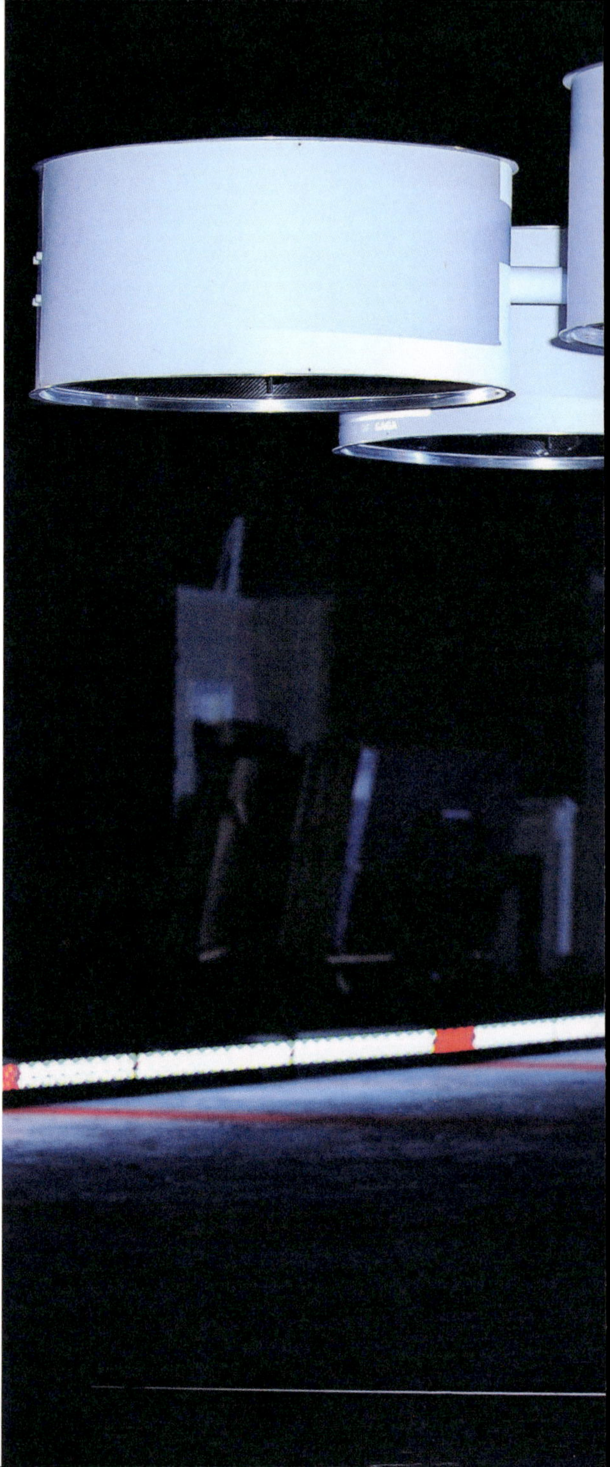

Lady Gaga debuted "the world's first flying dress", dubbed the TechHaus Volantis, as she took flight in 2014.

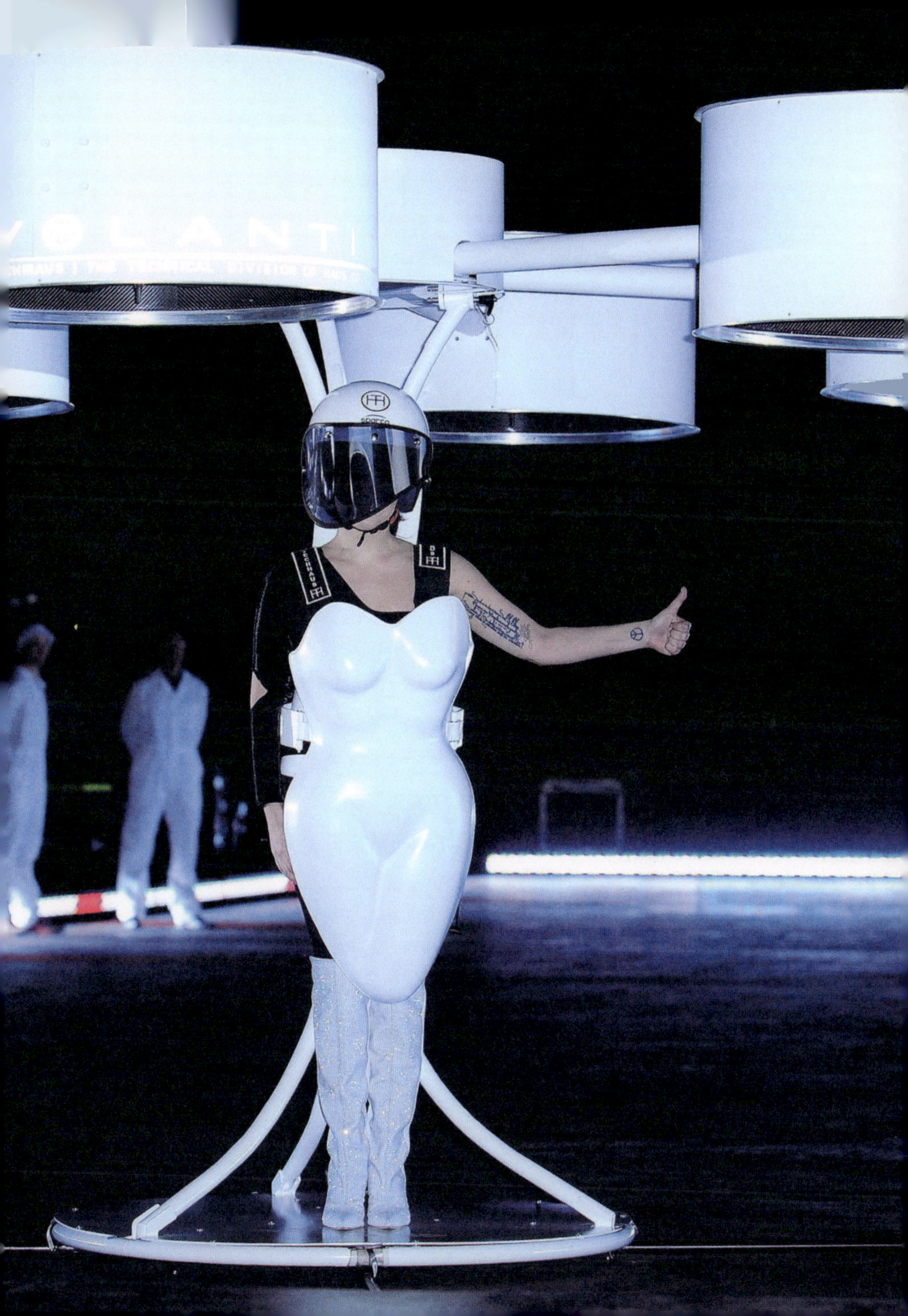
VOLANTI

For the actual tour itself, Lady Gaga wore pieces that verged on costume – some of the most extreme looks she's ever worn, such as giant inflatable pieces that took up space and transformed her into a majestic creature. She was reportedly inspired by the clothing and personal style of the original club kids when it came to her wardrobe for this particular tour. Club kids of the nineties in New York and London would typically make their own out-of-this-world outfits using what they had and found objects. Performance artists like the London-based Leigh Bowery (1961–94) led the movement, with colourful and surreal make-up and hair to match. Another one of Gaga's highly memorable moments included a holographic silver inflatable spiked dress designed by Jack Irving. In order to keep the structure of the dress, an air ventilation system was used to pump air into it. Gaga purposely used the look to her advantage, stepping out of the car with it not inflated and pushing a button to have the spikes go up in front of the waiting paparazzi.

The costumes for Lady Gaga's ArtRave: The Artpop Ball tour were overseen by fashion director Brandon Maxwell and costume designer Perry Meek, with a dose of heavy-hitting high fashion woven in. Maxwell would later launch his career as a fashion designer, but he got his start working on Gaga's team, later spearheading some of her most iconic looks of all time (more on that later). She opened the show wearing an Atelier Versace golden rococo-style angel costume replete with wings by Living Art of Armando and a shining gazing ball designed by the artist Jeff Koons. Her opening looks changed slightly based on the different cities she visited and the rest of her tour outfits had an equally extreme angle.

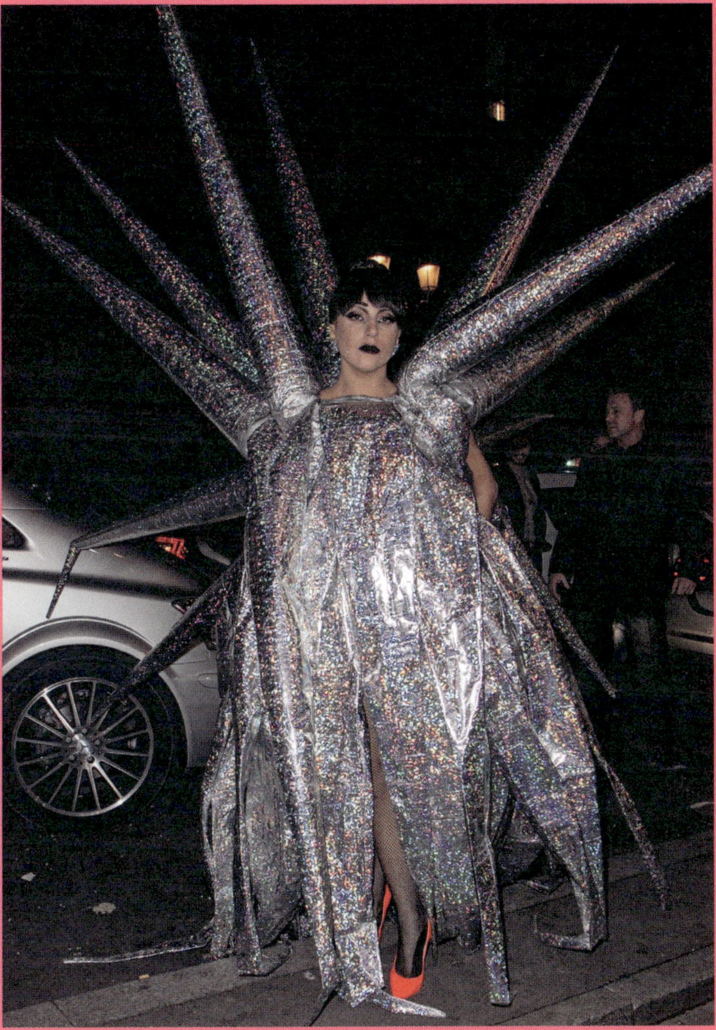

ABOVE Gaga has always supported emerging designers. Here, she wears a Jack Irving inflatable dress.

OVERLEAF In her *ARTPOP* era, Lady Gaga started working with the stylist Brandon Maxwell, who put her in this Atelier Versace golden rococo-style angel costume.

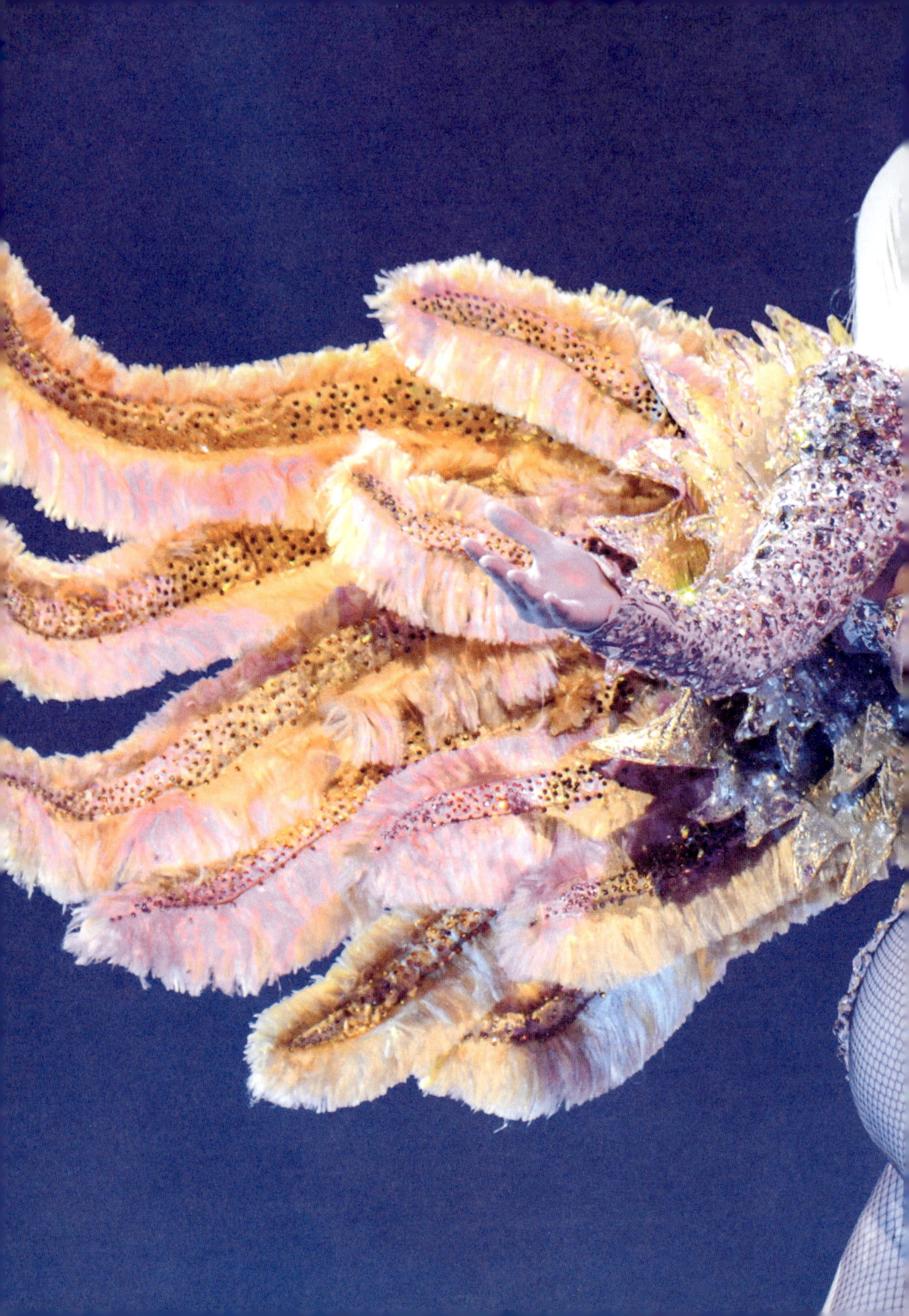

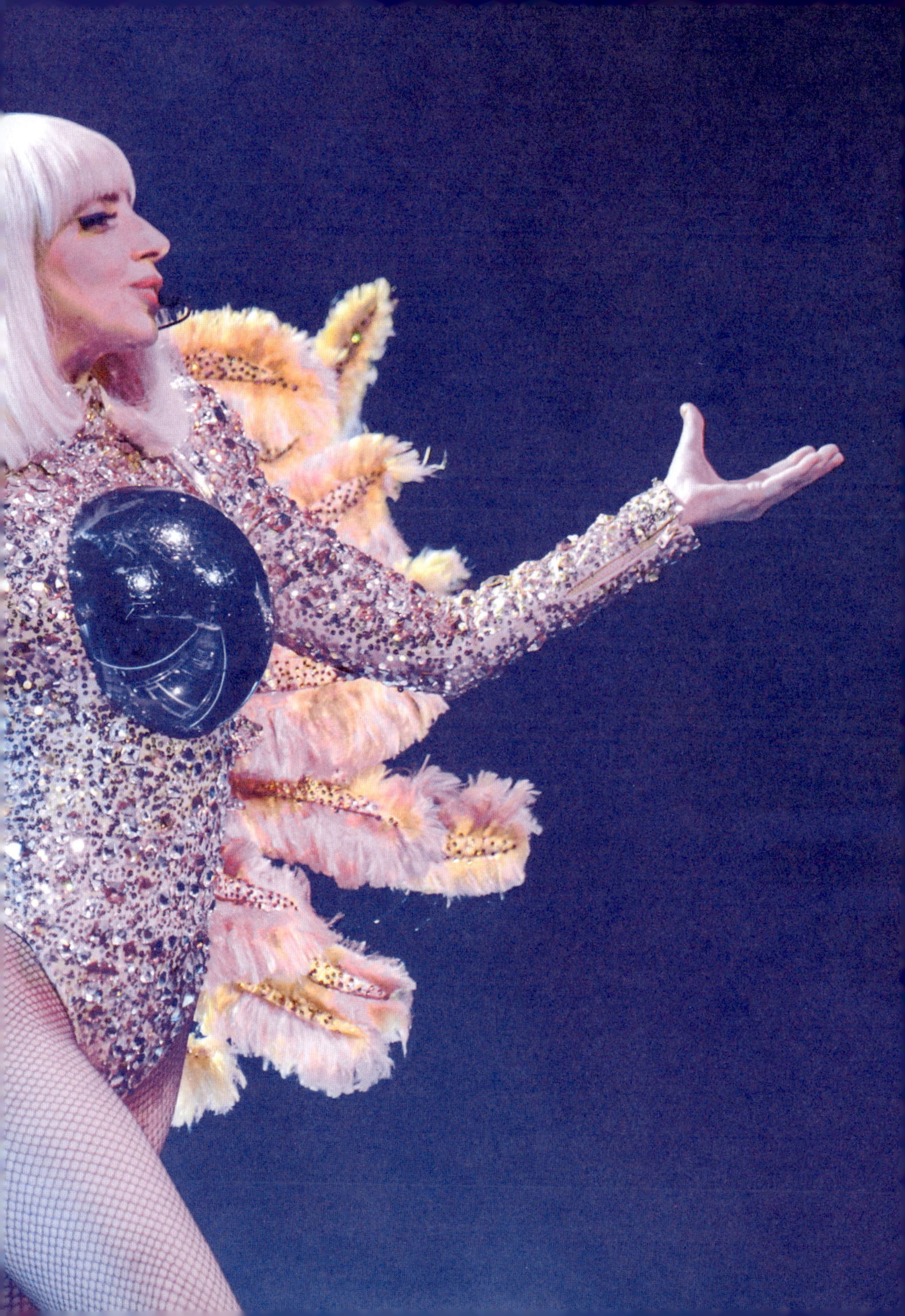

"I don't really care if people say I look beautiful*, or people say I look* sexy*, or people say I look* desirable.

It's not really the point, because I'm an artist and I'm enjoying expressing my music through my clothes."

LADY GAGA

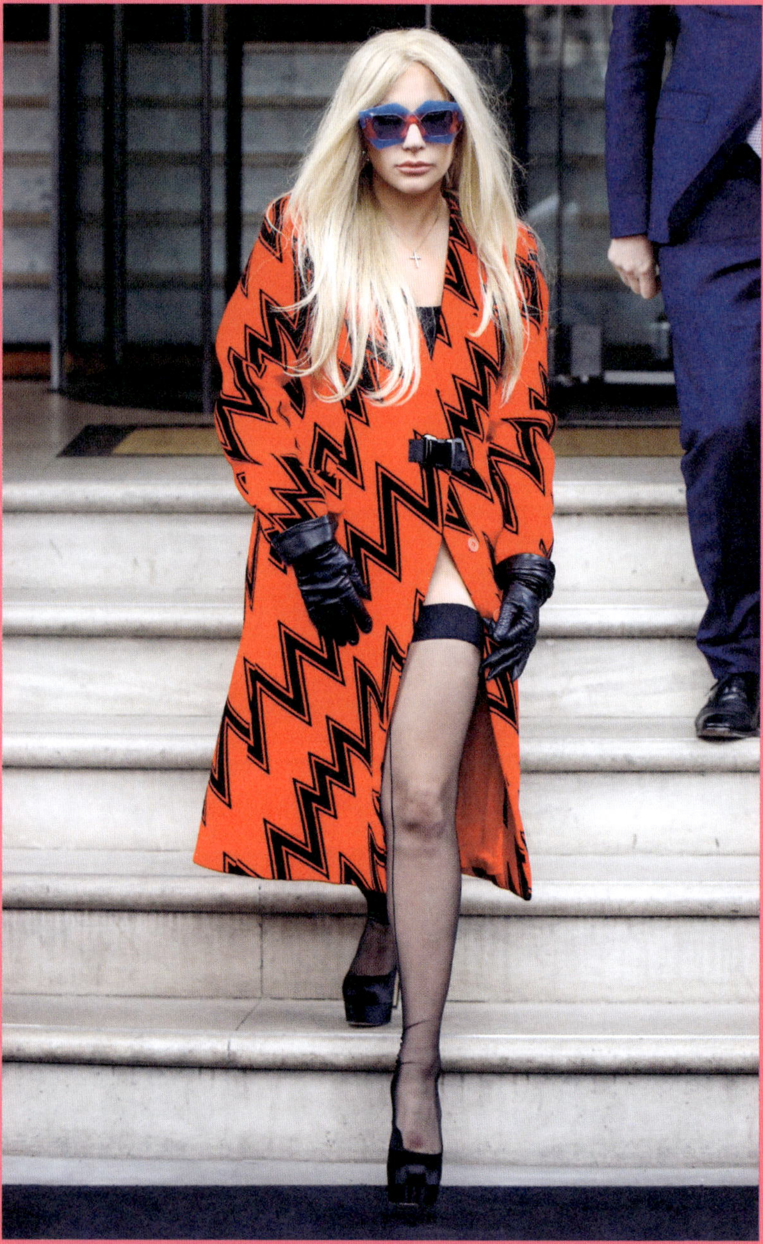

With a massive beehive swathe of hair, Lady Gaga transformed her typical look of underwear into a vintage-inspired seashell bikini set with black fishnet tights. Her other outfits for the rest of the set during this tour included a mash-up of Gaga classics that broke the boundaries and challenged the conventional ideals of fashion. Glitzy bodysuits, retro, futuristic-inspired gowns by Versace and plenty of latex were all in the mix. Most memorable were the aforementioned inflatable dresses and tentacle-like headpieces. Different versions of these were created by Vex Clothing and Dayne Henderson. From inky black to candy pastel shades of baby blue and powder pink, these art-driven looks had major stage presence and reinforced the concept of camp.

"I don't really care if people say I look beautiful, or people say I look sexy, or people say I look desirable," Gaga said in an interview in 2011 with Gayle King on SiriusXM. "It's not really the point, because I'm an artist and I'm enjoying expressing my music through my clothes. I make all sorts of wild decisions, and that's just part of who I am."

The ArtRave: The Artpop Ball tour continued into 2014, but around the same time, Lady Gaga started to shift her appearance into something more demure and sophisticated for other performances, awards shows and when she was out and about. It made perfect sense: as an artist, Gaga uses her fashion to express herself and transform. What good would that be if she was always the same?

Nearing the end of her *ARTPOP* tour of 2014, Gaga started experimenting with more mainstream and demure fashion for certain occasions.

In 2014, she also released a collaborative album (*Cheek to Cheek*) with the classic singer Tony Bennett, most well-known for his music in the 1980s. This showed her versatility as an artist, going fast almost in the entirely opposite direction away from the avant garde. To go along with Bennett's more traditional, family-friendly branding, Gaga easily transitioned into looks that were less controversial – pretty glittering gold gowns, long white dresses and sometimes even beige sweater sets. "When I came into this with Tony, he didn't say, 'You've got to take off all the crazy outfits and just sing,'" she told *Parade* in 2014. "He said, 'Be yourself.'" She also told *Yahoo Style*, "If you think about it, jazz is the most rebellious form of music. It's totally different from my previous message where there was an intention behind each look. Jazz brings out the fighter in me. The type of clothes that I've been wearing is less form fitting. Other days, I'll wear something more corseted and glamorous. Right now I'm wearing a leather jacket that my sister [Natali Germanotta] made me with Cheek to Cheek painted on the back and piercings and bleached brows."

At the time, it may have felt like the end of an era, but maybe above all else it also proved just how devoted Gaga is to her craft: of rising into something entirely new again and again and again.

While collaborating with the late singer Tony Bennett, Gaga changed her aesthetic to be more in line with Old Hollywood style.

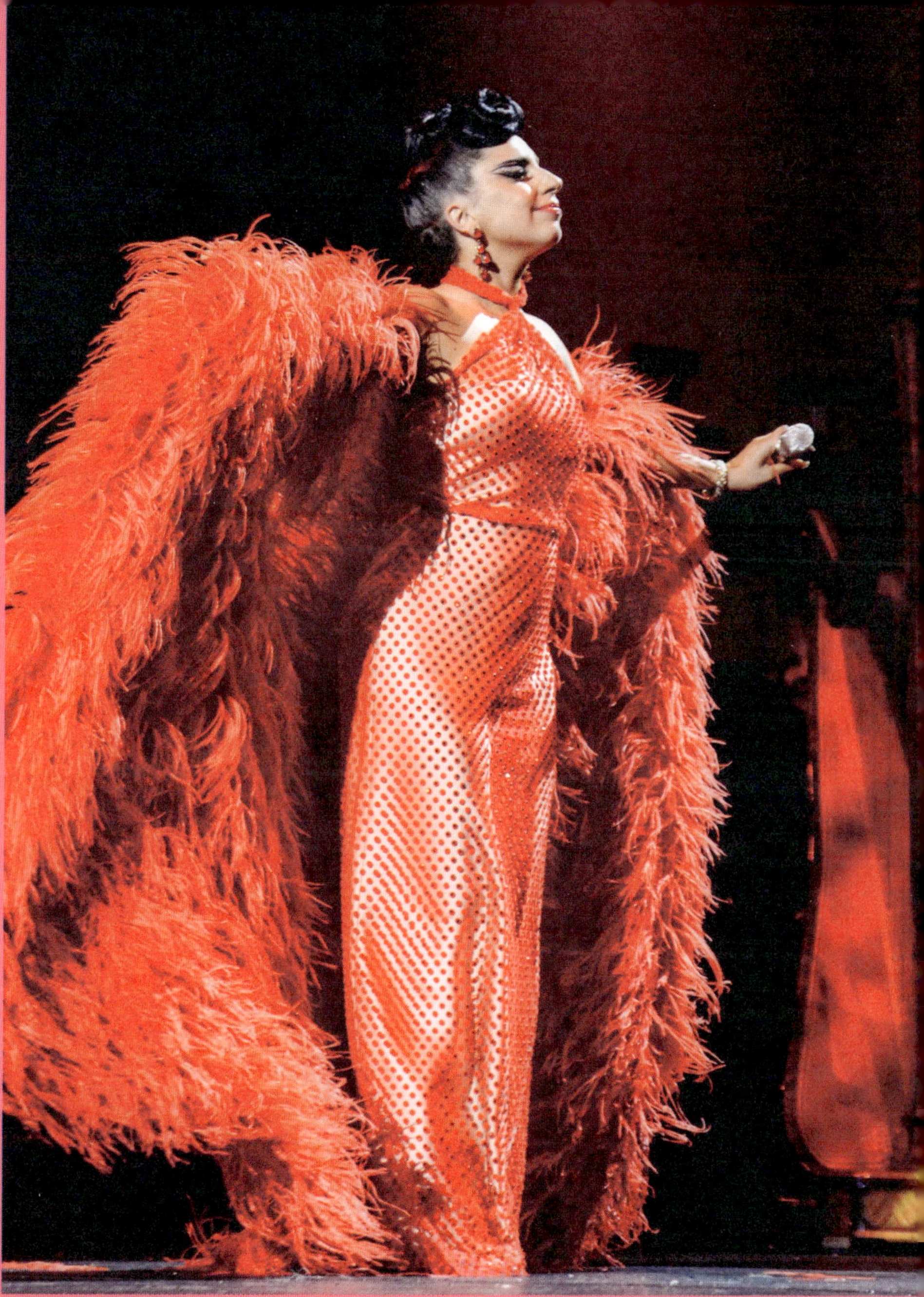

"*Jazz* is the most **rebellious** form of music ... Jazz **brings out** the **fighter** in me.

The type of clothes that I've been wearing is less form fitting. Other days, I'll wear something more corseted and glamorous."

LADY GAGA

A Star

CHAPTER 3

is Born

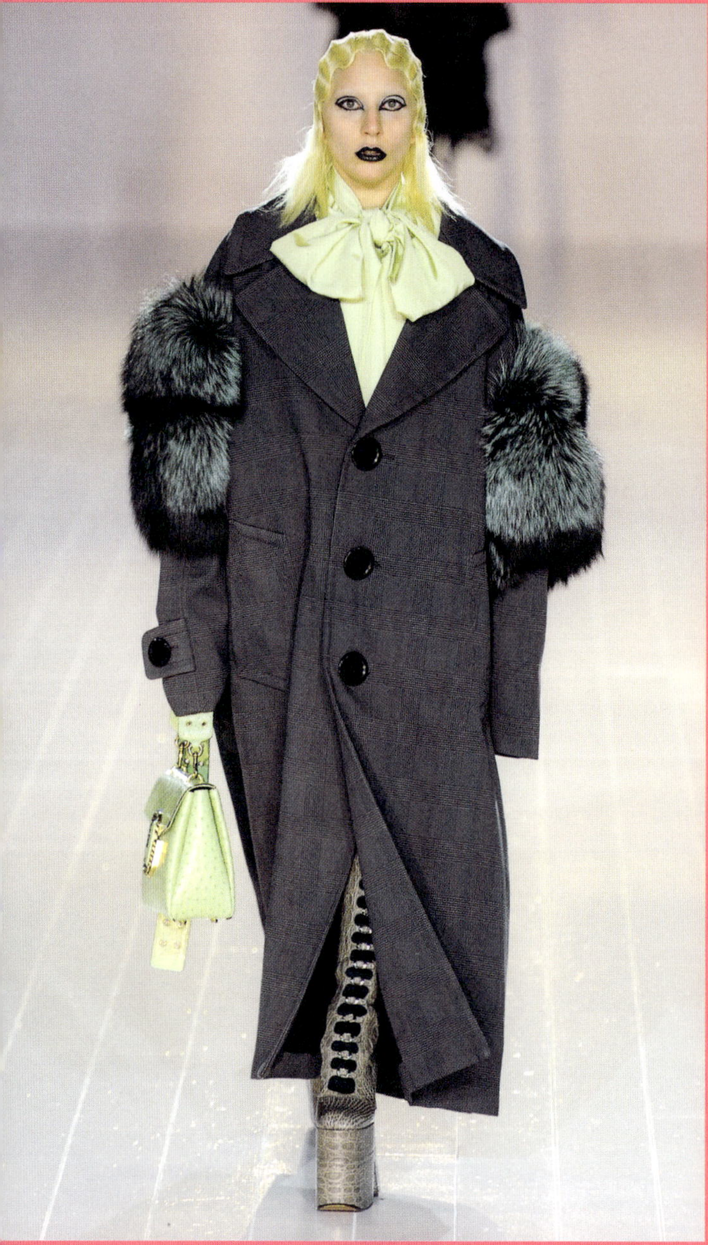

Transcendent fashion

The year was 2016 and Lady Gaga officially arrived as a mainstream major fashion influence. Walking the Marc Jacobs runway in an oversized Victorian-looking coat with a massive bow blouse and huge stomping Kiki heels, Gaga made her debut as a runway model.

The duo previously collaborated when Jacobs dressed her for the 2016 Grammys, inspired by David Bowie no less (more on that later). With a vintage finger wave hairdo, black glossy lipstick and bleached brows, Gaga was every bit as over-the-top as ever and the industry crowd was clearly excited and surprised to see her as a face on the runway alongside favourite models du jour, Binx Walton and Anna Cleveland.

"I told Marc I was disappointed the shoes weren't taller," Gaga joked backstage.

In 2016, Gaga made her runway debut walking for Marc Jacobs.

Off the runway, Lady Gaga continued to evolve her style into something that was less camp and more streamlined, honouring her own authenticity with subtle hints of surreal quirks that only she could pull off. For example, when she wore a custom white Azzedine Alaïa gown to the 2015 Oscars, styled with a pair of coral red wide leather gloves that gave the look that element of wonder and surprise that she's so well-known for.

Or when she honoured David Bowie, one of the artists she has said she has always looked up to, at the 2016 Grammys. Wearing the same shade of signature orange flame-hued hair from Bowie's Ziggy Stardust era, she performed 'Fame', 'Let's Dance' and 'Fashion' alongside guitarist and longtime Bowie collaborator, Nile Rodgers. She wore a bright cobalt blue suit embellished and embroidered by Marc Jacobs, which in its own way also paid tribute to the late, fashionable, eccentric Bowie.

For the 2015 Oscars, Lady Gaga wore a stunning Alaïa gown styled with a pair of coral red wide leather gloves.

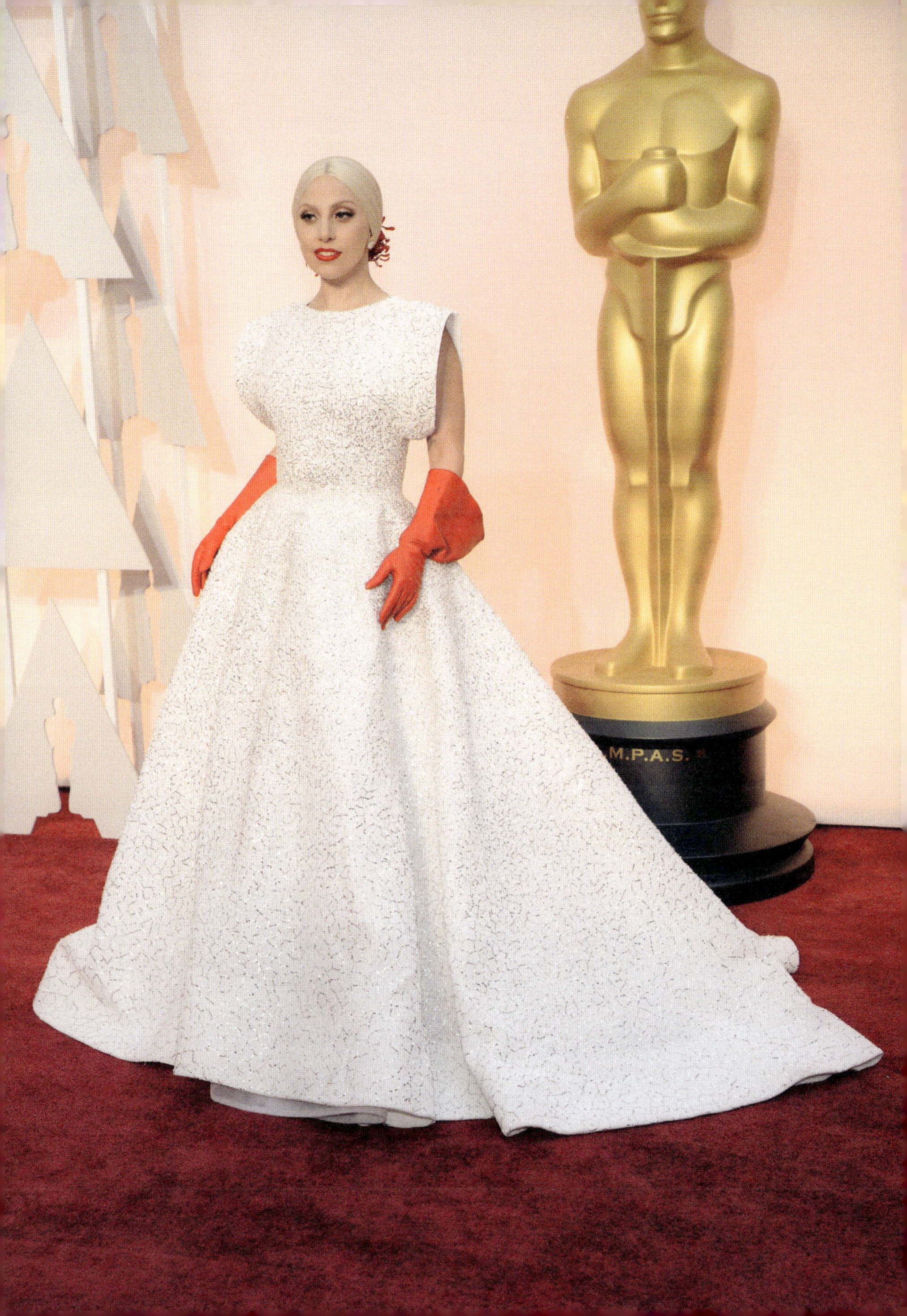
M.P.A.S.

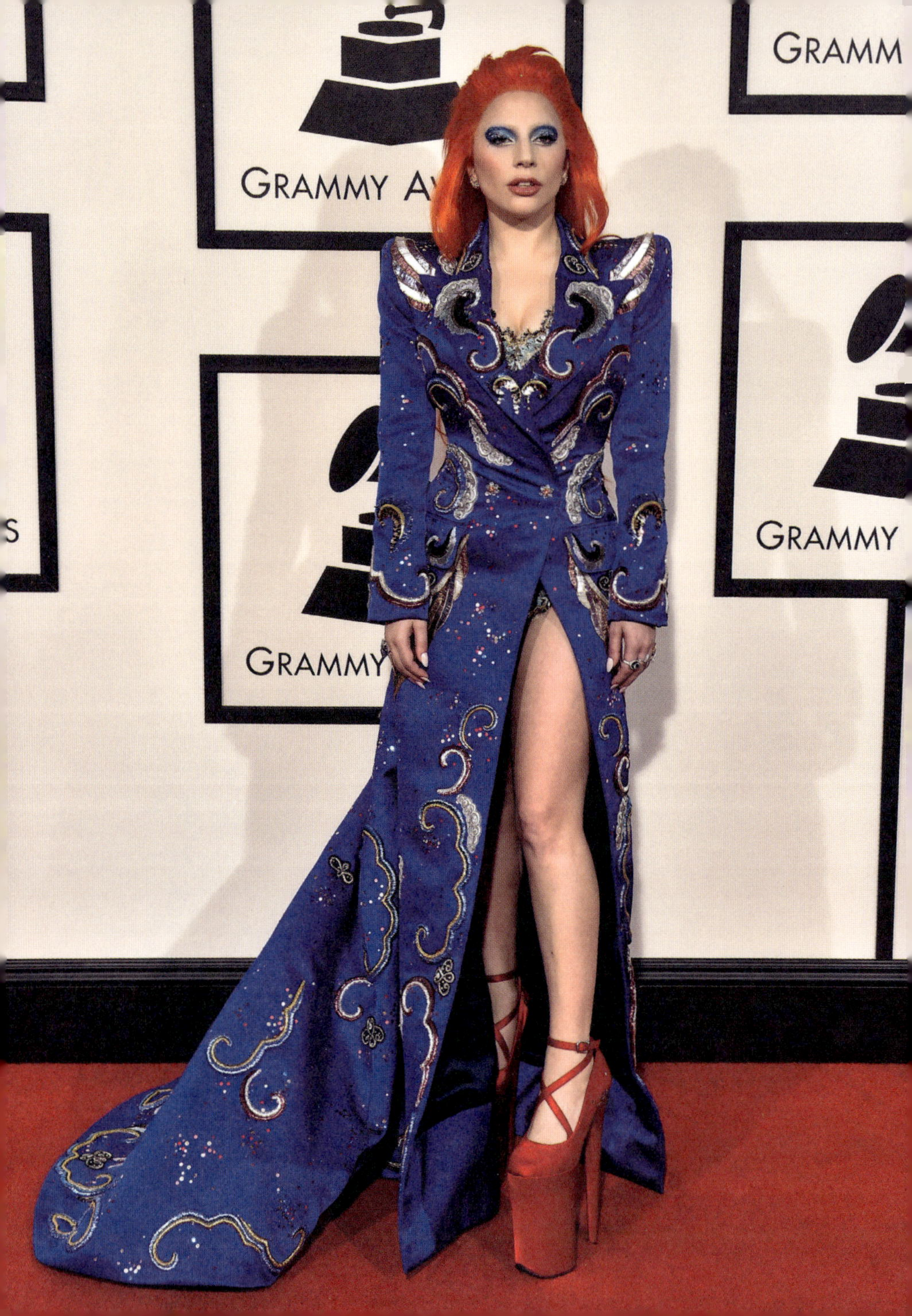
GRAMM
GRAMMY A
GRAMMY
GRAMMY

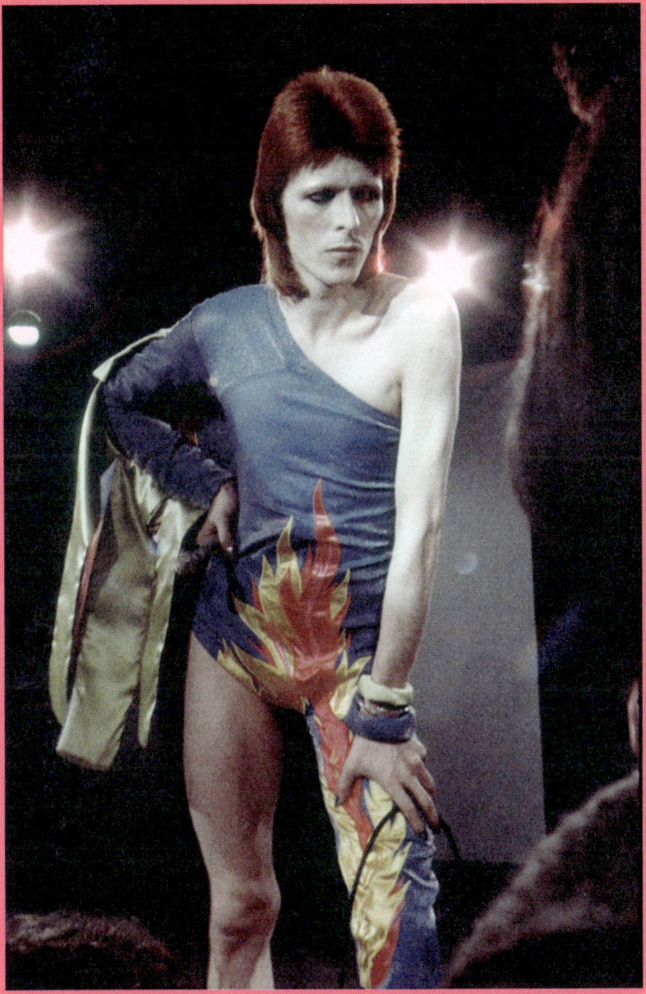

ABOVE Gaga was particularly inspired by David Bowie's Ziggy Stardust era, when the singer had bright orange hair and wore towering platforms and patterned bodysuits.

OPPOSITE Lady Gaga has said she's inspired by David Bowie. At the 2016 Grammys, she wore a look devoted to him; the music legend had passed in January of that year.

Toning it down

In 2016, Lady Gaga entered her *Joanne* era. This was the year she released the *Joanne* album, her fifth studio album, which rejected the upbeat pop sound she was known for in favour of a softer, more toned-down sound with country elements and a major focus on her voice. As such, Gaga also altered her sense of fashion to fit her new character.

At the centre of it all was a muted, rose-coloured pink hat with a cowboy silhouette and a slightly seventies wide brim. Designed by milliner Gladys Tamez, Gaga seemingly wore different variations of the pale pink hat with everything from jeans to gowns, from casual daily outings to important performances. The hat singlehandedly defined the new era of Lady Gaga, one that was softer and more approachable. The hat itself even appeared on the album cover. "Gaga told me she loves pink," Tamez told *People*. "I brought several samples, several designs and we agreed to have one, and then two and then more and more."

But even if she wasn't wearing inflatable fashion, she still found a way to add in her own Gaga staples. For example, she wore a version of the pink hat with a crystal trim and matching crystal crop top and hotpants to a *Saturday Night Live* performance in 2016. Elsewhere, in her daily life, Lady Gaga started wearing classic pieces with tinges of seventies glam. There were little pink leather moto jackets, regular blue jeans and oversized aviator sunglasses.

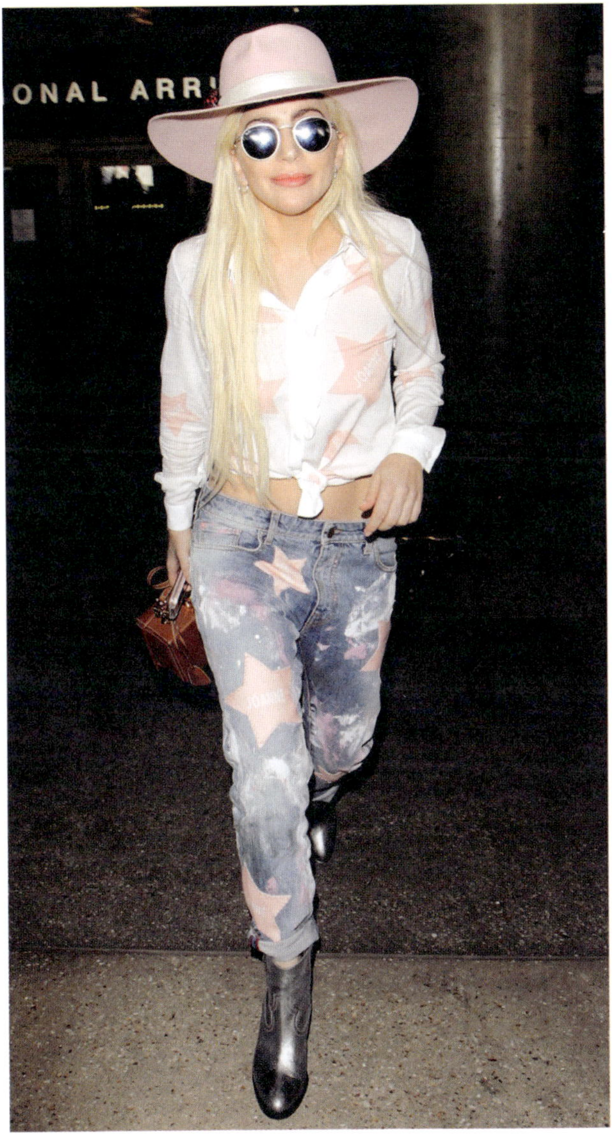

During her *Joanne* era, Gaga significantly toned down her look and wore lots of denim, button-down shirts and hats.

"I think something more subversive *is going on. Rather than suddenly becoming* conventional*,*

Lady Gaga is, in fact, turning a certain convention on *its head.*"

VANESSA FRIEDMAN, THE *NEW YORK TIMES*' FASHION CRITIC

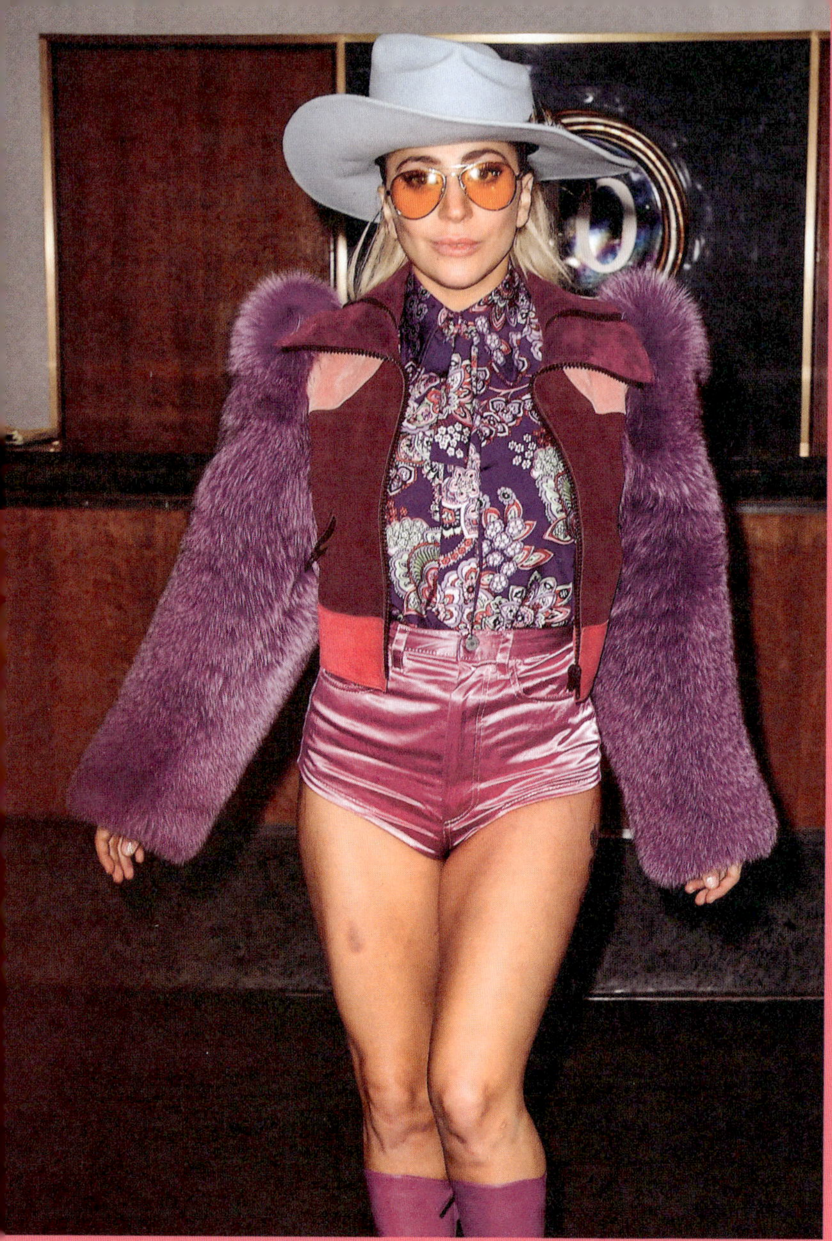

Lady Gaga proved that she still has a wild streak during her *Joanne* era, wearing bright pops of colour and fun textures with her now-signature hotpants.

She gravitated toward loungy, oversized trench coats and loose-fitting suits in neutral shades and also indulged in lots of pieces that might have been plucked from the wardrobes of the country superstars – like tiny denim cut-off shorts or white T-shirts with the sleeves rolled up. In some ways, it felt like Gaga was using fashion as a way to spotlight her new sound first and foremost.

While in the past Lady Gaga gravitated toward some of the most avant-garde designers of all time, such as Alexander McQueen and Thierry Mugler, in her *Joanne* era she opted for labels that were more down to earth. On one occasion she wore a long black fringe look designed by Alexander Wang, a designer who was then associated with downtown New York cool. Her biggest fans (known passionately as Little Monsters) still loved her over-the-top dramatic looks and so there were subtle nods to the extreme during the Joanne tour. Like the massive, floor-length, red Norma Kamali puffer jacket styled with a 10-foot-train, matching bow-bedecked boots and an art-worthy mask that covered half of her face.

Gaga's shift away from all-extreme-all-the-time has certainly been the fascination of the general public, fans and even the biggest players in the industry alike. In 2016, Vanessa Friedman, The *New York Times*' fashion critic wrote of the star's recent style shift: "I think something more subversive is going on. Rather than suddenly becoming conventional, Lady Gaga is, in fact, turning a certain convention on its head. She is challenging a dearly held tenet of celebrity that says that whatever you wear, you must be the dominant brand in the relationship: Your look must trump anyone else's look." Gaga is not a muse, but an enabler, according to the *NYT*.

Superdom

Lady Gaga transcended stardom when she performed as the sole artist for the 2017 Super Bowl and, with it, came a return to the classic Gaga aesthetic. She worked with her stylist Brandon Maxwell to choose custom looks from Atelier Versace that were glitzy and glittery enough to see from the massive stage. Maxell told *Vogue* that the wardrobe for the half-time show "was always about celebrating all that she has done in this first decade of her career," adding, "They know not only how to design functional costumes that work well for performance, but also that would deliver visually on the spectacle and excitement that a stage like the Super Bowl half-time show deserves."

Gaga started out the evening in a glittering leotard with shoulder pads paired with matching boots and fishnet tights and had several outfit changes throughout the performance, each one speaking to the looks her fans know her best for. She added in her Netflix documentary, *Gaga: Five Foot Two*, "I've never really done a lifetime achievement award or performance that was meant to celebrate my career and I feel like this is that moment. The truth is there really isn't anything bigger than this, so I better enjoy it today because it's not going to happen again."

OPPOSITE Lady Gaga made her Met Gala debut in 2015, wearing an Alexander Wang-designed Balenciaga gown.

OVERLEAF Fans got to see a raw version of Gaga in her 2017 Netflix documentary, *Gaga: Five Foot Two*, wearing plenty of denim shorts and white T-shirts.

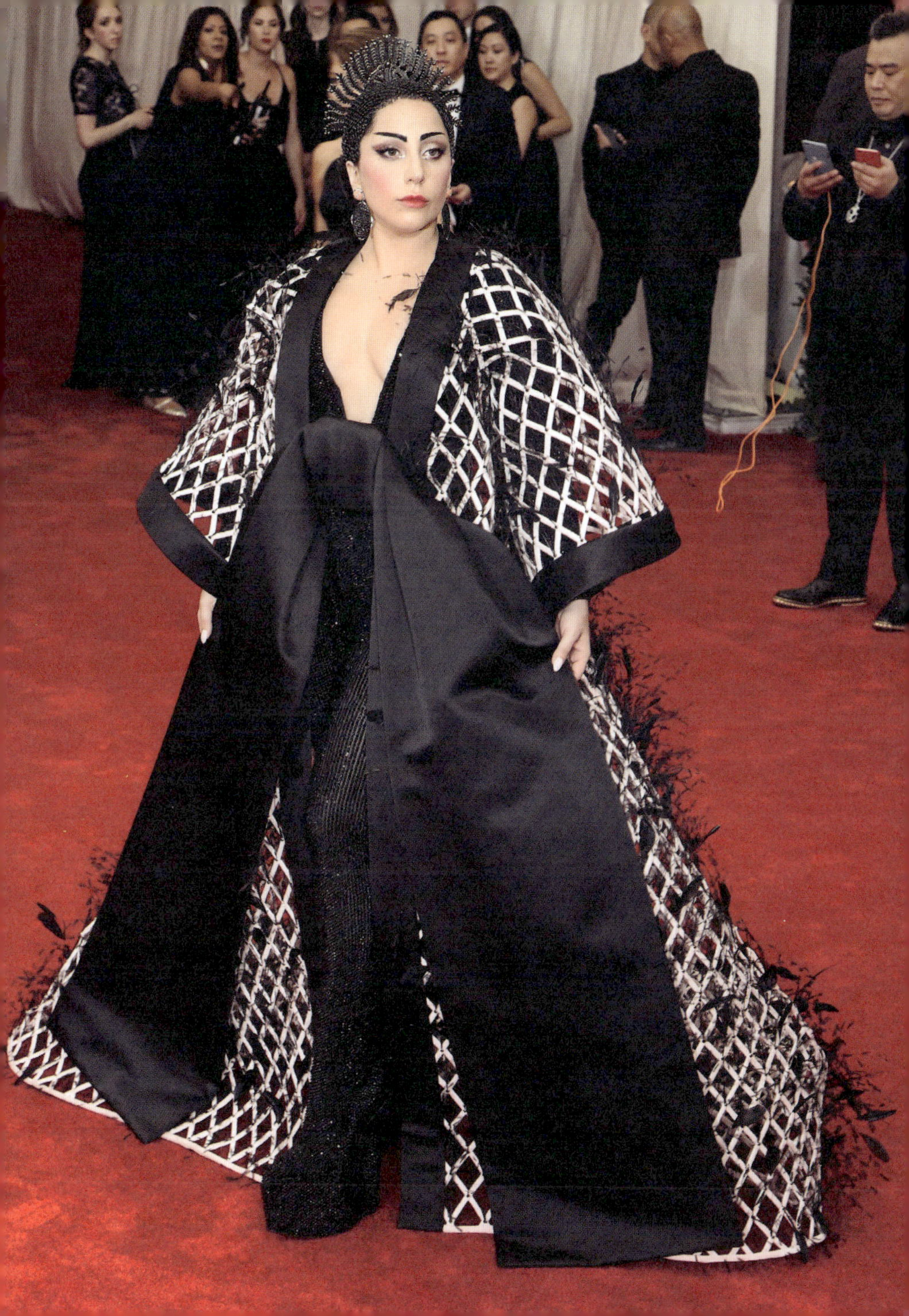

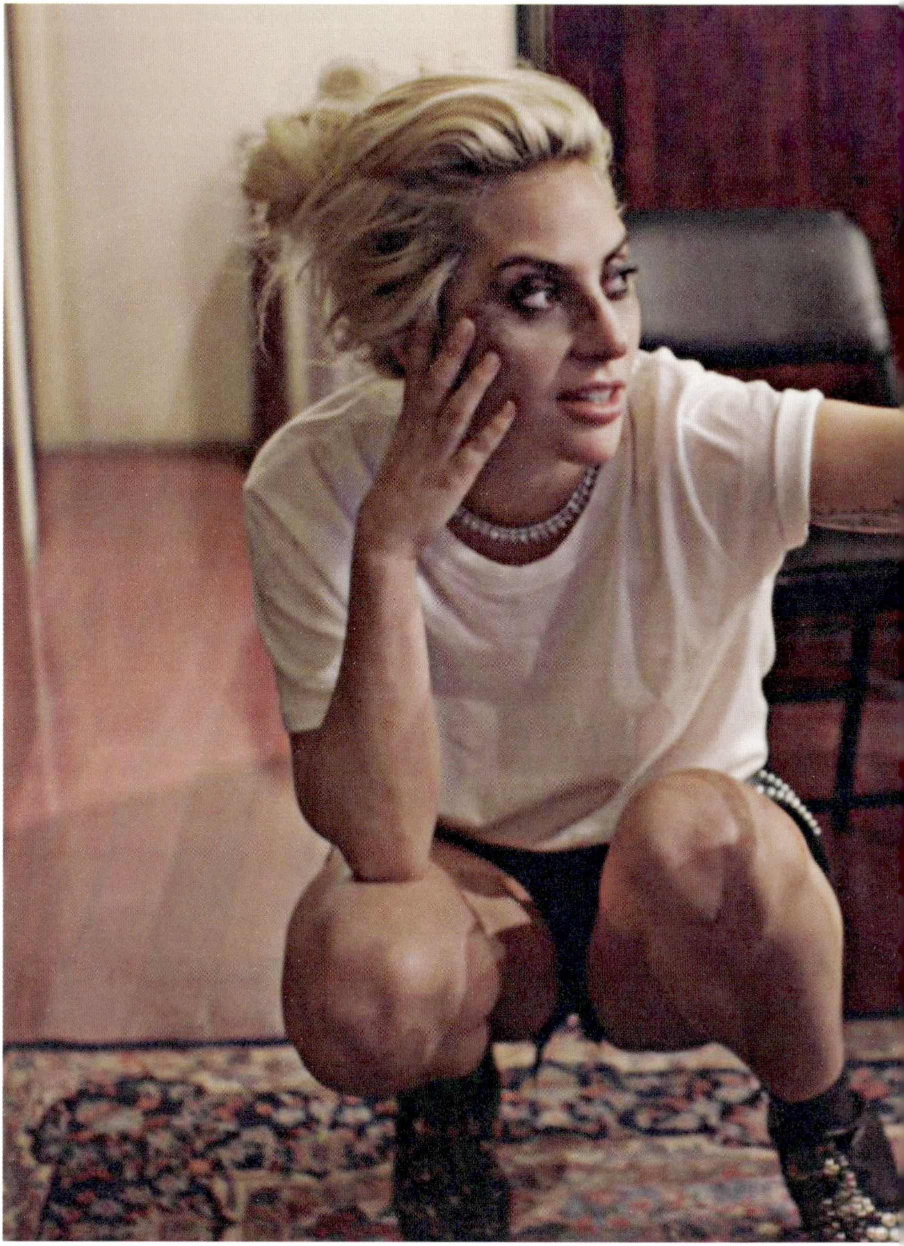

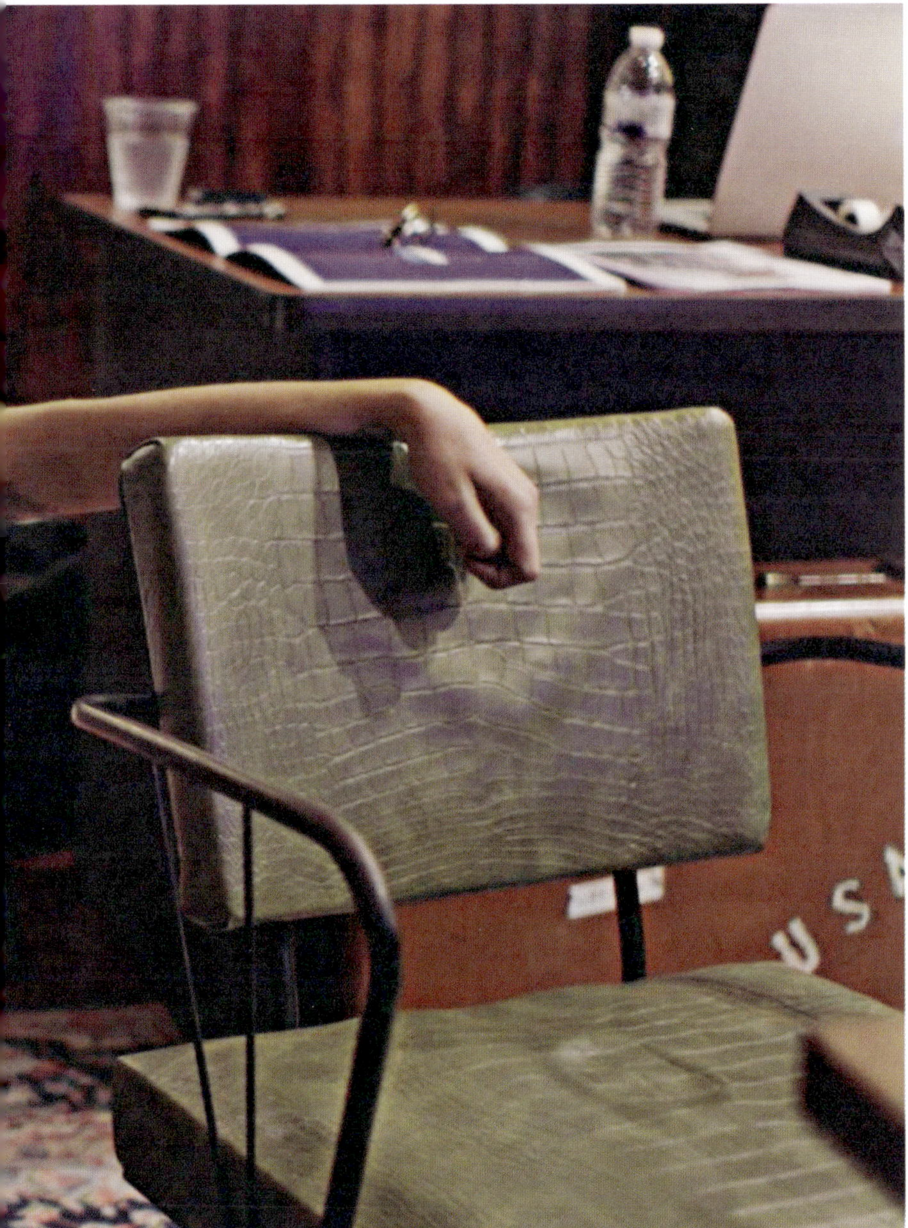
USA

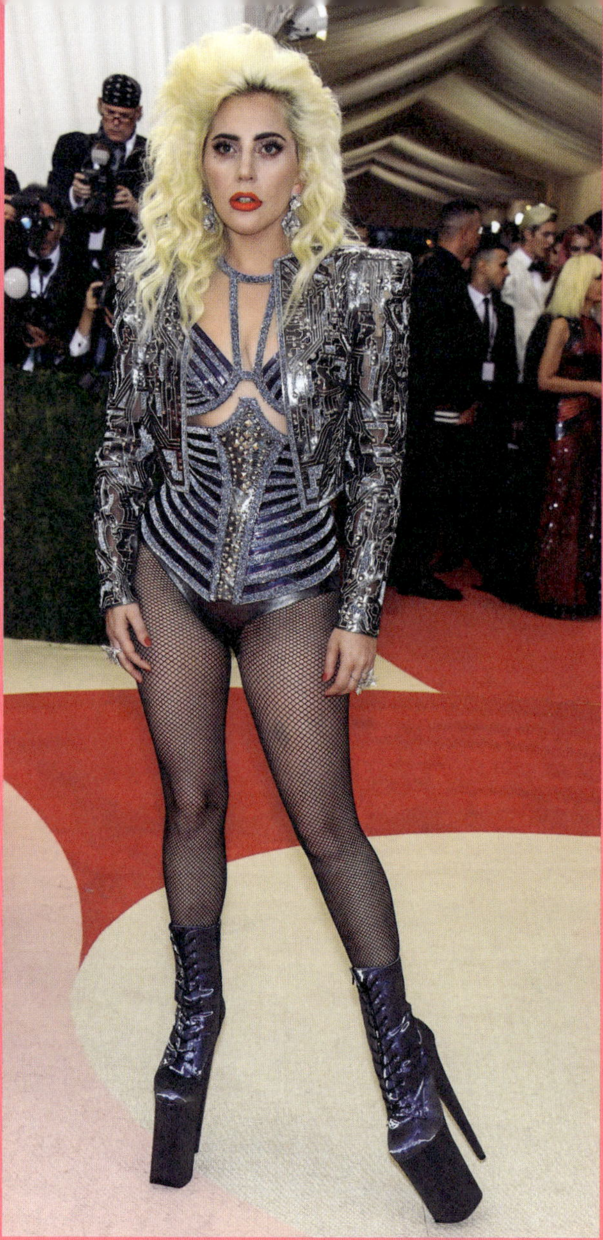

Lady Gaga returned to the Met Gala red carpet in 2016, wearing a futuristic-looking leotard designed by Versace, with sky-high Pleasers boots and fishnet stockings.

Gaga herself has been very transparent about the inspiration the concept of fame has on her and her body of work, as well as the countless performers who have inspired her along the way, both in terms of her music and her way of putting herself together visually. "It's not a secret that I have been inspired by tons of people," she told *Vogue* in 2011, "David Bowie and Prince being the most paramount in terms of live performance."

As a music icon who is also heavily in the fashion space, it's no wonder Lady Gaga attended the Met Gala – fashion's biggest night out where celebs, designers and heavy hitters of the art, political and tech worlds come together to celebrate and support the museum's latest exhibition. She first attended the event in 2010 as a performer, skipping the red carpet fanfare, but really shined in the spotlight in 2015, when she attended for the second time.

China: Through the Looking Glass served as the 2015 theme for the Met Gala and Lady Gaga wore an incredibly dramatic black and gold custom cape dress designed by Alexander Wang for Balenciaga. Her stylist and fashion director Brandon Maxwell spearheaded the look. Gaga wore black hair covered in crystals, with huge art deco drop earrings. "Alex and Gaga are both iconic New York figures," Maxwell wrote for *T Magazine*. "I've been friends with Alex for a while, and when it came time to think about the Met Gala, Alex called and asked if Gaga would be his date. I thought they'd be a great match because they are similar in so many ways and, surprisingly, hadn't previously collaborated. Knowing both of their minds, which are both so vast, diverse and energetic, I knew that if they joined forces the outcome would be amazing."

Gaga returned to the Met Gala carpet a year later, in 2016, to honour the theme of "Manus x Machina: Fashion in an Age of Technology". By this point, she was one of the most anticipated red carpet guests for fashion lovers and commentators alike. Going back to her roots and her signature style, she wore a futuristic-looking leotard designed by Versace, with sky-high Pleasers boots and fishnet stockings. To match the theme, which focused heavily on tech, she wore a sculptural long-sleeved leotard made of laser-cut leather and layered with gunmetal and crystals on top.

But Lady Gaga's biggest Met Gala moment was one that would go down in history, cementing her as a fashion star for the ages. For the 2019 Met Gala, the theme couldn't have fit Gaga better. Dubbed "Camp: Notes on Fashion", the idea was inspired by Susan Sontag's 1964 essay *Notes on 'Camp'*, which interrogates the concept of camp. For the occasion, Gaga staged a red carpet debut like no one had ever seen before, which involved multiple outfit changes verging on performance art. Walking arm in arm with her stylist Brandon Maxwell, she began the journey by walking three New York City blocks to the venue in a fuchsia flowing dress with a 25-foot-train designed by Maxwell. On her head, she wore a matching pink hair bow.

OPPOSITE In 2016, Gaga still leaned into the aesthetic of her early work, choosing a geometric metallic dress for a night out, as seen here.

OVERLEAF Lady Gaga made history at the 2019 Met Gala, styled by Brandon Maxwell.

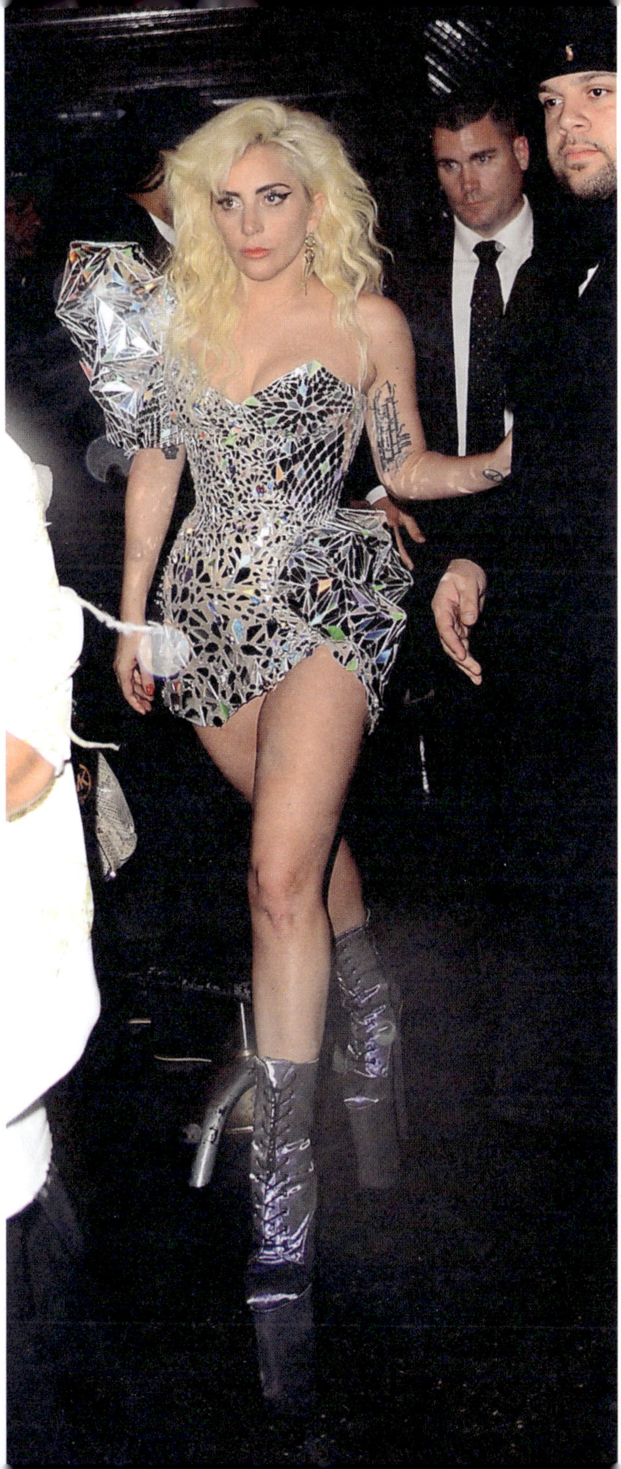

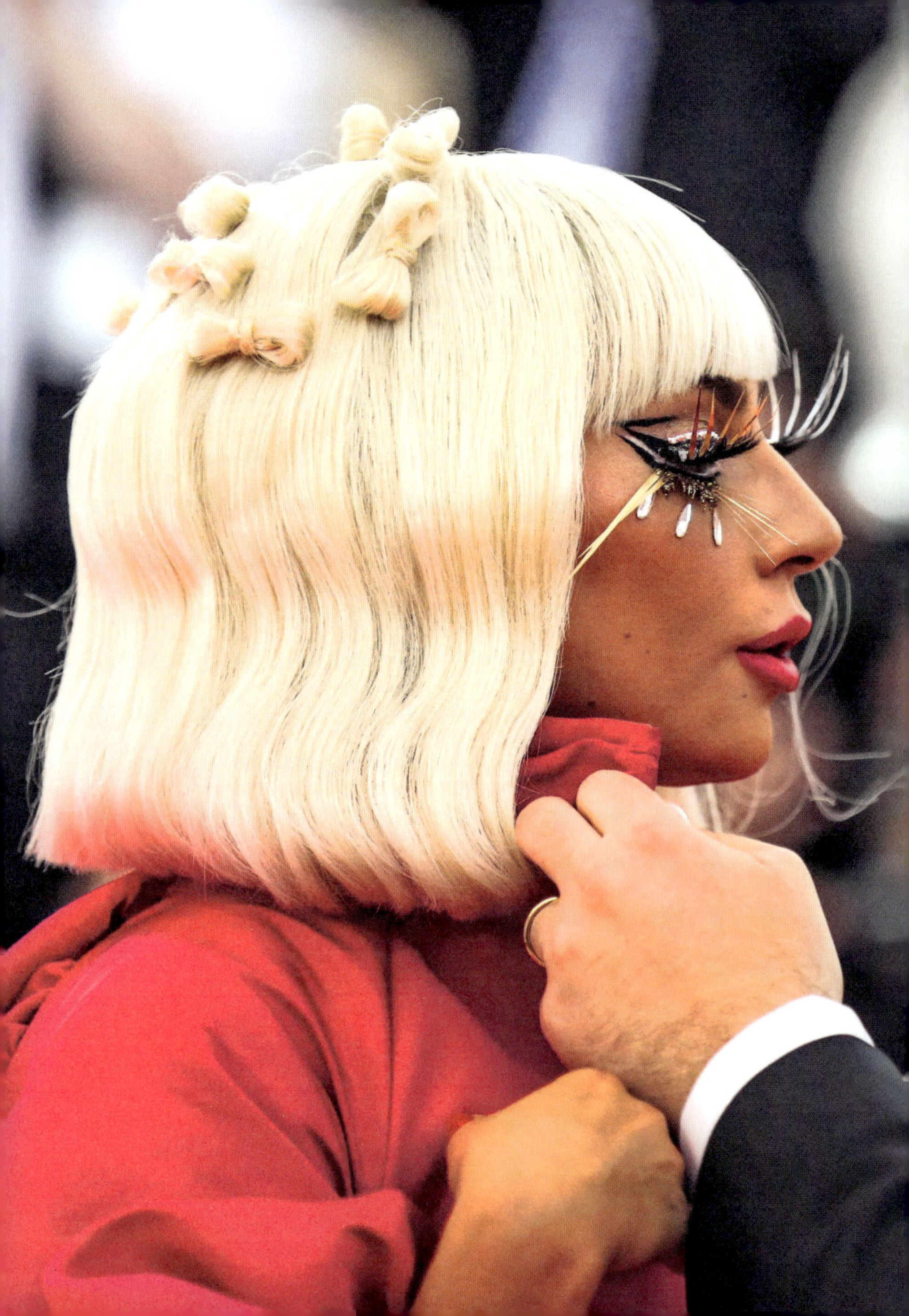

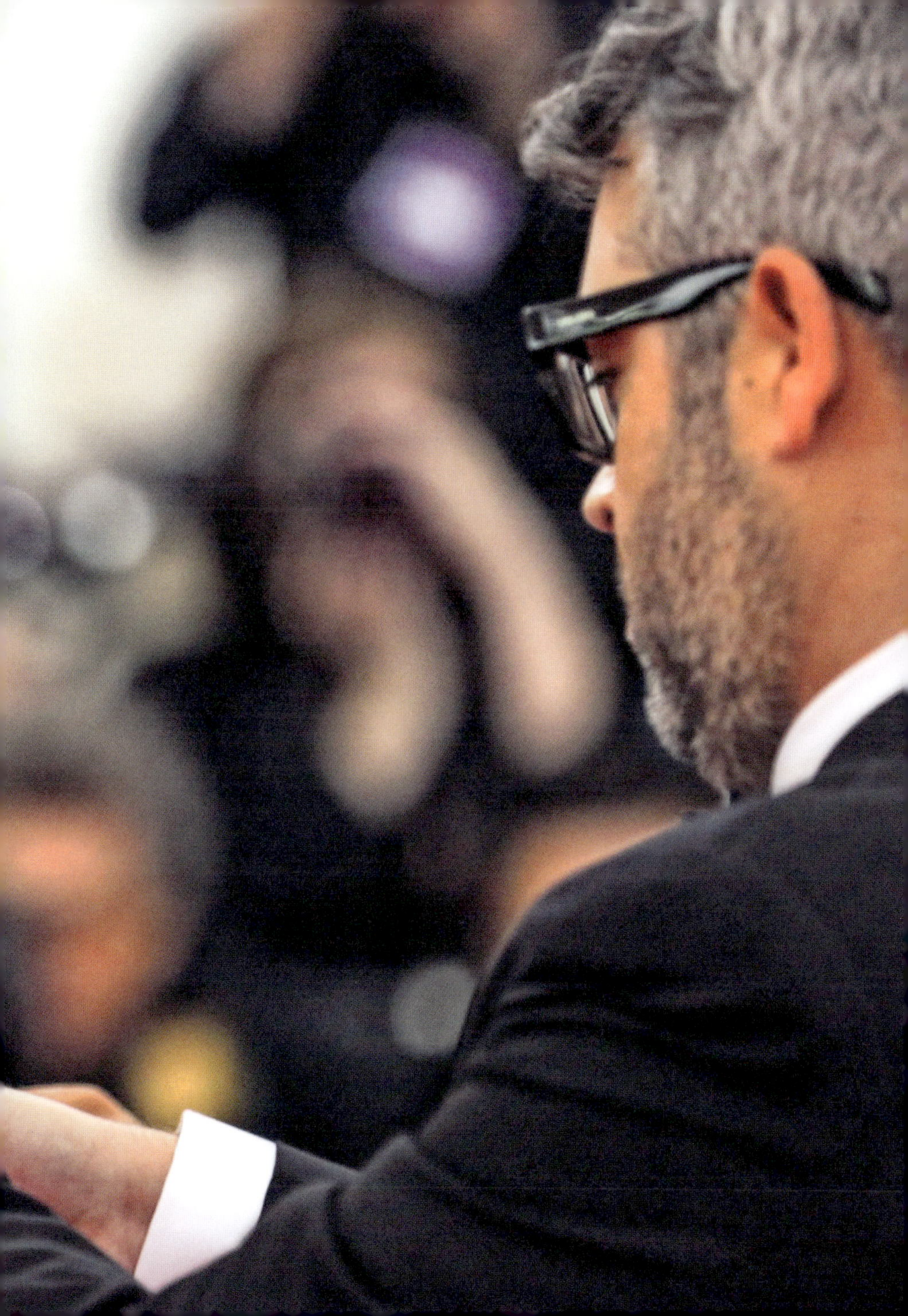

"I know intrinsically *that I have a* camp soul, *I knew because we're such a* family

and the way that we
work together
as a creative
collective, that what
we would **create**
together would
be camp."

LADY GAGA ON WORKING WITH BRANDON MAXWELL

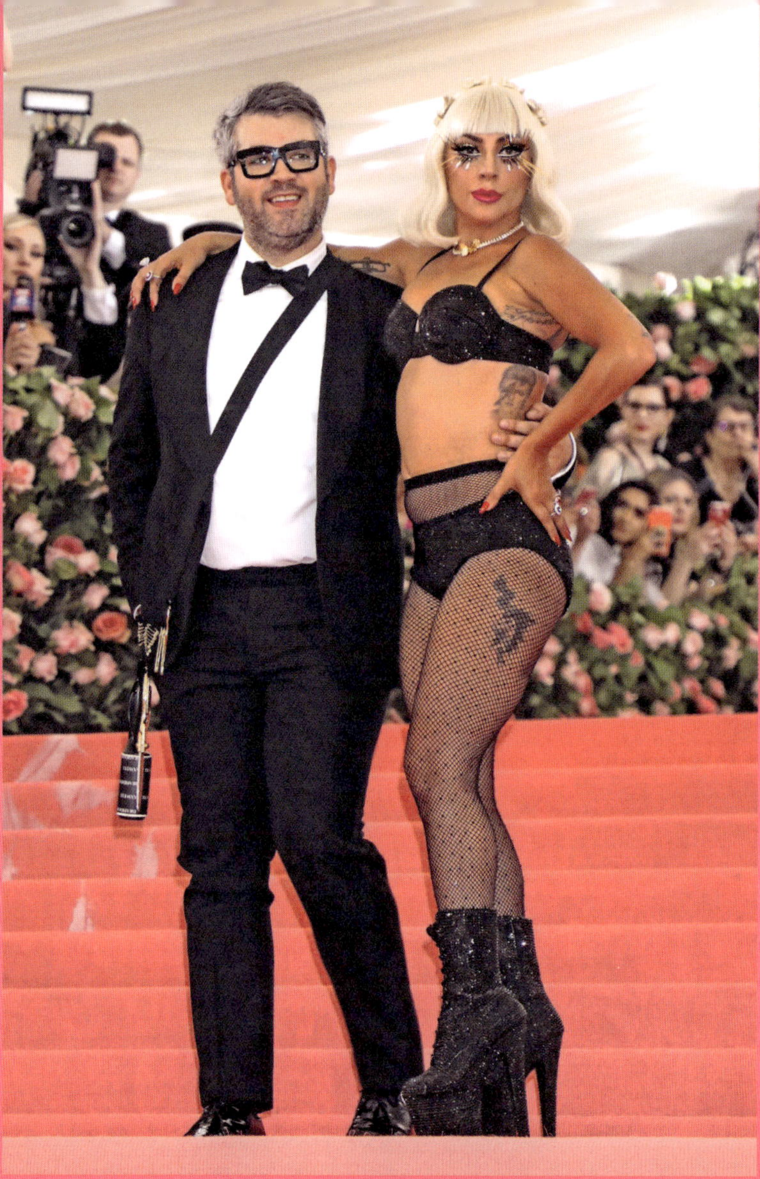

ABOVE Lady Gaga's red carpet moment at the 2019 Met Gala consisted of multiple theatrical outfit changes, the first of its kind ever to be seen there.

OVERLEAF The bold pink dress Gaga wore to the 2019 Met Gala fitted the theme – camp – perfectly.

Gaga and Maxwell worked together to create a performance of a lifetime that involved multiple outfit changes on the red carpet in front of reporters, editors, paparazzi and *Vogue*'s Anna Wintour herself. With helping hands, Gaga's pink dress came off to reveal a strapless structured black gown with a matching black umbrella. Next came a streamlined pink slip dress complete with oversized black sunglasses and a bedazzled telephone bag designed by Judith Leiber. Finally, Gaga's slip dress came off to reveal her classic black underwear set and fishnets, paired with Tiffany & Co. jewellery, glittering "Pleaser" boots and a wagon full of pink cowboy hats and champagne. "I know intrinsically that I have a camp soul," she told *Vogue* of collaborating with Maxwell. "I knew because we're such a family and the way that we work together as a creative collective, that what we would create together would be camp."

Of course, Lady Gaga isn't just a musical artist and her deeper foray into acting also allowed for her to experiment with fashion on a very different level. Her first big role was in *American Horror Story: Hotel*, which was released in 2015. The miniseries was inspired by old hotel horror films and real hotels in downtown Los Angeles. Gaga starred as Elizabeth Johnson, better known as The Countess. The visuals in *AHS* are always striking and Gaga is seen with opulent updos, swanning around in floor-length, vampy gowns. Later, she would return to the franchise with a role in *American Horror Story: Roanoke*, which was released in 2016. She took on the guest role of Scáthach, a witch with a very dramatic, almost zombie-like medieval look.

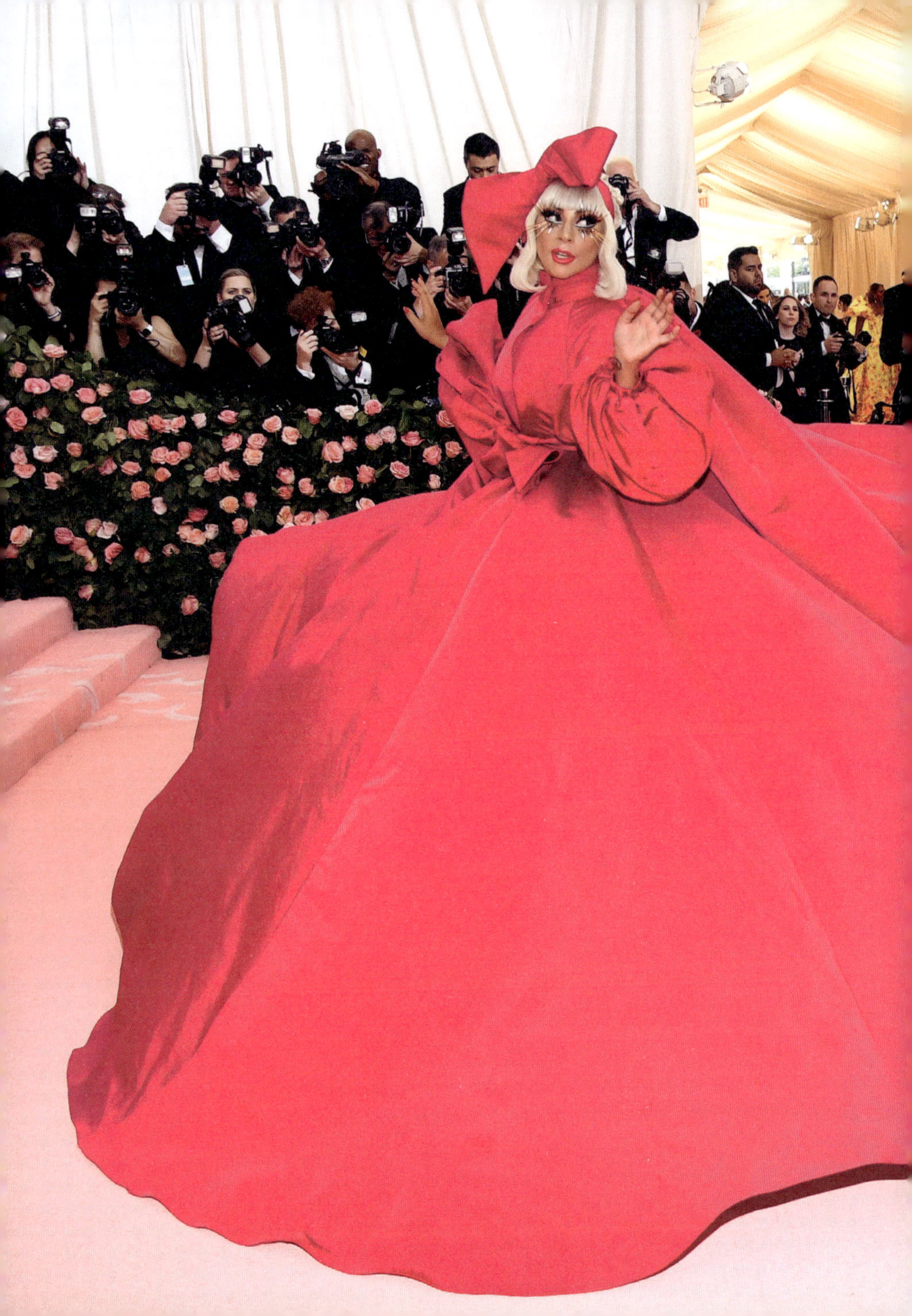

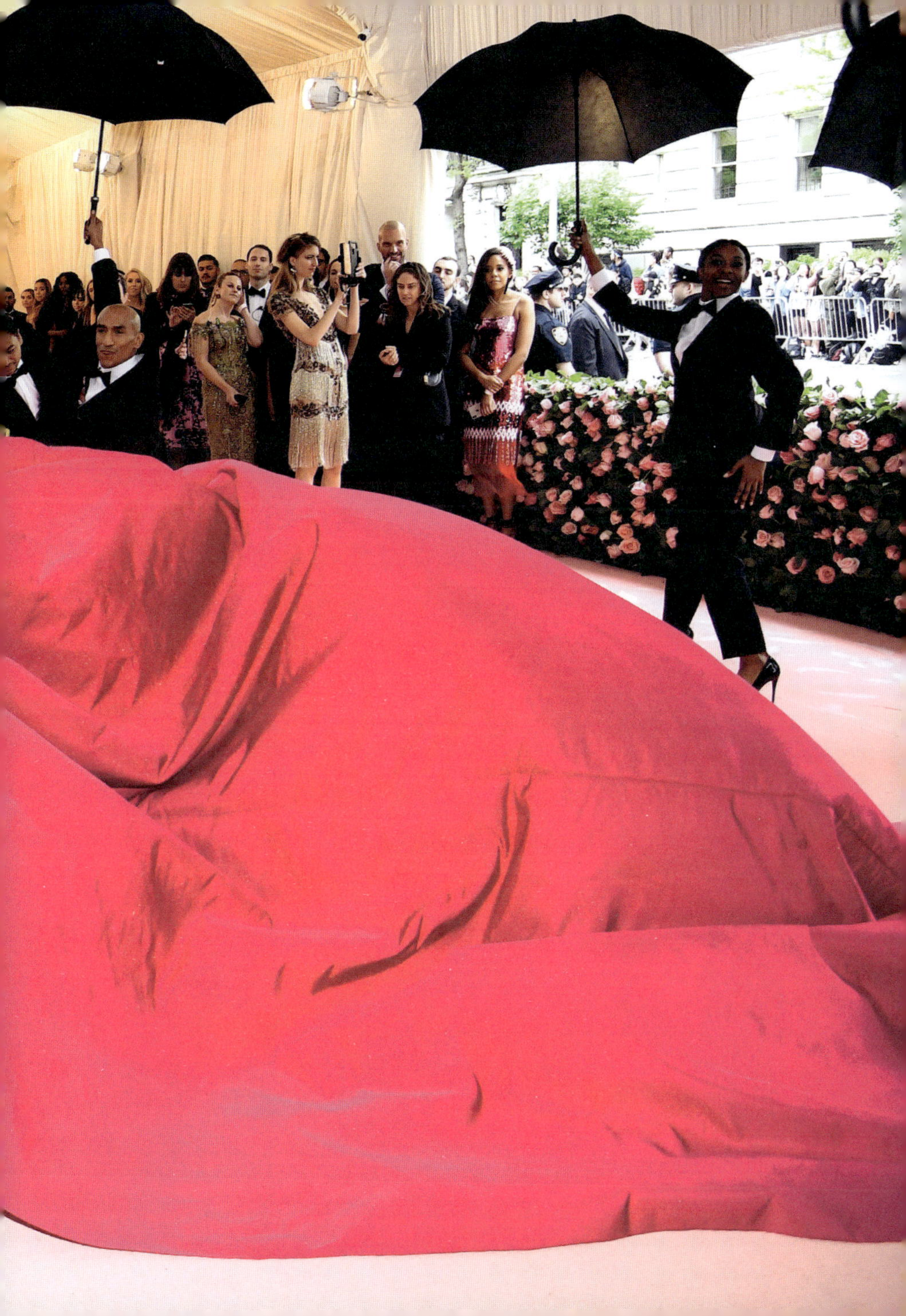

That Hollywood glow

But Lady Gaga's biggest fashion and film moment to date would come in 2018, when she starred in *A Star is Born* alongside Bradley Cooper. The film was based on the original 1937 romantic drama and its remakes. In it, Gaga is shown as a talented young artist who dresses in down-to-earth, everyday outfits that speak of her vulnerability and young musician lifestyle. She wears a lot of jeans, T-shirts and pieces that have a rocker vibe, such as wide-brim hats, leather boots, striped pants, animal prints and sheer blouses.

Mirroring her real life, it felt as if Gaga truly emerged as a new kind of star in playing this role in a major Hollywood movie. As such, her personal wardrobe experienced its own kind of fashion twist, cementing a new era that perfectly matched the look of a budding Hollywood starlet. During the promotional tour for *A Star is Born*, Gaga put an emphasis on lots of beautiful, slinky gowns that showed off their quality and craftsmanship without outshining her personality.

OPPOSITE In *A Star Is Born* (2018), Lady Gaga wore a toned-down uniform fit for a rising songstress.

OVERLEAF The outfits in *A Star Is Born* recalled some of the looks Gaga wore in her own *Joanne* era, with a more tomboyish element.

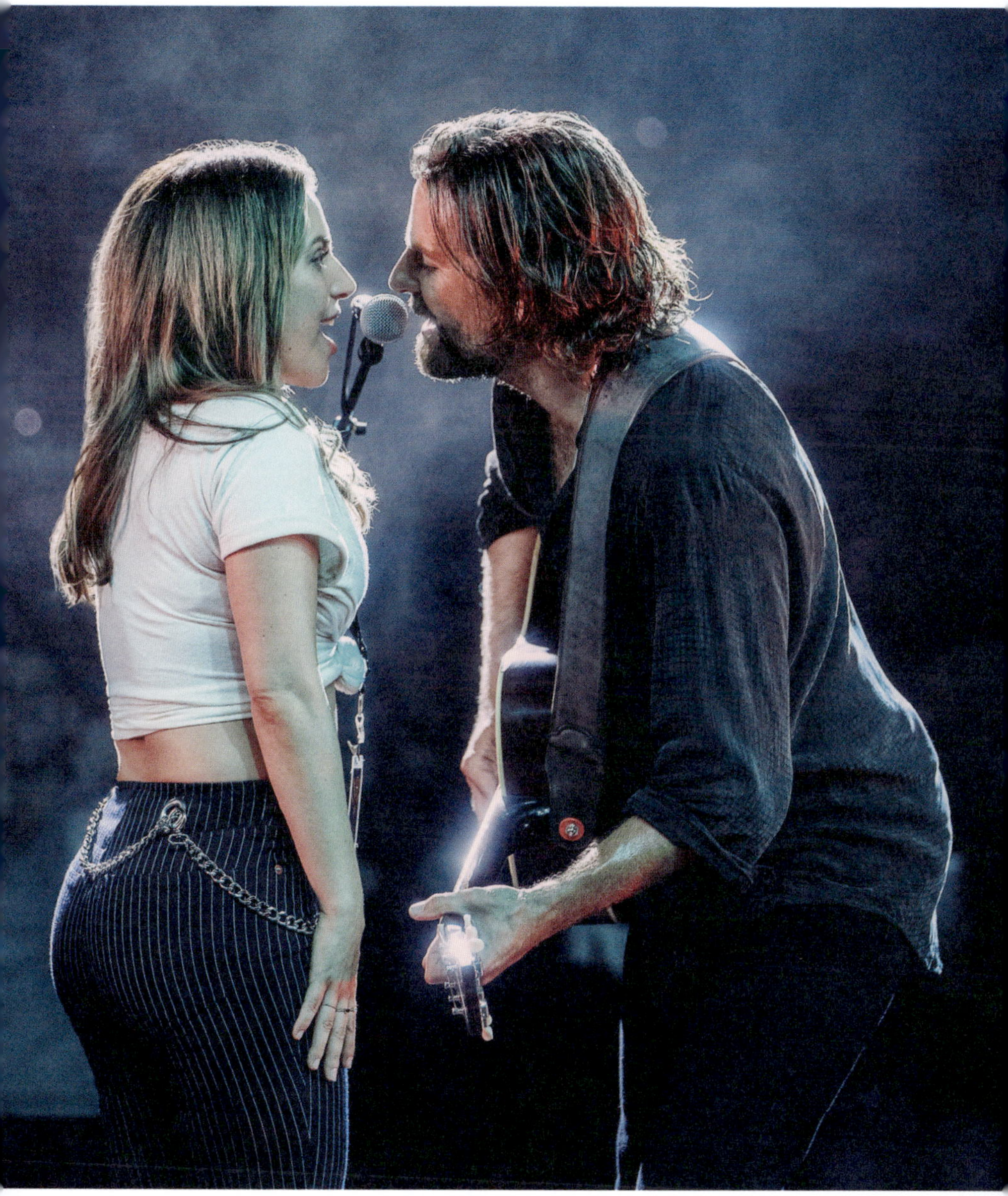

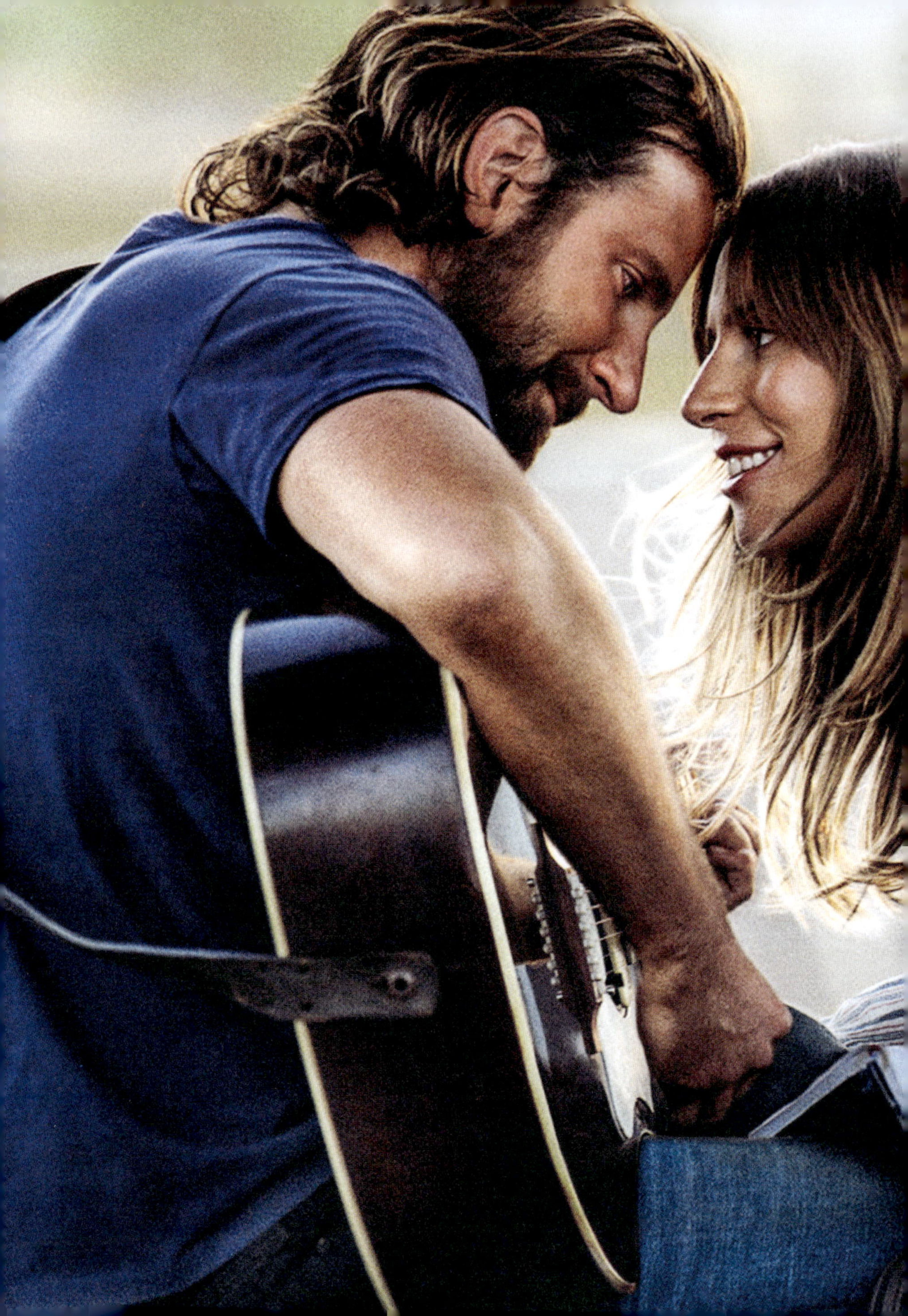

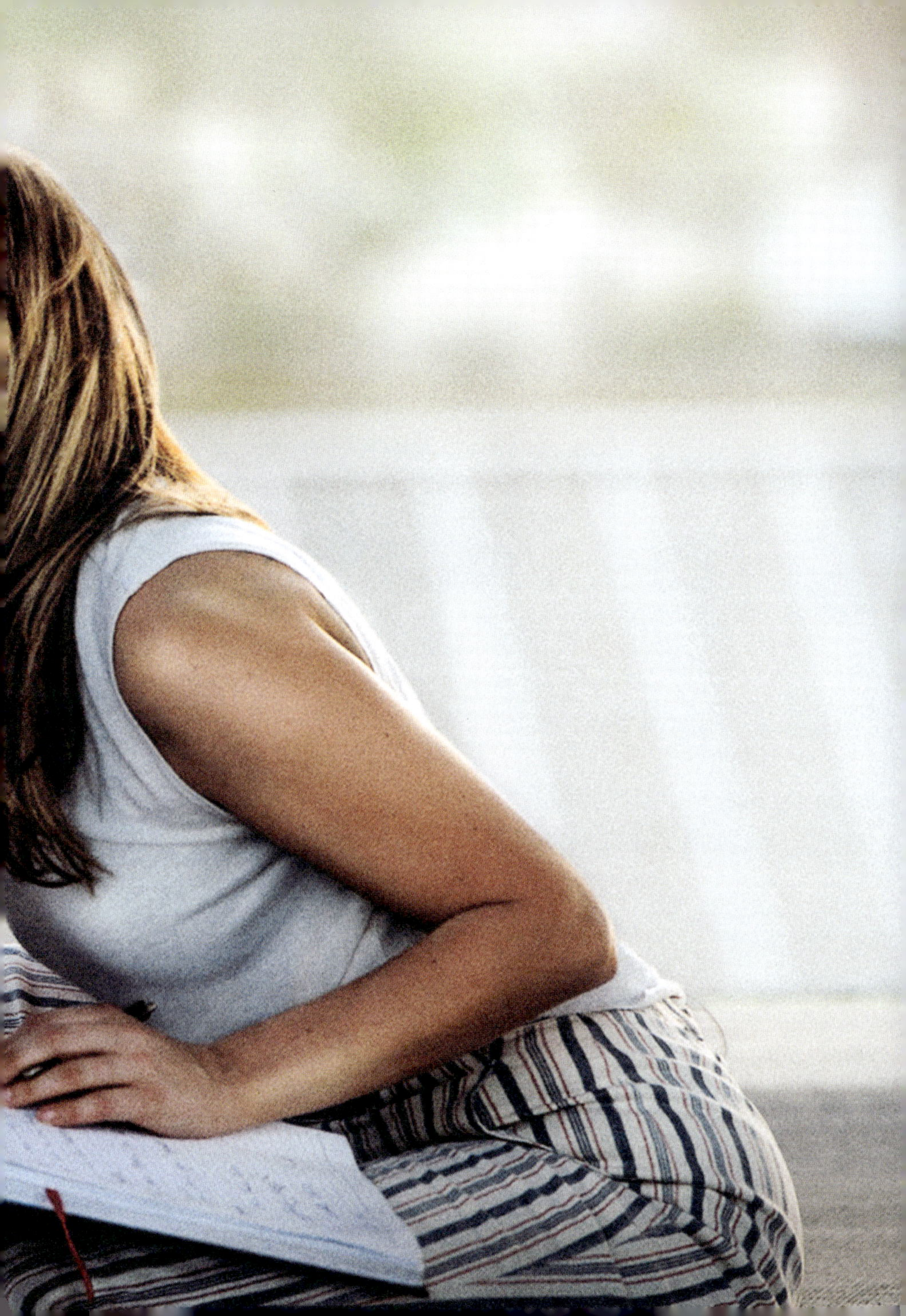

During this time, Lady Gaga often wore her hair swept back into glamorous updos, with classic, minimal make-up and glittering fine jewellery. She opted for gowns from brands she'd worked with in the past, but toned it all down in terms of colour, cut and shape. For one appearance, she wore an off-the-shoulder velvet gown in a lush, red wine colour by Ralph & Russo. Another time, she opted for a champagne sequined strapless dress by Armani Privé. Ditching her usual Pleasers and black fishnet tights, she instead chose plain stilettos or strappy heeled sandals.

Low key looks aside, when Gaga did want to make a statement during her promotional period of *A Star is Born*, she held nothing back. Take, for example, when she wore a cloud-like fluffy pink feathered gown to the Venice Film Festival. Or the Shakespearean-inspired dress she wore to the London premiere of the film, complete with a neck ruff, puff sleeves and a golden corset. The Alexander McQueen creation from 2013 showed that even if Gaga's look has evolved over the years, she's still not afraid to go to the depths of high fashion.

During this time, Gaga maximized traditional red carpet style, seen here wearing a feathered Valentino Couture look.

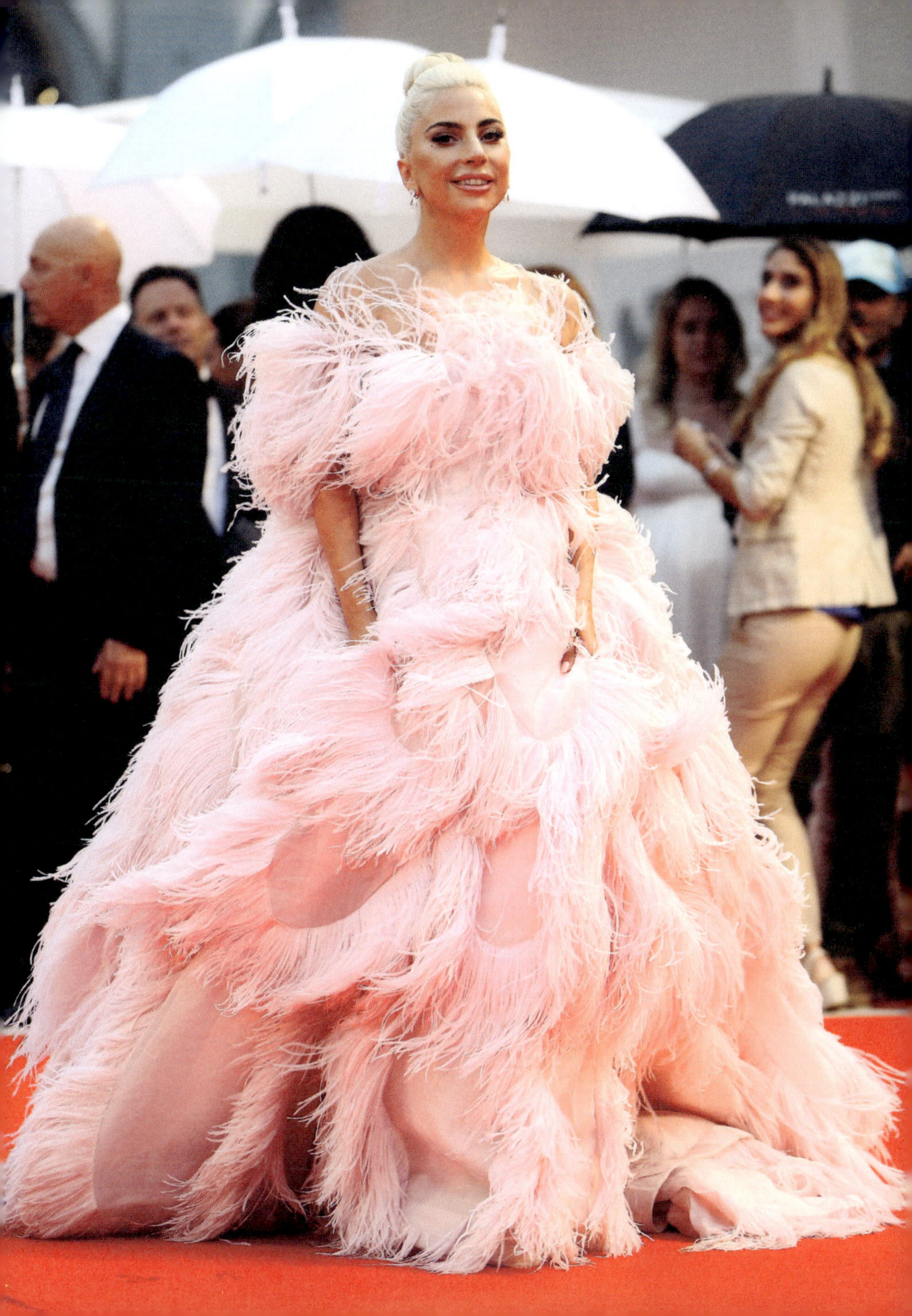

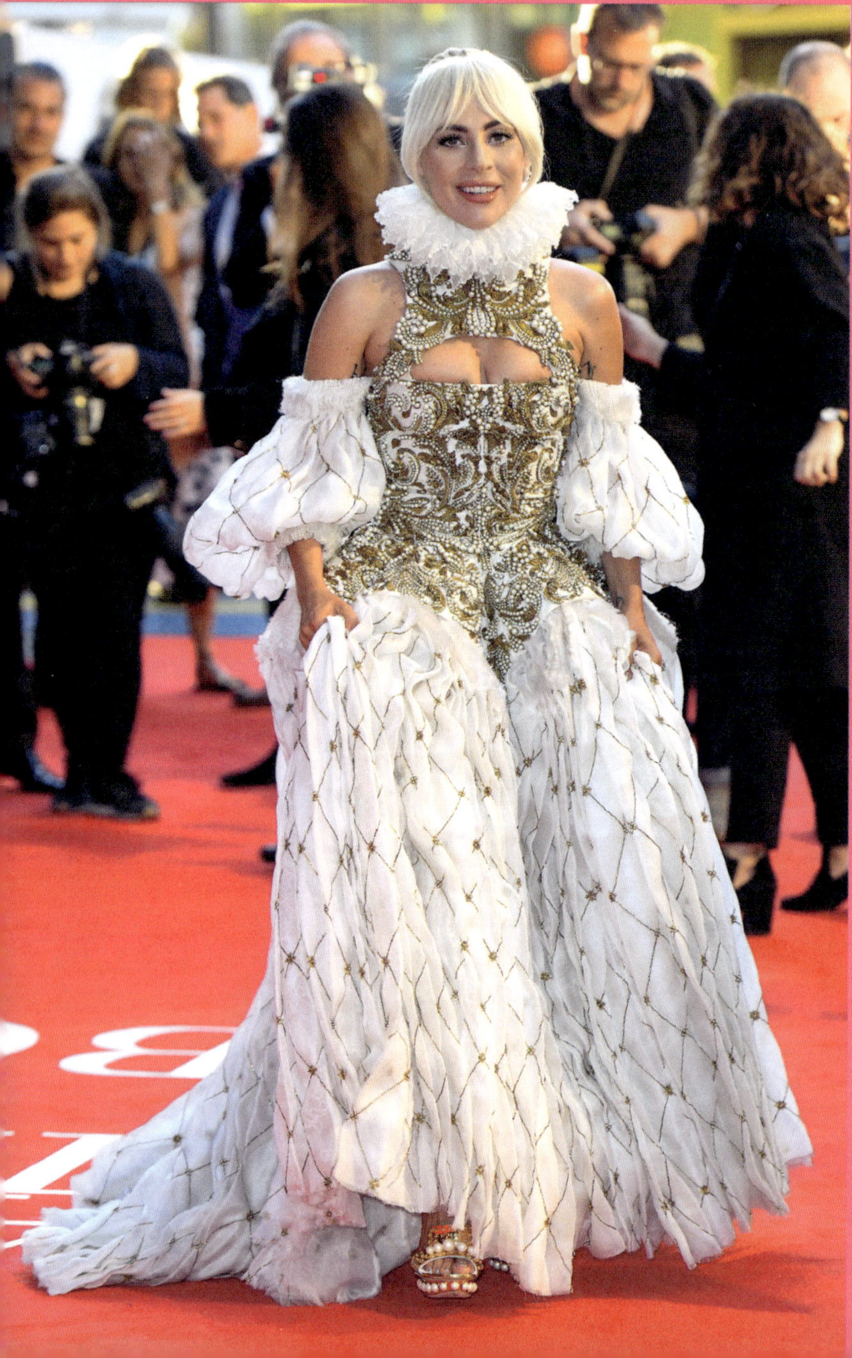

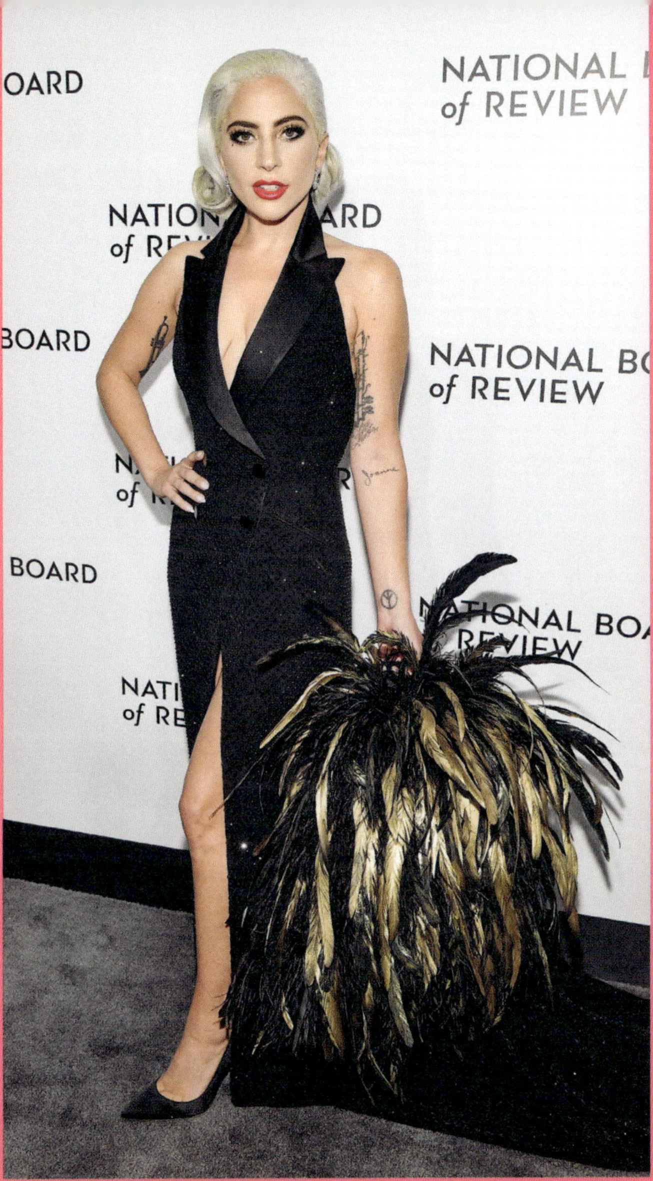

ABOVE On the red carpet, Lady Gaga also experiments with elements of suiting and menswear, as seen here.

OPPOSITE Gaga wore an extreme Alexander McQueen gown to the UK premiere of *A Star Is Born* in 2018.

In 2021, Lady Gaga transformed once again for her role in *House of Gucci*. Playing the part of Patrizia Reggiani in the 1970s through to the 1990s, in the film, Gaga wears a melange of oversized sunglasses, chunky furs, dramatic dresses and flashy gold jewellery. Janty Yates was responsible for the costumes in the film and pulled directly from the Gucci archives. Gaga's outfits in *House of Gucci* couldn't be more different to her sense of fashion in *A Star is Born*. Here, we see her as a larger-than-life personality who uses fashion to express herself and stand out. Even in scenes where she is skiing on the slopes, she is covered in gold jewellery and accessories that pop. She wears sequins, big hair, tight lace dresses, polka dots and plenty of leather and Gucci logos. "I was either in my hotel room, living and speaking as Reggiani, or I was on set, living and speaking as her," she told British *Vogue* in 2021. "I had some psychological difficulty at one point toward the end of filming."

Lady Gaga in *House of Gucci* is a fashion lover's dream – especially when it comes to vintage. Beyond the Gucci archives, Yates scoured the earth for rare, standout pieces for the star and other characters in the film, finding pieces on eBay, Etsy and even Gaga's own personal vintage archive. Five seamstresses worked behind the scenes to make custom looks for Gaga. Overall, she had a whopping 54 different outfits in the film and according to Yates, nothing was repeated, not even a single piece of jewellery. Because of the range of dates that the film covered, from the 1970s to the 1990s, there's a huge variety in the kind of fashion Gaga carried off and you get to see her in a little bit of everything, even a handmade lace wedding dress.

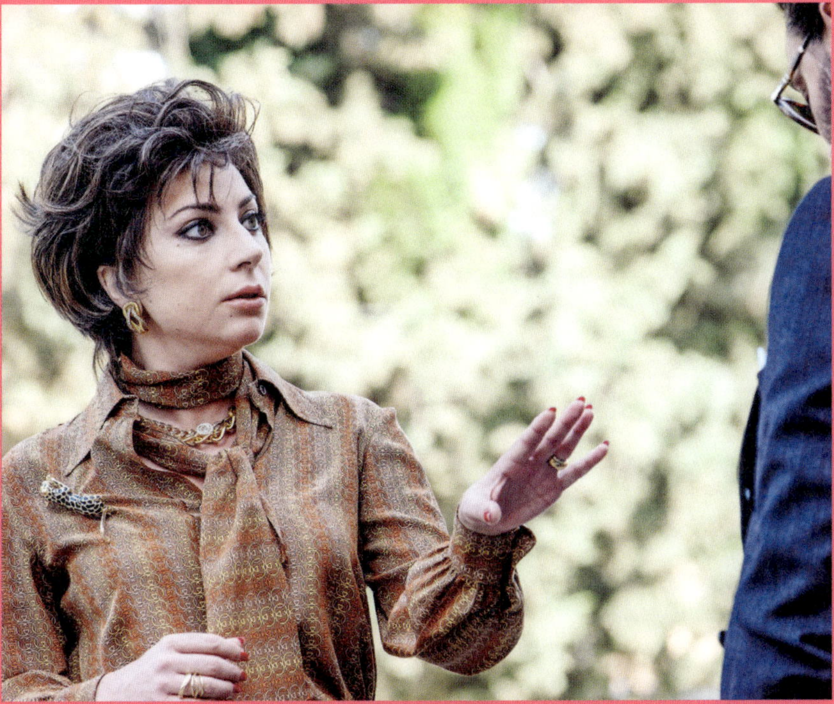

ABOVE In her next Hollywood role, Lady Gaga starred in *House of Gucci* (2021) as Patrizia Reggiani, wearing lots of vintage Italian fashion.

OVERLEAF As Patrizia Reggiani, Gaga leaned into dramatic accessories and lots of jewellery.

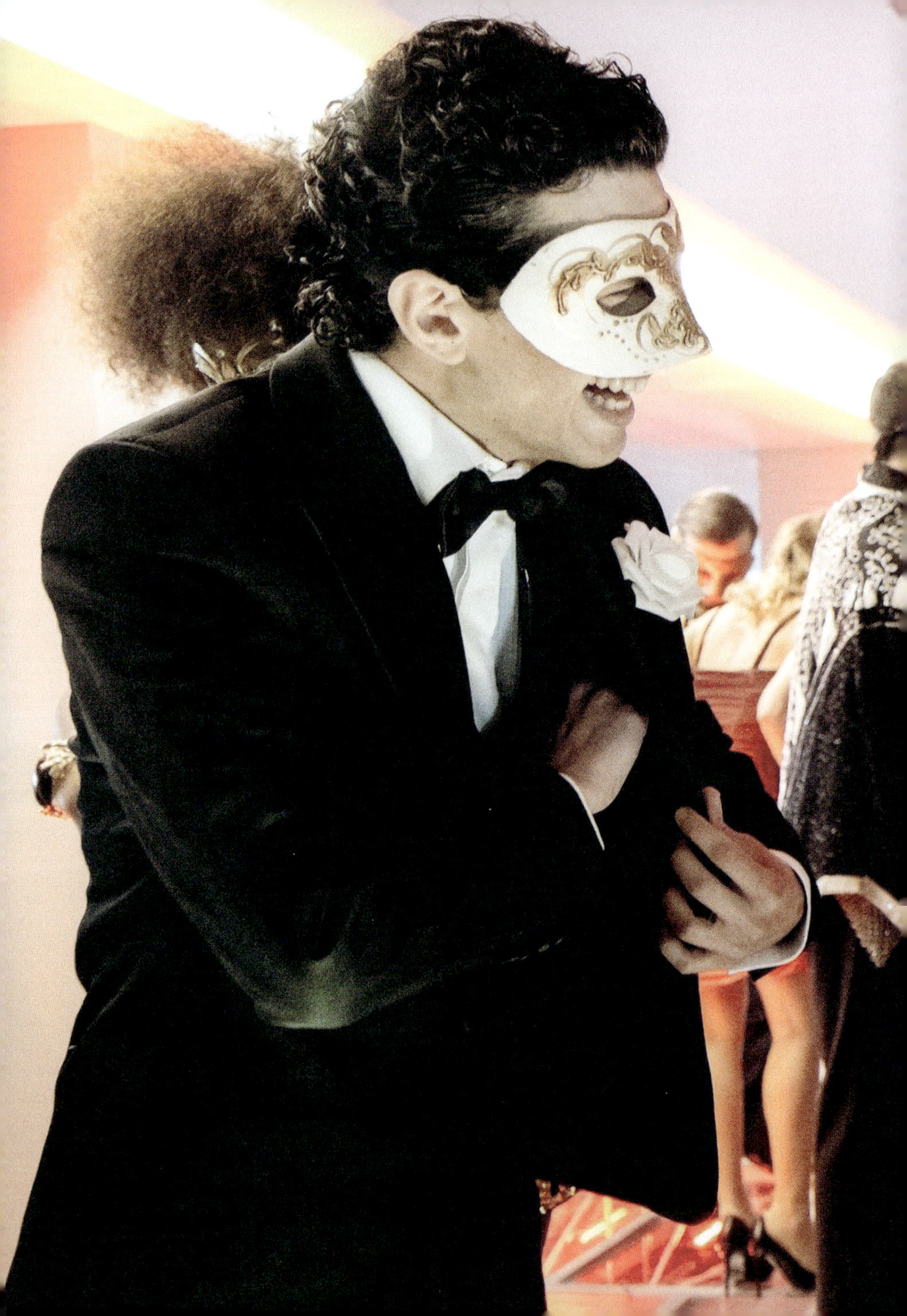

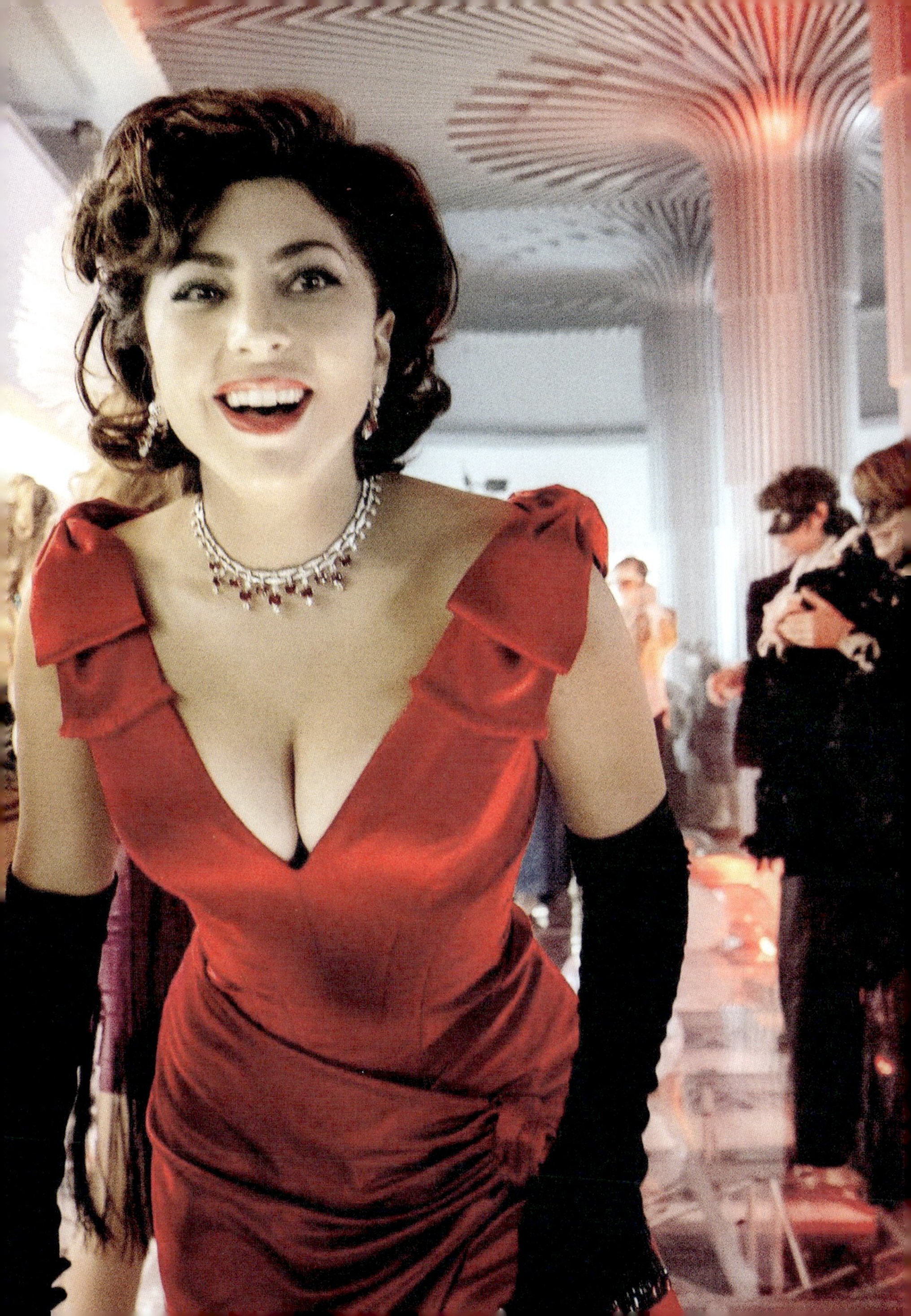

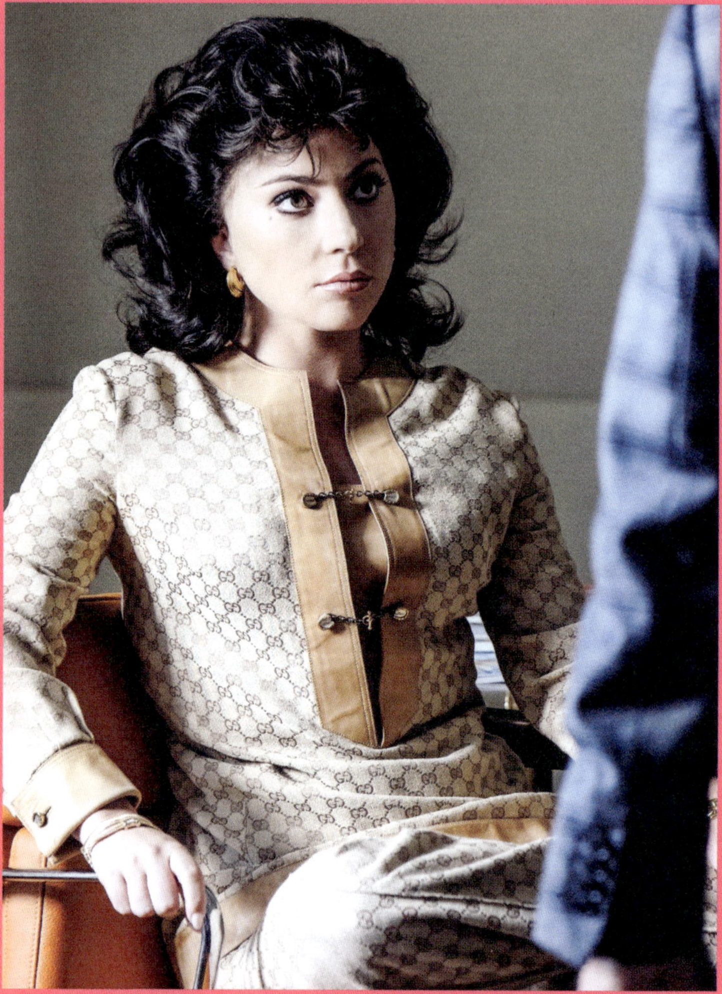

ABOVE Gaga wore lots of vintage Gucci straight from the archives for her role as Patrizia Reggiani in *House of Gucci*.

OVERLEAF While promoting *House of Gucci* on the red carpet, Lady Gaga seamlessly kept her own sense of personal style, with dramatic silhouettes and bright colours fit for Hollywood royalty.

"We didn't want her to be a Joan Collins from *Dynasty* type – what we were aiming for was more in the style of Gina Lollobrigida," Yates told The *New York Times*. "Knowing L.G.'s [Lady Gaga's] penchant for extremes, I was initially a little nervous about that. But L.G. said she really wanted to dress like her Italian mother did at that time, so we took that as a jumping-off point. Jewelry was very important, for example; we layered up two necklaces here, four bracelets there, we used tons of accessories."

For her press tour for *House of Gucci,* Lady Gaga leaned into her character and chose lots of dramatic gowns with modern glamour. She wore lots of Italian brands including Gucci, Versace and Valentino, and opted for floor-length silhouettes with lots of big diamond jewellery. Perhaps most stunning of all was the outfit she wore to the worldwide premiere of the film in London in 2021. Wearing a sheer, diaphanous purple gown with black crystal sleeves underneath and black fishnet stockings, she glowed against the darkness of the red carpet. The entire outfit was created by Gucci.

For the remainder of the press tour, Gaga alternated between demure looks during the day consisting of beautifully-cut coats by Celine and more eye-popping fashion spectaculars for her evening events. Gaga seemed very much at home dressing up in looks that her onscreen character would have loved too. Think leopard print, hoop earrings, big sunglasses, platform heels and form-fitting dresses with built-in details like corsets and bustiers. Whereas in *A Star is Born* it was about a toned-down sort of realness, *House of Gucci* is all about beautiful artifice. And with Salma Hayek, Al Pacino, Adam Driver and Jared Leto as co-stars, dramatically classic red carpet looks that fit the bill of the Hollywood elite were the go-to.

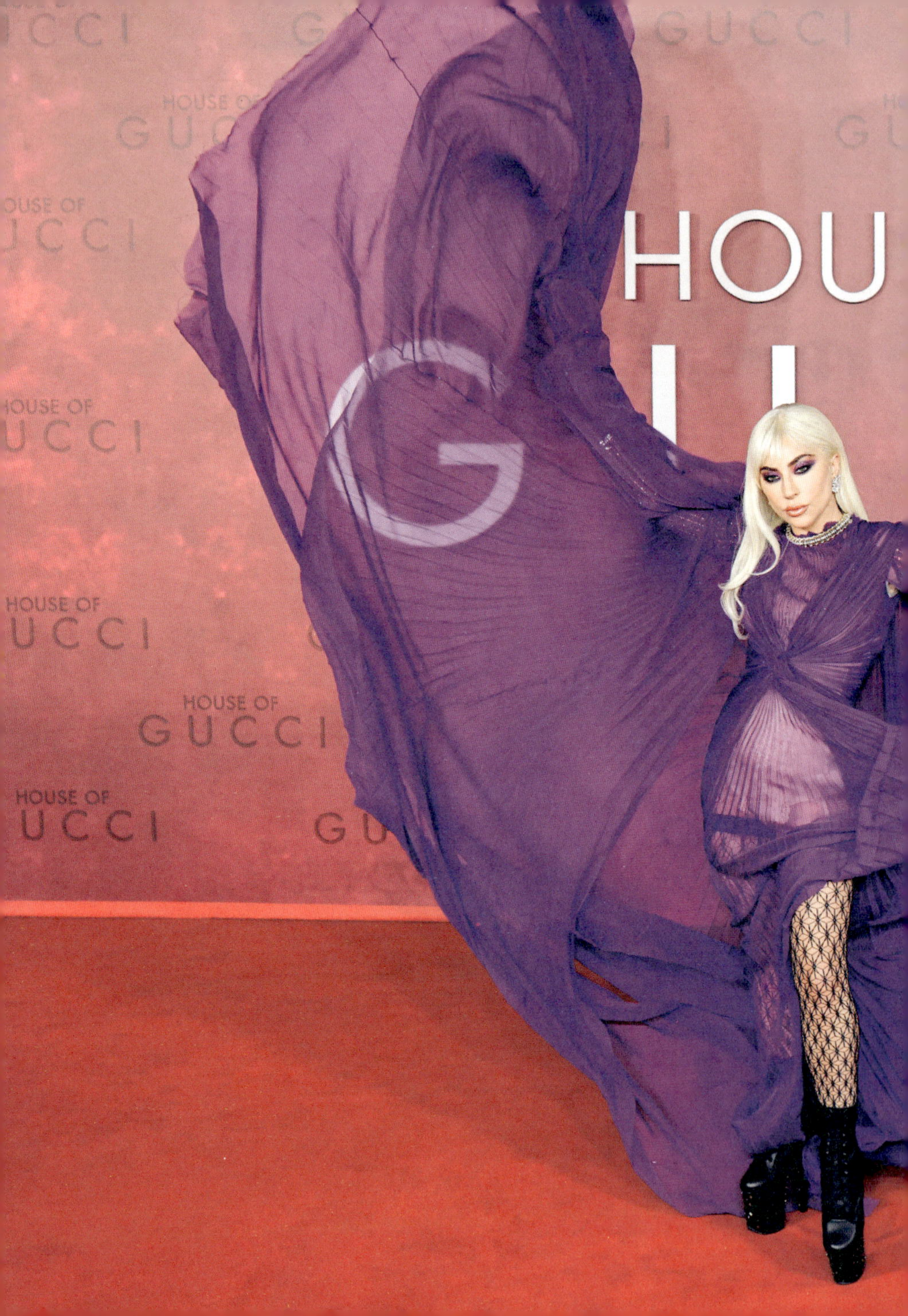
HOUSE OF
GUCCI

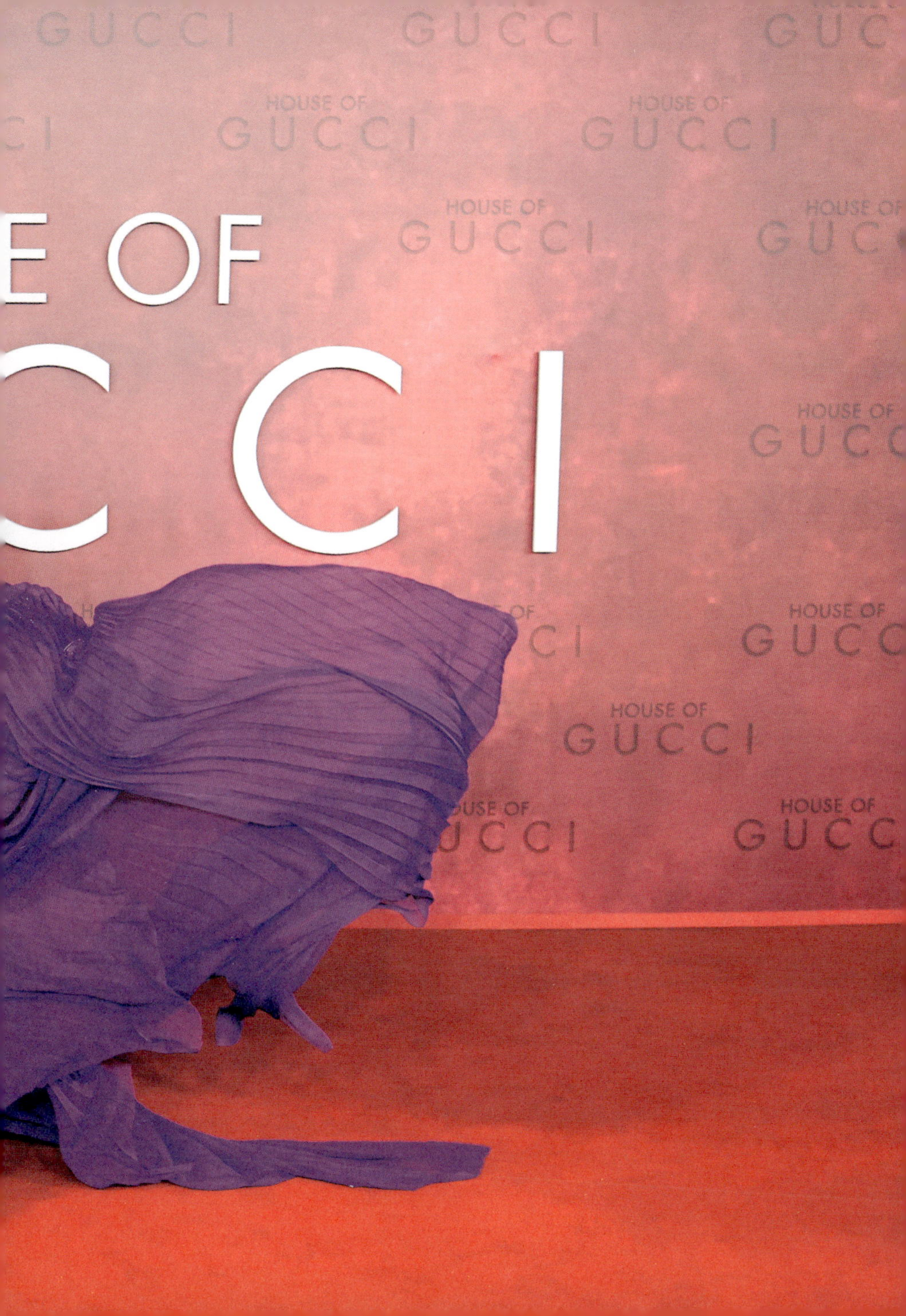
HOUSE OF
GUCCI
E OF
CCI

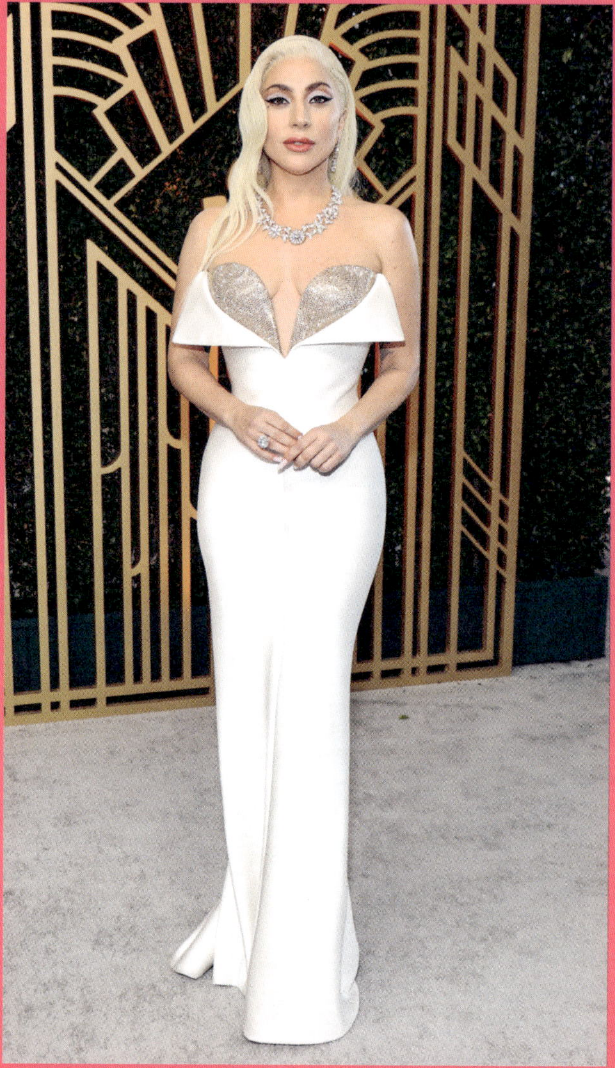

ABOVE At the 2022 Screen Actors Guild (SAG) Awards, Gaga opted for a streamlined, sculptural white gown by Armani Privé.

OPPOSITE Lady Gaga stunned on 2022 Critics Choice Awards red carpet in a gold and black Gucci gown.

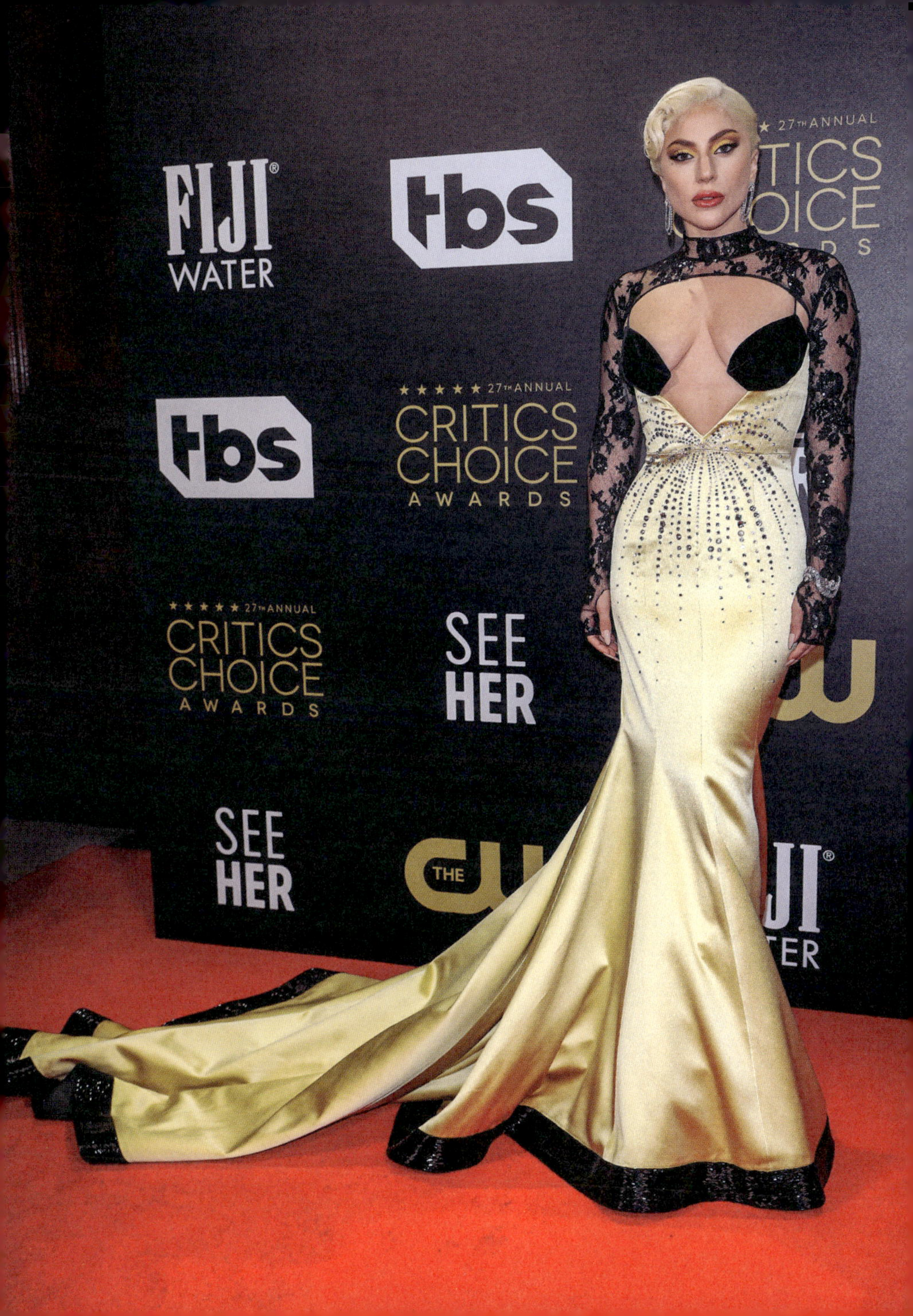
FIJI WATER
tbs
27TH ANNUAL CRITICS CHOICE AWARDS
SEE HER
THE CW

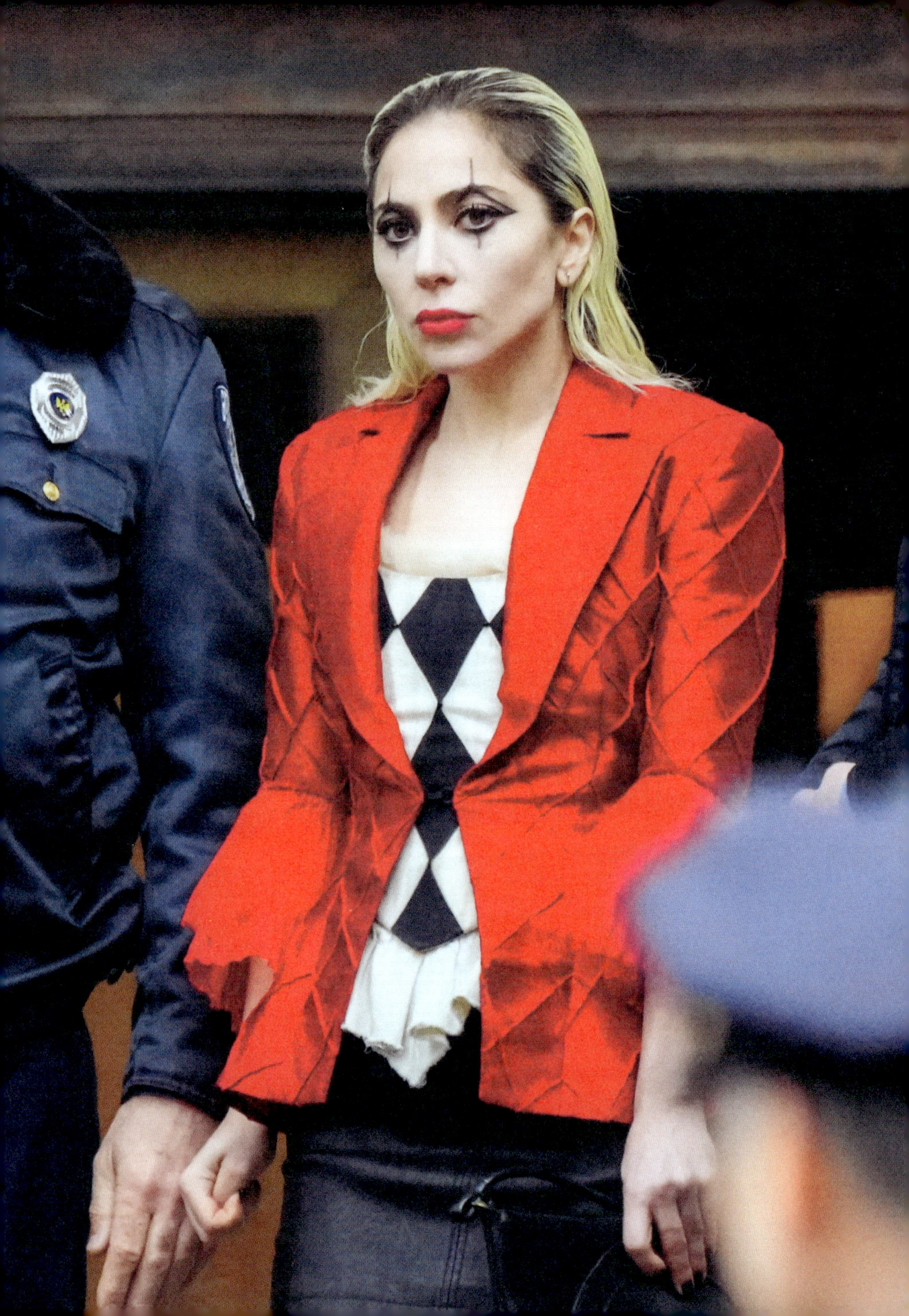

Taking a break between filming, working on upcoming albums and being a fashion icon, Gaga enjoyed a historic fashion moment when she wore Schiaparelli couture designed by Daniel Roseberry to perform at President Biden's inauguration in 2021. The dress was patriotic, with a bright, billowing, cherry-red skirt and navy-blue bodice. To accessorize, she donned a giant golden dove pin by the brand. The dress was also reportedly bulletproof. "Singing in a Schiaparelli bulletproof dress. I don't know if people know this about me, but if I weren't who I am today, I would have been a combat journalist. That was one of my dreams," she told British *Vogue*.

Continuing her streak of Hollywood hits, Lady Gaga starred in *Joker: Folie à Deux* in 2024. The iconic costume designer Arianne Phillips was behind Gaga's wardrobe for the film. Given Phillips did the costumes for the 1999 thriller-drama *Girl, Interrupted*, she was more than up to the task of creating imaginative looks for Gaga. According to her, Gaga envisioned her character Lee Quinzel (an inmate of Gotham City's Arkham State Hospital, also known as Harley Quinn) as someone who was obsessed with musical theatre, which contributed aesthetically to the costumes in the movie.

Gaga starred in the film *Joker: Folie à Deux* in 2024, wearing a maximalist medley to suit her character, Harley "Lee" Quinzel.

"Arianne Phillips and I worked on styling this film together; We had this tall order, because there's this idea that people have of Harley Quinn, and we wanted to create something completely new."

LADY GAGA ON WORKING ON *JOKER: FOLIE A DEUX*

Gaga's elegant black Celine look brought Old Hollywood glamour to the actress's method dressing.

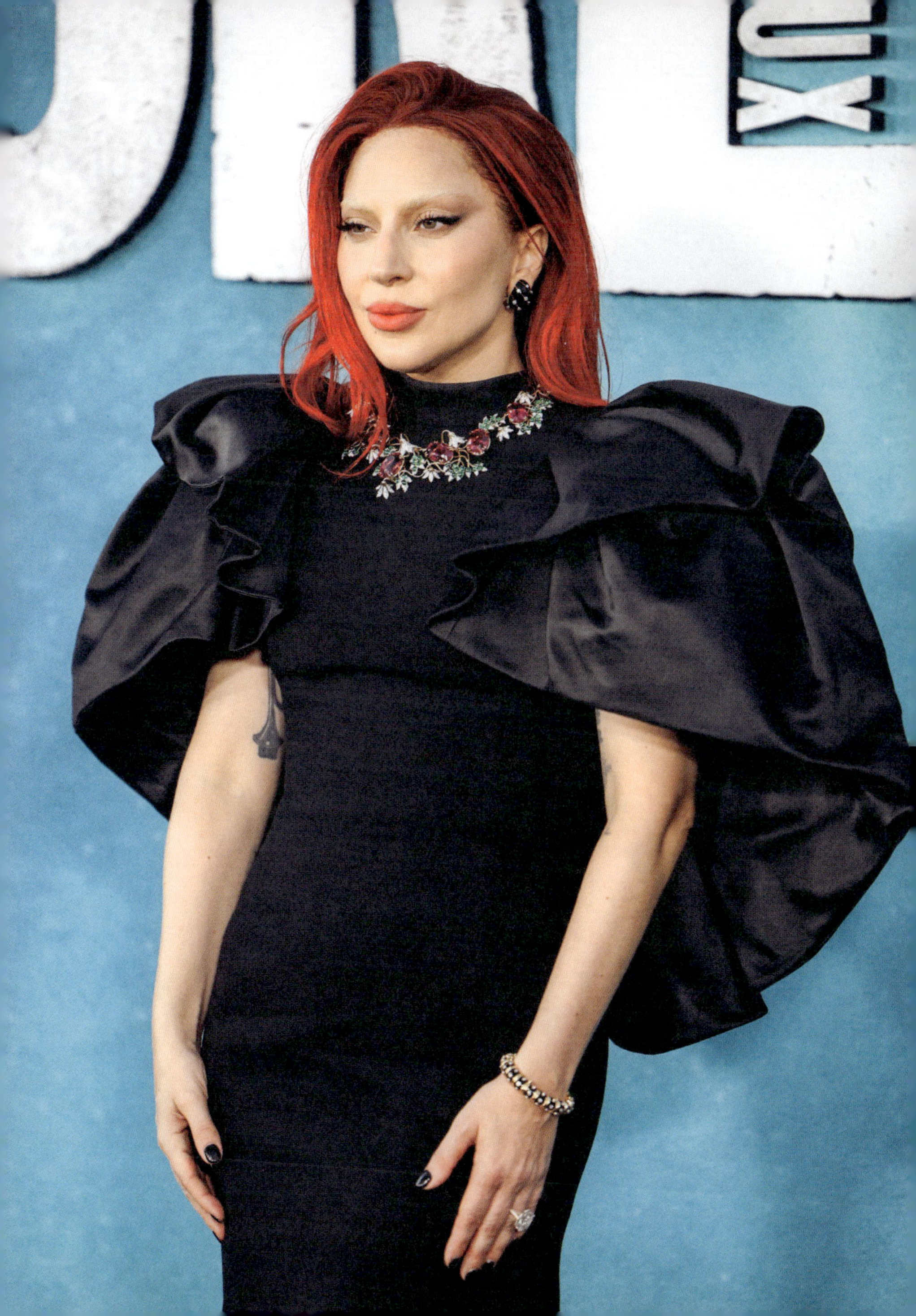

For *Joker: Folie à Deux*, Phillips dressed Gaga in a mix of silhouettes inspired by vintage shapes of the late sixties and seventies, with lots of red, black and white and punkish details mixed with a big dose of femininity, inspired by the original comic. "I had this idea that Lee was a reflection of what was happening at the time when New York City was at its lowest place," Philips told *Variety*. "Gotham is a dark, gritty, dangerous place and the art wave and punk movement was emerging. So I wanted her to have hospital-issue pants, almost like a scrub, a men's tank, but you could feel the femininity of her bra underneath. I wanted her to have a big cozy sweater for the volume to feel big enough that she could wrap herself in it."

The result was a reworked, Gaga-ified version of the classic Harley Quinn. Gaga has also said she worked collaboratively with Phillips when it came to the costumes. "It was a really special, exciting experience delivering the movie to the world," she told *Vogue*. "Arianne Phillips and I worked on styling this film together; We had this tall order, because there's this idea that people have of Harley Quinn, and we wanted to create something completely new. The clothes were kind of immature, indicative of a younger mind."

Off screen, Gaga wore lots of punky black and white pieces, with towering Marc Jacobs Kiki boots.

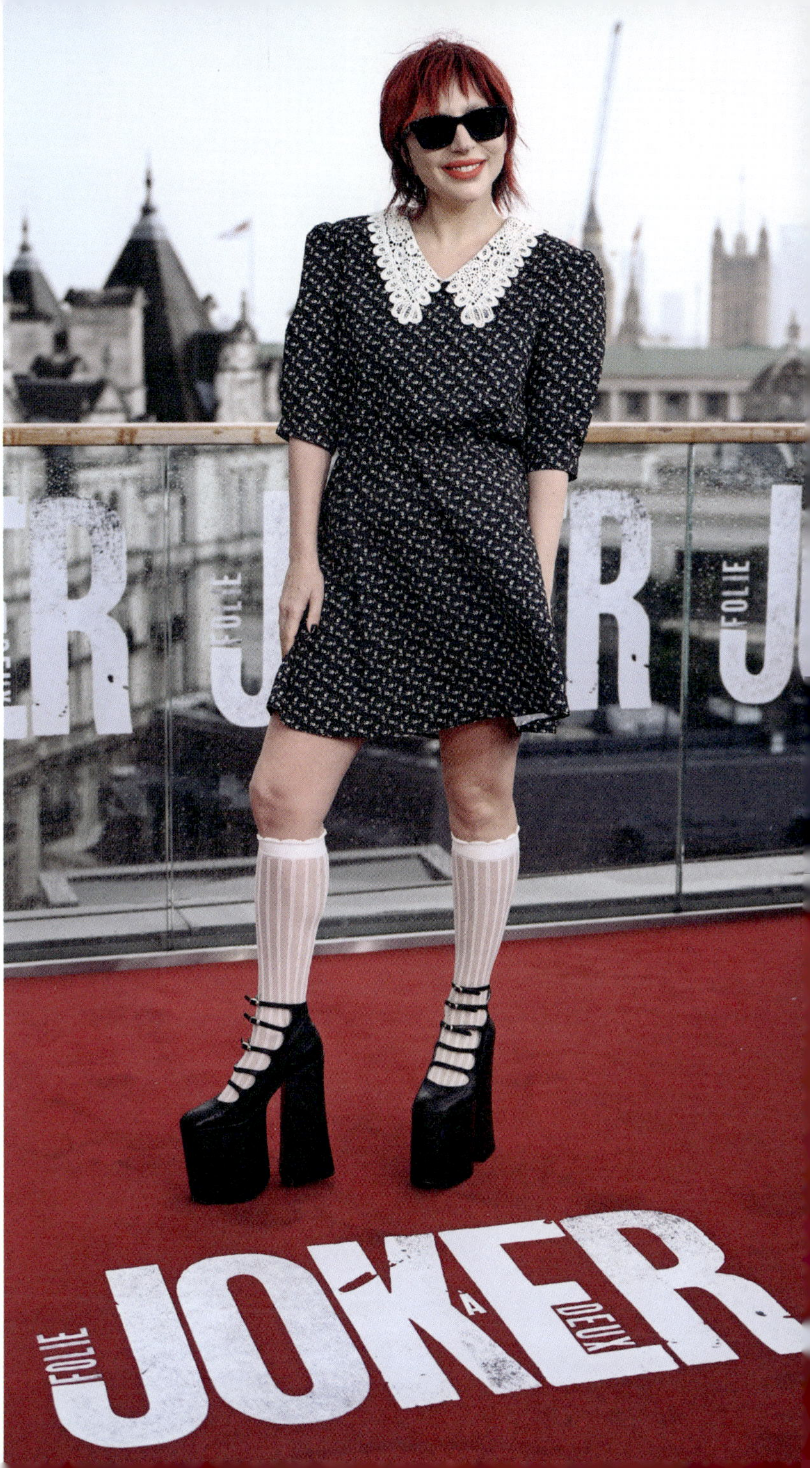
FOLIE
JOKER
À
DEUX

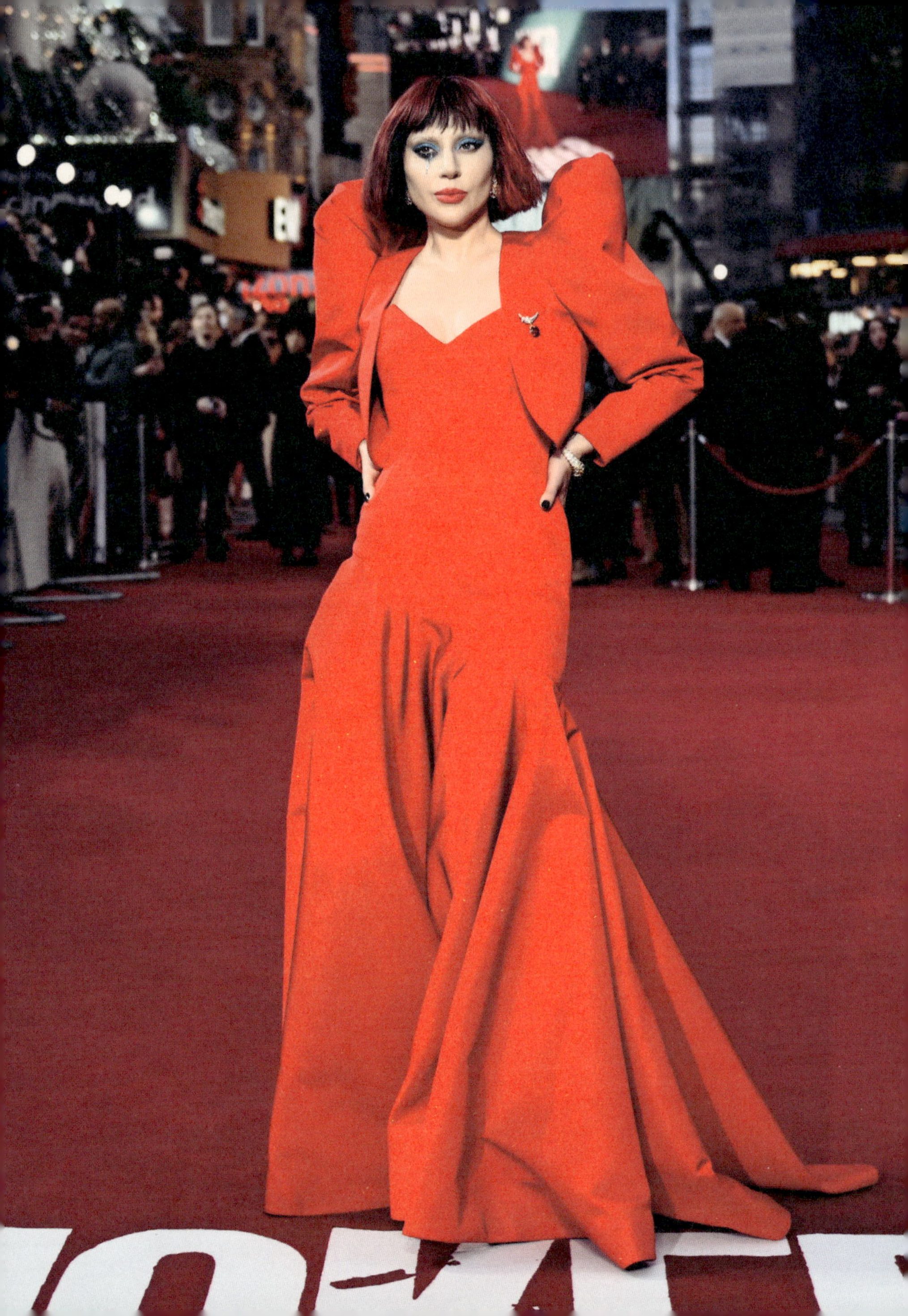

For her London premiere of the film, she opted for a cherry-red dress and matching extreme puff-sleeve bolero designed by Hedi Slimane for Celine. Slimane, who also has an extensive history as a photographer, lensed her for the cover of her 2009 album, *The Fame Monster*. Many called Gaga's dedication to the role during her press tour a form of method dressing. For much of the promotional period before the film, she mostly wore her hair dyed red, with brownish roots and punkish, choppy bangs. Many of her outfits played with the idea of mimicking her role in the film – for example, showing harlequin prints or motifs in an unexpected way. From Dior haute couture to vintage, she played with stripes, dramatic shapes and playful prints. Lady Gaga has always mastered playing different characters and she proved to stay perfectly in character through her *Joker* era.

Red, black and white were the trio of colours Lady Gaga gravitated toward while on tour to promote *Joker: Folie à Deux.*

Lady Gaga

CHAPTER 4

Classics

Gaga as fashion lore

Few celebrities love fashion the way that Lady Gaga does. She personally has a huge archive of clothes, ranging from high-end designer to rare vintage and everything in-between. It's been said that she stores her fashion archive in a 40,000-square-foot (3,700-square-metre) warehouse in Los Angeles. "I don't wear fashion, I am fashion," she told *Yahoo Style* in 2014. "I don't mean that to sound arrogant or rude or anything like that but you know when you just love something so much it just hurts. Like when the topstitching is just perfect. The beading is exquisite. It's like a love affair. Those clothes are so special. I have another relationship with fashion that goes beyond just wearing clothes."

And yet, through all the evolution and adaptation of fashion, Gaga has a sense of style that is instantly recognizable, whether she's wearing toned-down Americana classics or her over-the-top looks injected with a hefty dose of art-fuelled avant-garde attitude. Toeing the line between something more conservative and a vision of out-there edginess, she picks and pulls from her own archive of rotating staples to reintroduce classics in her world. Think underwear as outerwear, towering stilettos, leotards and, in other cases, the casual white T-shirt and cut-off "Daisy Duke" denim shorts.

Even if Gaga is wearing something classic, she'll give it her own spin, such as when she matched her baby blue Valentino Couture gown to her hair for the 2019 Golden Globes.

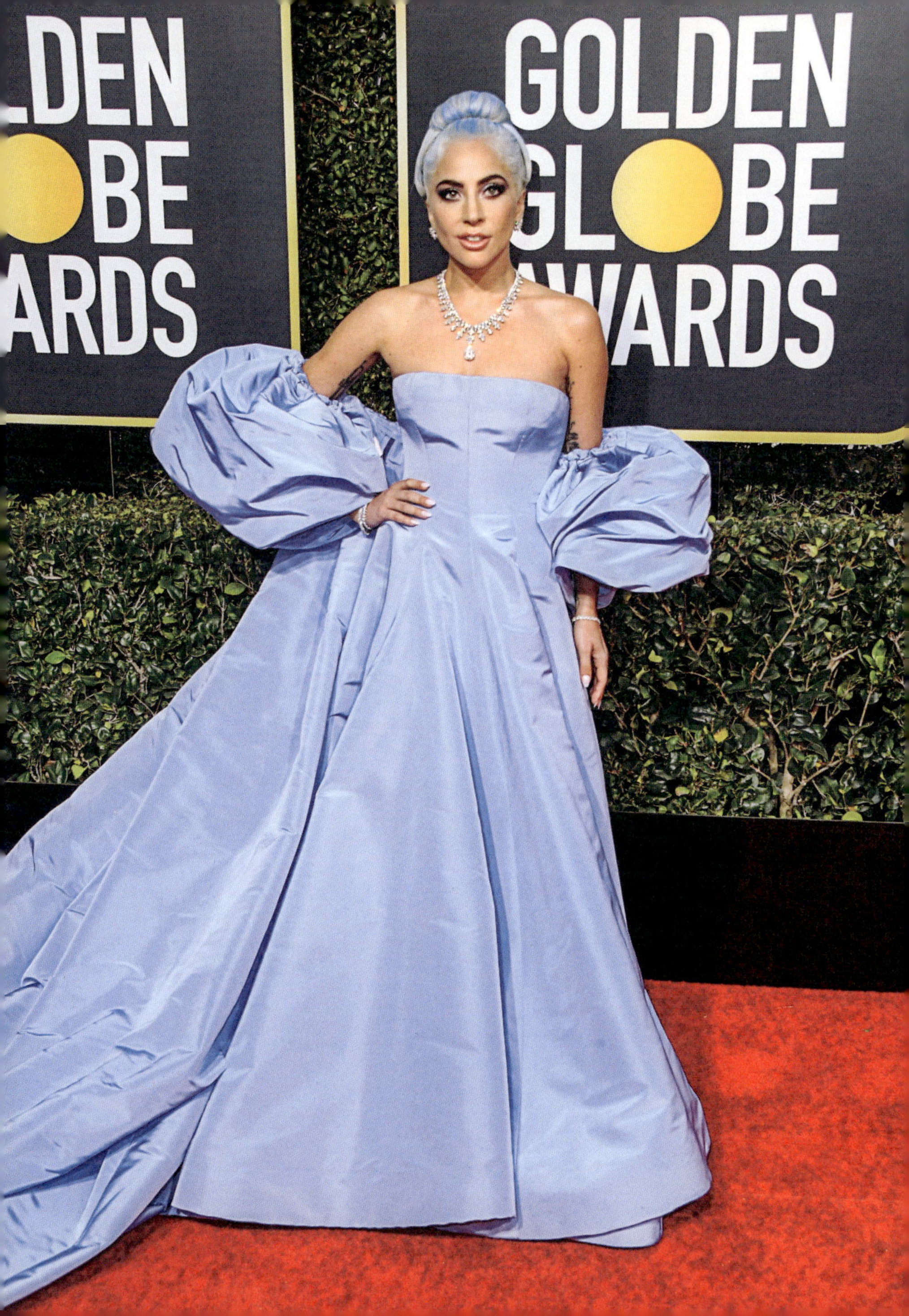
GOLDEN
GLOBE
AWARDS

"I don't wear fashion,
I am fashion.
I don't mean that to
sound arrogant
or rude or anything
like that but

you know when you just love something *so much* it *just hurts."*

LADY GAGA

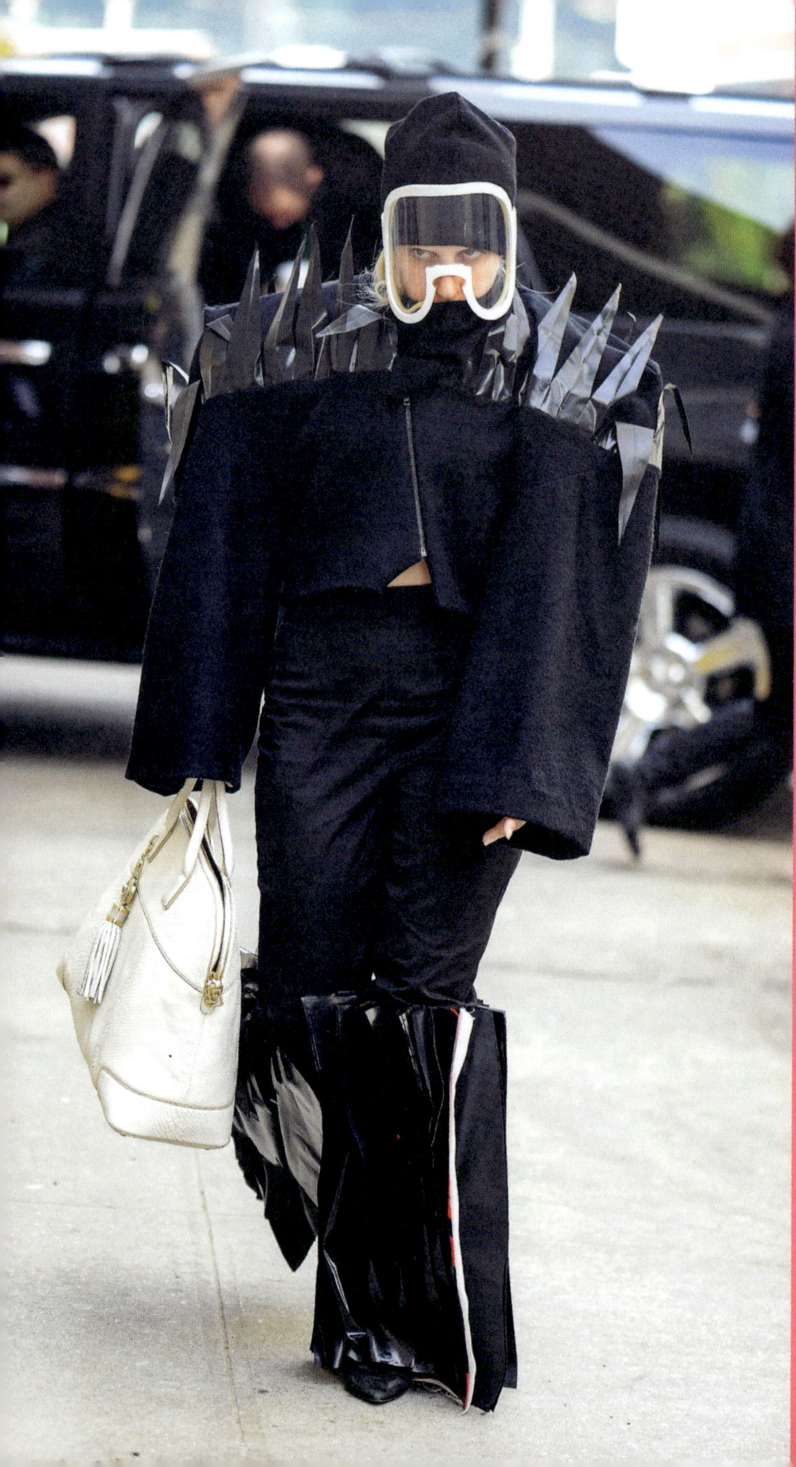

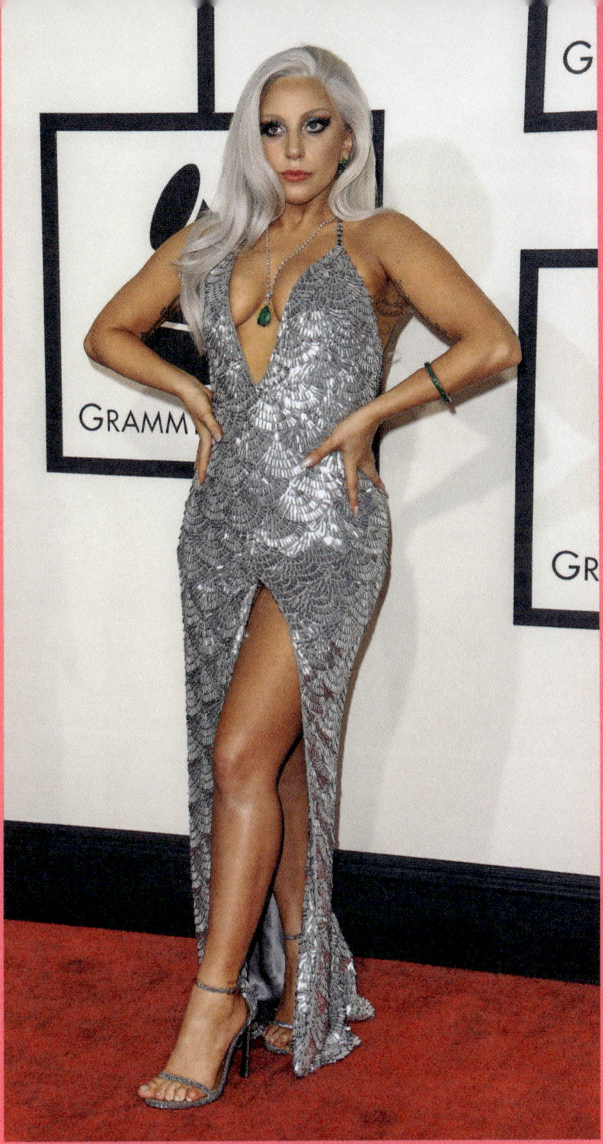

ABOVE Gaga has proved she's a style chameleon, mastering edgy pieces on the street and high fashion on the red carpet, as seen here at the 2015 Grammys.

OPPOSITE Gaga's early looks, as seen here in 2014, still influence her personal style no matter what.

Some might say that Lady Gaga is one of the very few celebrities to take dressing for the red carpet to the next level by adding an element of performance art or surprise, even in the subtlest of ways. That's classic Gaga, after all. One example of this is the time she attended the 2019 Golden Globes and walked the red carpet wearing a powdery blue Valentino couture gown, with her hair done in the exact same shade of soft blue.

In 2022, Lady Gaga proved her commitment to extreme style by going back to her roots in terms of pushing the boundaries of wearability. For her Chromatica Ball tour, she chose looks that her biggest fans and devotees to fashion would deeply appreciate. She opened the tour wearing a gothic, all-black look: an archival sculptural piece from Gareth Pugh's spring 2007 collection. Previously, Gaga engaged in out-there fashion during her *ARTPOP* era, but this felt like a slightly darker, more elevated take than what she wore previously.

This time Gaga worked with three stylists – Nicola Formichetti, Tom Eerebout and Sandra Amador – to dream up her looks for the Chromatica Ball tour. *Chromatica*, for her, was an amalgamation of her past and present mental health issues combined with a new sort of fashion alter ego that pulls from both the present and the past. "*Chromatica* is not utopian or dystopian," Nicola Formichetti told *Vogue*. "It's how Gaga sees the world. It's very, very upbeat, but it's realistic in its message, and she speaks about a lot of deeply personal things. So there is this interplay of light and dark. We needed something that wasn't running from the past – actually, we wanted to embrace the past – to show that Gaga is on her path towards healing."

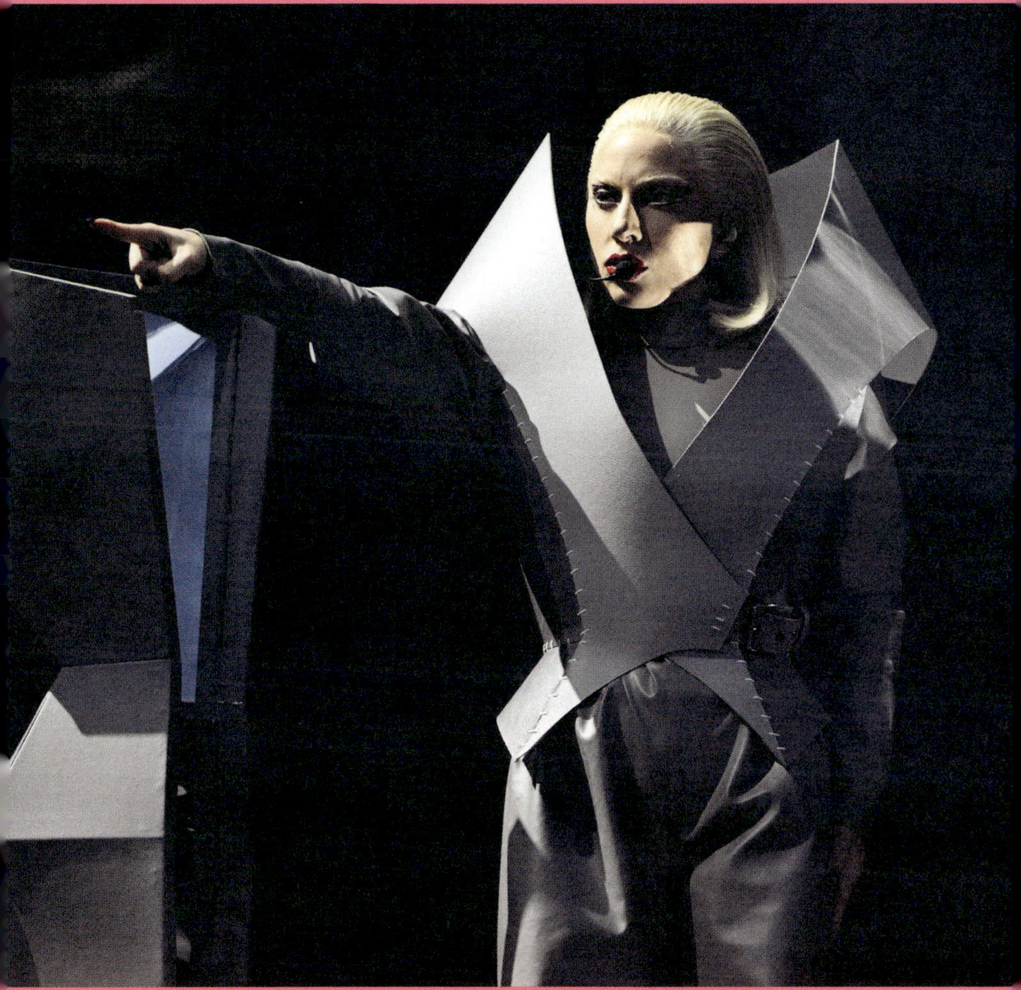

ABOVE For her Chromatica Ball tour in 2022, Gaga went back to her roots of extreme fashion, choosing sculptural, experimental looks.

OVERLEAF Lady Gaga worked with three stylists for her Chromatica Ball tour: Nicola Formichetti, Tom Eerebout and Sandra Amador, each dreaming up outfits that were more experimental than the last.

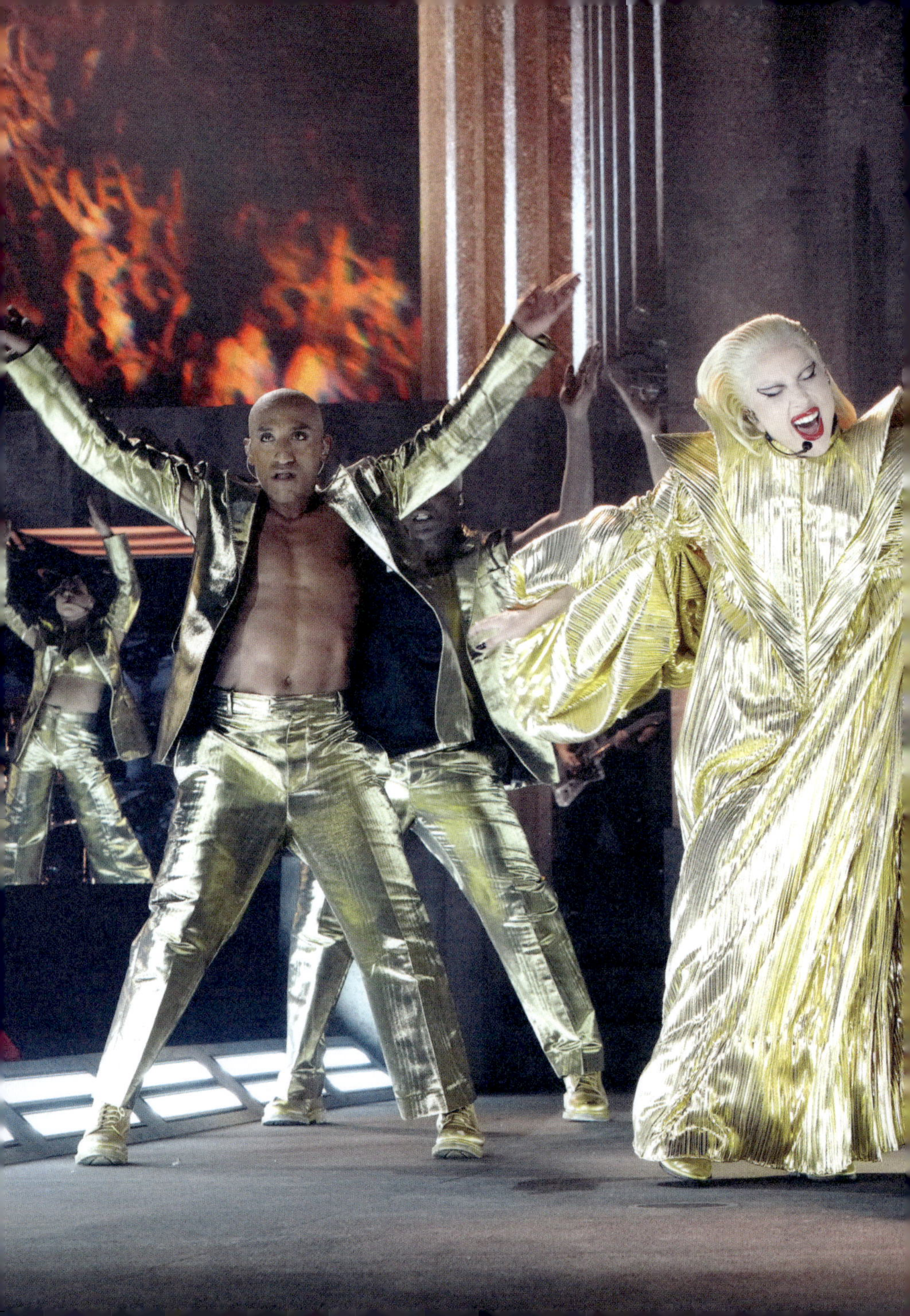

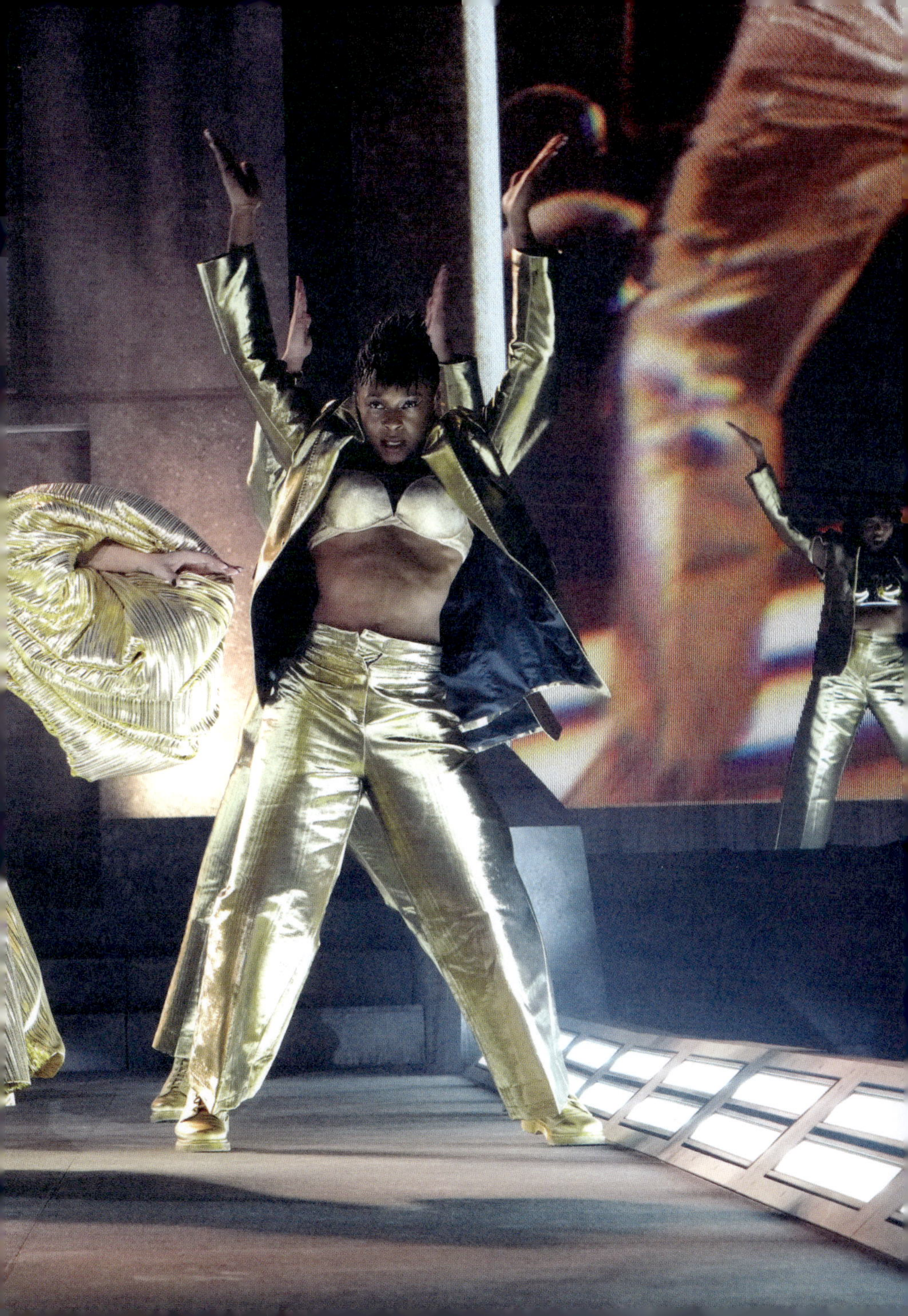

That also meant leather, latex by her favourite brand, Vex, and both her signature Pleaser stiletto boots as well as some punkish gothic platform boots from Demonia. But there were some subtle differences too, of course. In her early career, Gaga was famous for her over-the-top wigs, hair accessories, sunglasses and ornamentation. During her *Joanne* era, she went for a softer, toned-down look. And when she played singer-songwriter Ally in *A Star is Born*, she transformed with an old Hollywood glam look to match. *Chromatica* felt new, in a different sort of way. "Gaga wanted to own the roots of her past [in pop]," Formichetti told *Vogue*. "And we wanted to show that through fashion, as well. Before, we used to kind of hide her. Gaga was this mystery, with the wigs, the sunglasses, the makeup. She was an enigma. We still have that element, of course, but she's much stronger, and you can really see more of her in everything. You start seeing more of her face, her skin."

Nothing was off the table for the Chromatica Ball tour, including emerging designers. For one look, Gaga sported a custom latex bodysuit by Dead Lotus Couture with a Xtian de Medici bug headpiece. In a throwback to one of her most memorable stage moments of all time (when she fake-bled on stage at the MTV VMAS in 2009) she appeared to bleed in a latex bodysuit by Vex Clothing and Yummy Latex Clothing.

OVERLEAF Lady Gaga took inspiration for some of her favourite high fashion moments from the likes of Thierry Mugler and more for the Chromatica Ball tour. Here, she wears a custom latex bodysuit by Dead Lotus Couture with an Xtian de Medici bug headpiece.

"Chromatica is not utopian or dystopian. It's how Gaga sees the world."

NICOLA FORMICHETTI

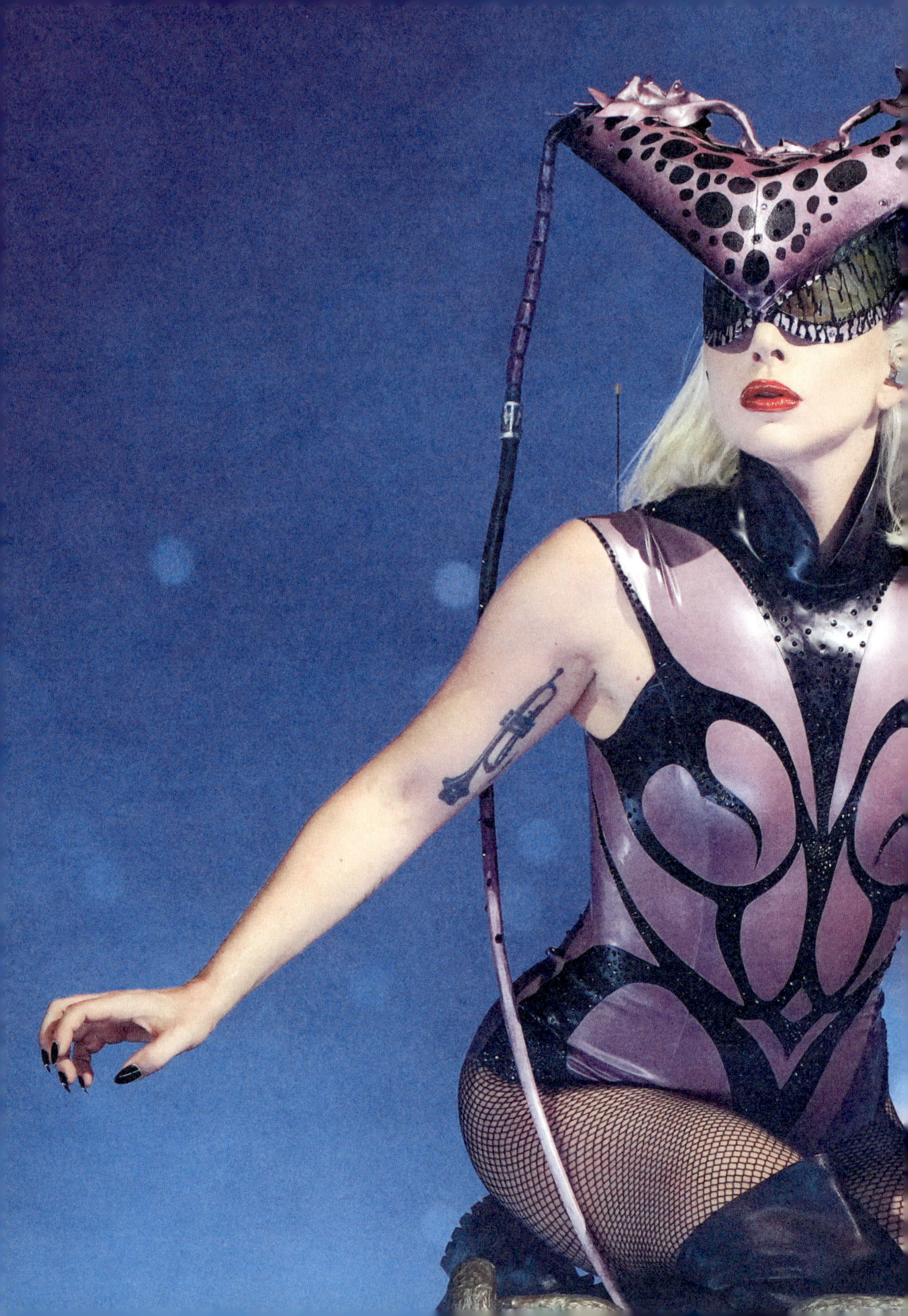

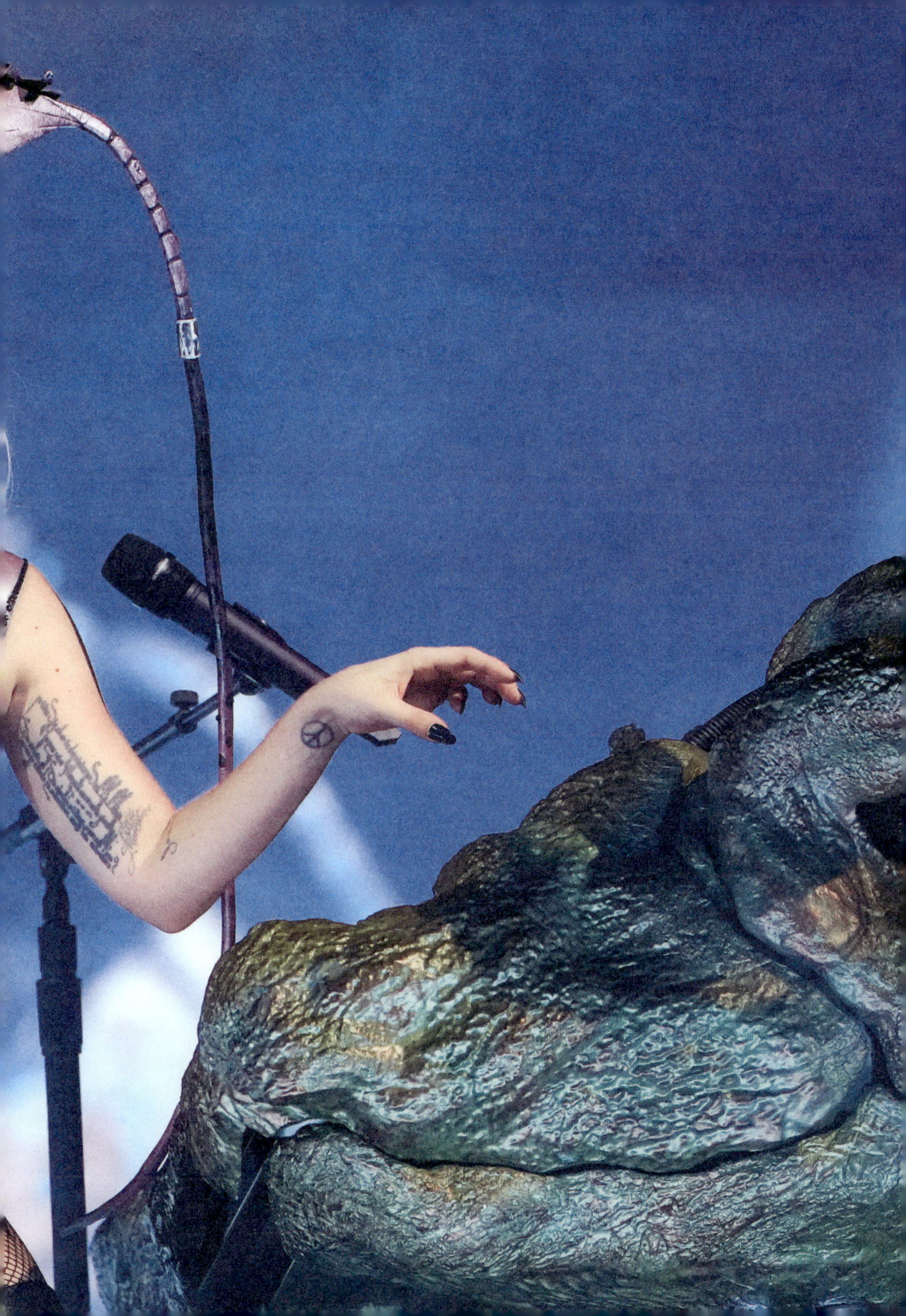

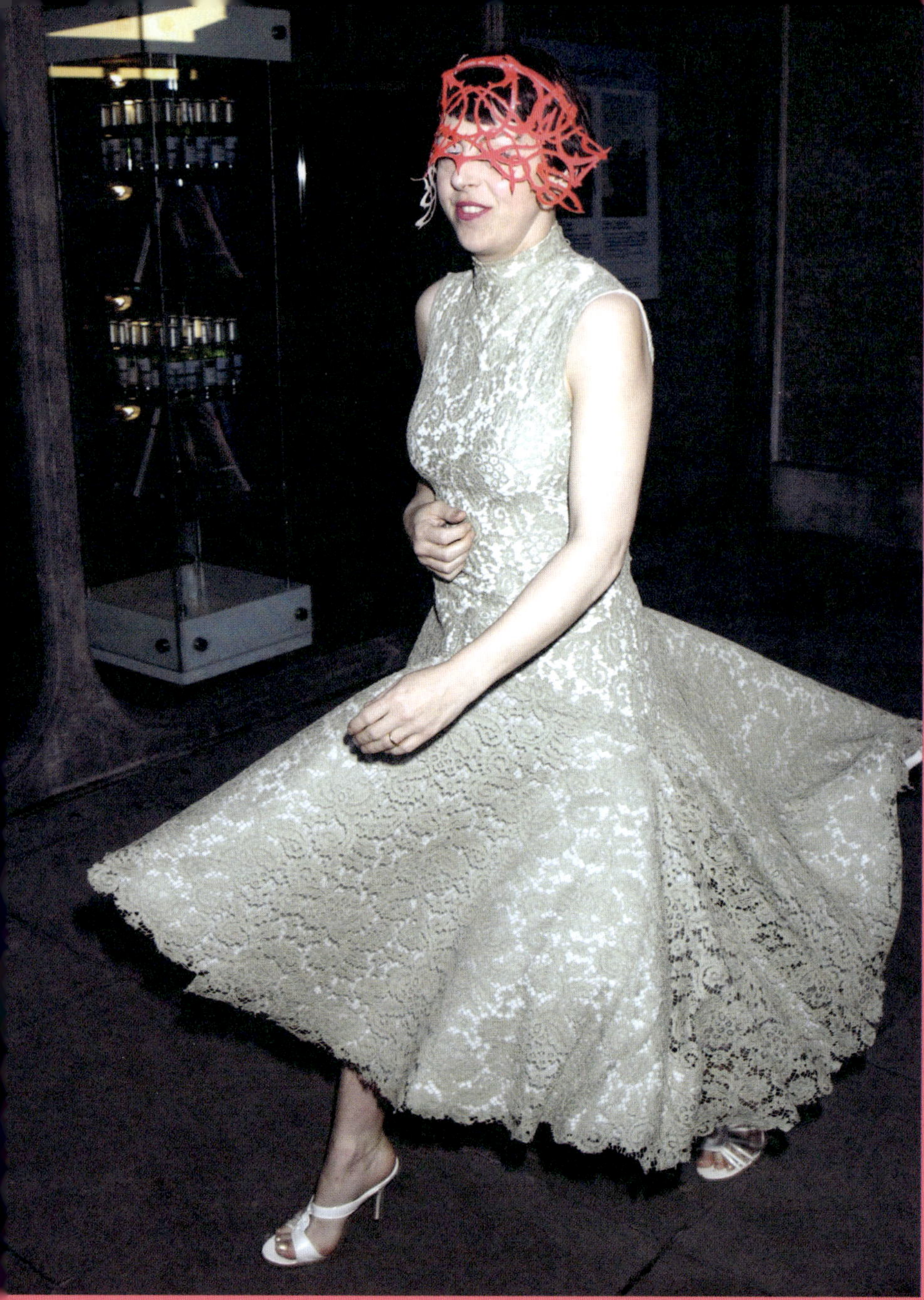

The Gaga-ification of fashion

Lady Gaga will never give up some of her forever staples. For those inspired by her look, there are subtle, easy ways to pay homage to it, even without an extensive, archive wardrobe filled with work from designers from Thierry Mugler to Alexander McQueen.

Gaga has been transparent that she's been inspired by other artists, but especially tastemakers in the late designer Alexander McQueen's circle. Early on in her career, she was compared to both Daphne Guinness and the late Isabella Blow, both eccentric English aristocrats who adored avant-garde fashion and had excellent taste in clothing and accessories. Both muses and friends of McQueen, they often wore and collected some of his most extreme work and celebrated talent in the art and fashion world. Blow was the muse of the milliner Philip Treacy. "The fashion community in general got me much earlier than everyone else. I felt truly embraced by this London cultural movement, that McQueen, Isabella, Daphne Guinness wing of the English crowd," Gaga told *Vogue* in 2011. "I remember when I first started doing photo shoots, people would say, 'My God, you look so much like Isabella Blow, it scares me.' And McQueen used to say,

Gaga has cited both Daphne Guinness and the late Isabella Blow (pictured here) as style inspirations.

"I felt truly embraced by this London cultural *movement, that McQueen, Isabella, Daphne* Guinness *wing of the English crowd"*

LADY GAGA

Daphne Guinness (pictured here) often wears towering heels and runway pieces by Alexander McQueen – it's no surprise Gaga is a fan.

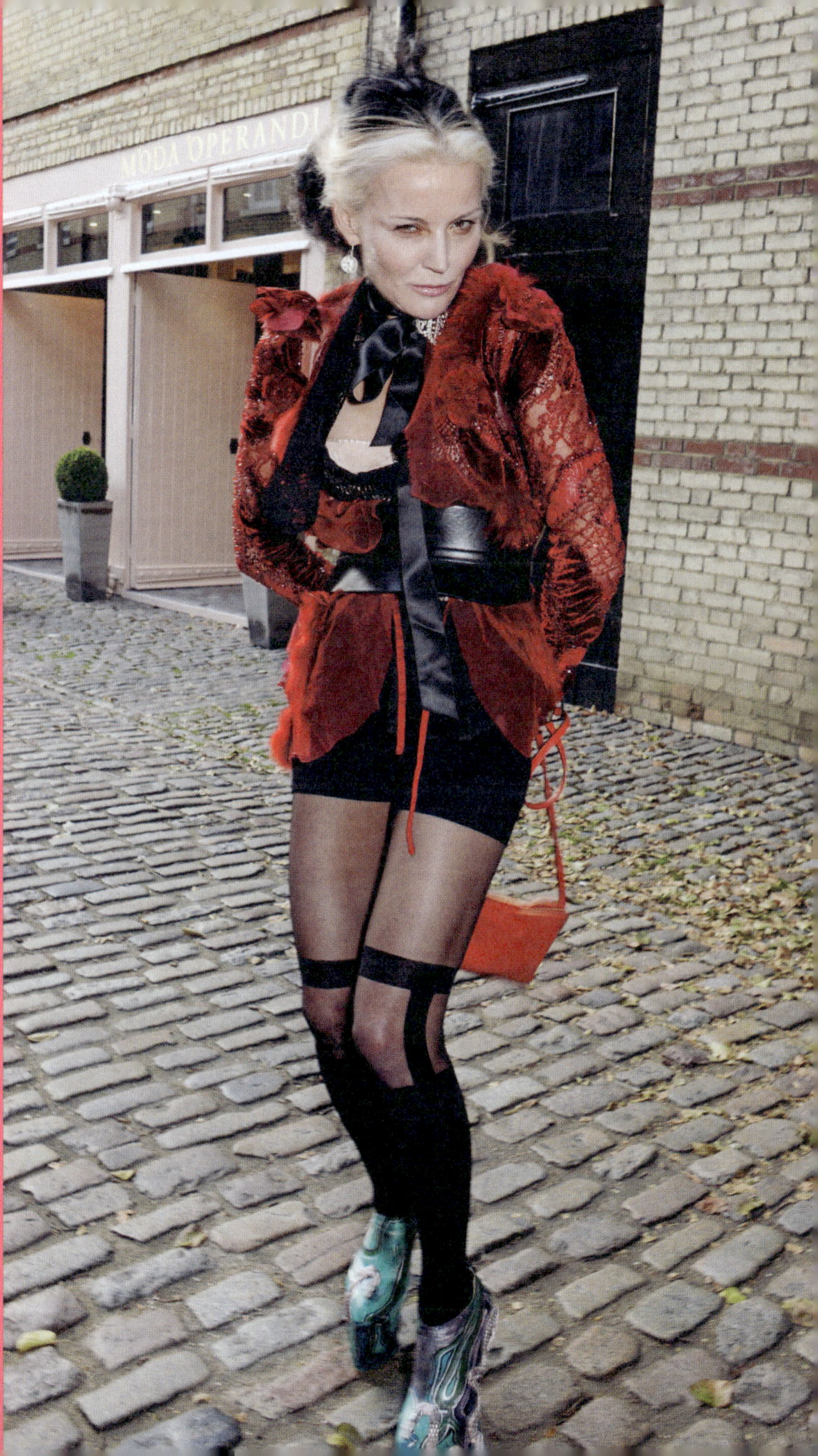
MODA OPERANDI

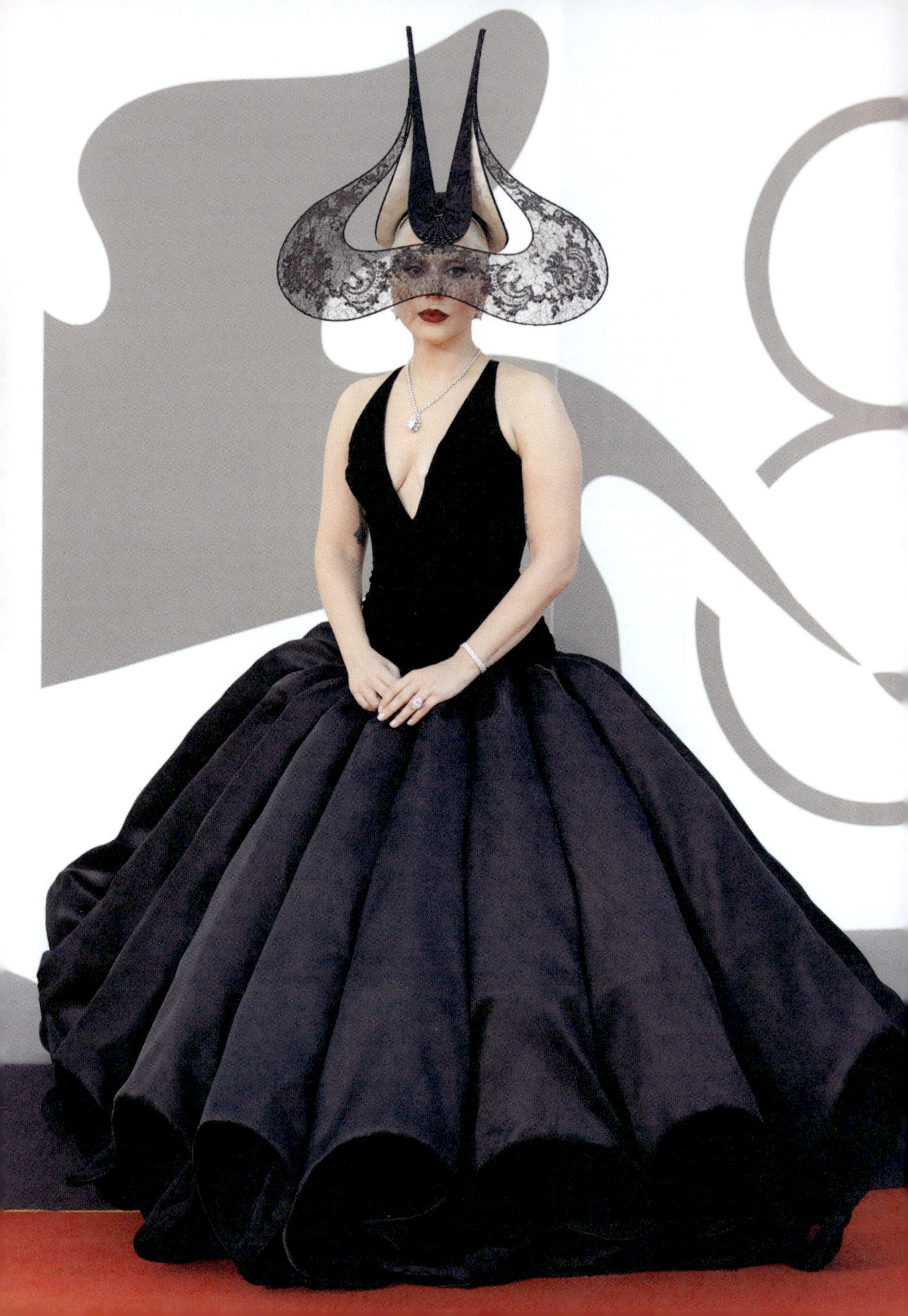

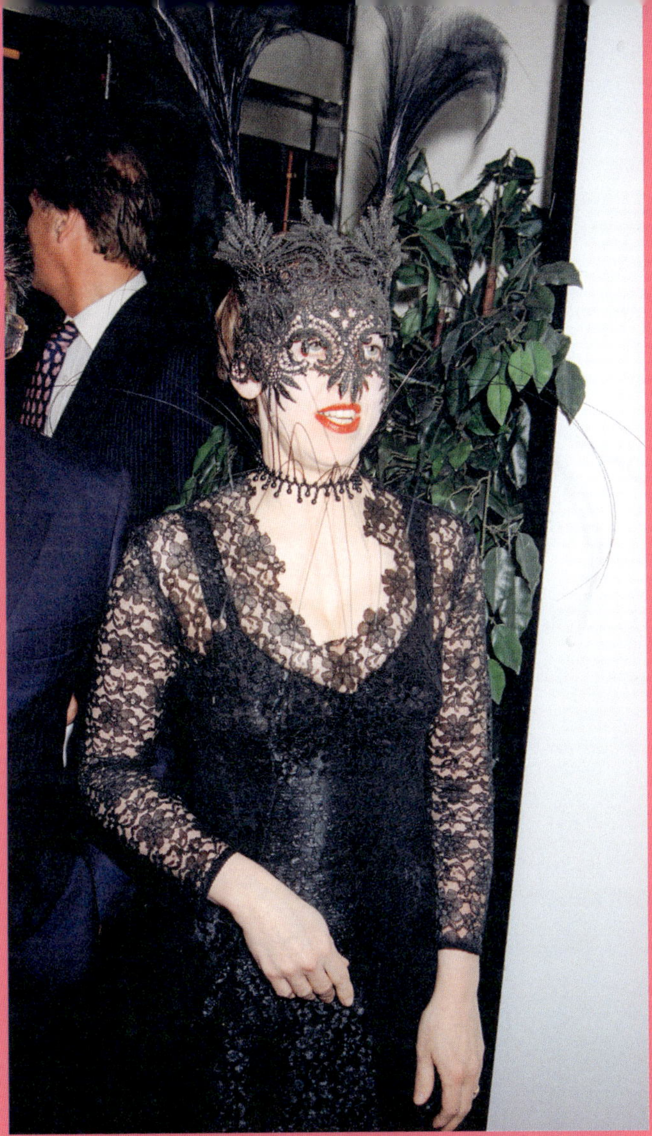

ABOVE Isabella Blow often wore headpieces designed by her close friend Philip Treacy.

OPPOSITE At the premiere of *Joker: Folie à Deux* at the 81st Venice Film Festival, Lady Gaga wore a black lace headpiece from Philip Treacy's Autumn/ Winter 2001 couture collection, first worn by Isabella Blow in 2002.

'Oh, my God, your boobs!' He actually grabbed both of them and said, 'Even your boobs are like hers!'"

Guinness often wore hugely tall heels and Blow usually wore an art-worthy hat or head topper. And Gaga emulated both to a certain degree. Taking things to a more literal level, at the red carpet premiere of *Joker: Folie à Deux* at the 81st Venice Film Festival on September 4, 2024, Gaga wore a black lace headpiece from Philip Treacy's Autumn/Winter 2001 couture collection, first worn by Blow in 2002. With her jet-black Dior couture gown with hugely sculptural pleats, the look was whimsical yet refined. The lace headpiece is theatrical in nature and swoops down in front of the wearer's eyes to make quite the statement.

In 2010, Gaga wore a glittering lobster headpiece that Treacy made for her. Previously, Isabella Blow wore a few similar styles of lobster head toppers created by Treacy, dating back as early as 1998. Likewise, Daphne Guinness has always had her expressive coif of icy white hair paired with a section of pitch black. Gaga frequently goes back to her own shade of platinum.

There are so many similarities between the wardrobes and tastes of these three women. Blow and Guinness were also close. In 2007, when Blow died in tragic circumstances, her impressive collection of designer fashion was put up for auction by Christie's but Daphne Guinness purchased the entire lot before it went on sale. Later, Blow's collection became the subject of the exhibition, "Isabella Blow: Fashion Galore" at Somerset House in London, 2013.

"I have another relationship *with* fashion *that* goes beyond *just* *wearing* clothes*"*

LADY GAGA

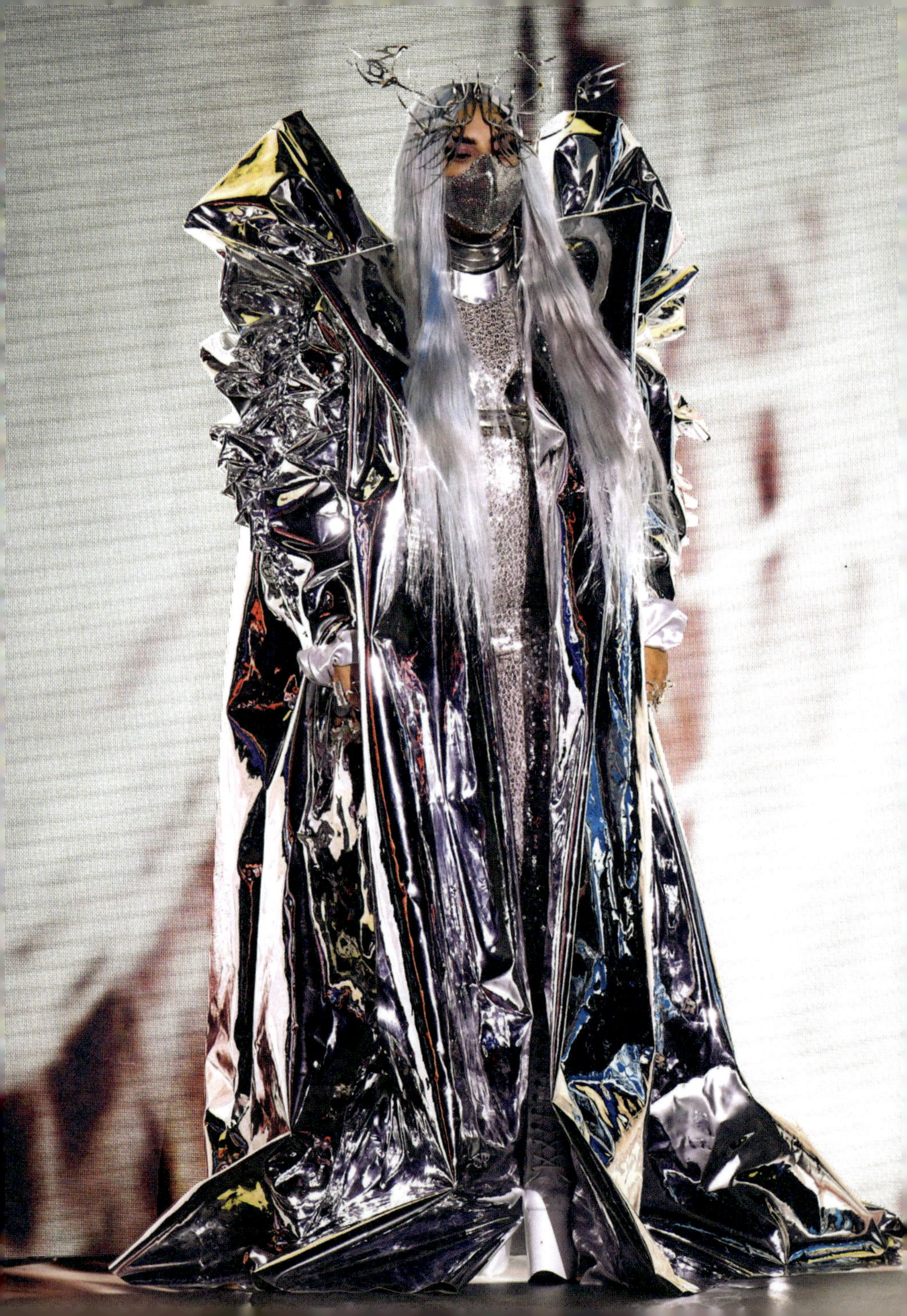

And the hat that Lady Gaga wore, given it was couture after all, likely came from Blow's collection. Great style is eternal and Gaga clearly sees the never-ending inspiration of visual language that both of these women created.

But perhaps one of the biggest signatures of Lady Gaga's style is the grand outfit change. One only has to watch a clip of her historic red carpet outfit change for the 2019 Met Gala to see that. The same goes with the Super Bowl, in which she had multiple outfit changes in succession as the sole performer on stage, with the exception of her troupe of backup dancers for the occasion. What would a Lady Gaga appearance be without the performance? Her Little Monsters crave the drama and she delivers.

For the 2020 MTV VMA awards, she went over-the-top with nine different outfit changes. It was the thick of the pandemic and COVID-19 had clearly affected the entertainment industry, but Gaga didn't let that deter her. With each outfit change, she wore a different protective face mask. Some of her standout looks of the night included pieces from both big household designer names as well as labels that were more up-and-coming. She opted for a bright, billowing kelly green Christopher John Rogers gown with a mask with horns and pearl jewelry for one look. For another, she wore a latex catsuit from Vex Clothing with all the edgy accessories to go with it.

Even with mask mandates during the global pandemic, Gaga found a creative way to make them a fashion statement.

Many of her looks touched on all the subcultural aesthetics she's explored in the past, from steampunk to raver, gothic Lolita, sci-fi and glam goddess and everything in-between. According to Lady Gaga, wearing the masks upfront was an intentional statement at the time in a world where wearing a mask during the pandemic was controversial to some people. Gaga has often infused tech into her fashion looks (like the time she debuted a flying dress at the SXSW Conference in 2013) and this was also an opportunity to do the same. During her performance of 'Rain on Me', the song lyrics were projected through her mask. The mask had a digital sensor to project whatever Gaga was singing. She also wore a kaleidoscopic rainbow of a dress by Iris van Herpen and a silver look that seemed to be a throwback to one of her earlier, art-worthy looks: an Area jacket, Conrad Muscarella headpiece and her signature Pleaser shoes.

Her longtime collaborator and stylist Nicola Formichetti was the one who styled her for the evening. "Obviously the looks for the red carpet and the speeches were much more sophisticated, and then the performance was '80s inspired, punk rock, Gaga," he told *Vogue*. "We wanted to show the whole spectrum of Gaga because she's not just one thing, and that's what I love about who she is. She can sing, dance, play the piano, be classic, avant-garde, or street, so we wanted to show all of that."

Nicola Formichetti styled Lady Gaga for the 2020 MTV Video Music Awards (VMAs), as seen here, in a rainbow of cyberpunk-inspired outfits.

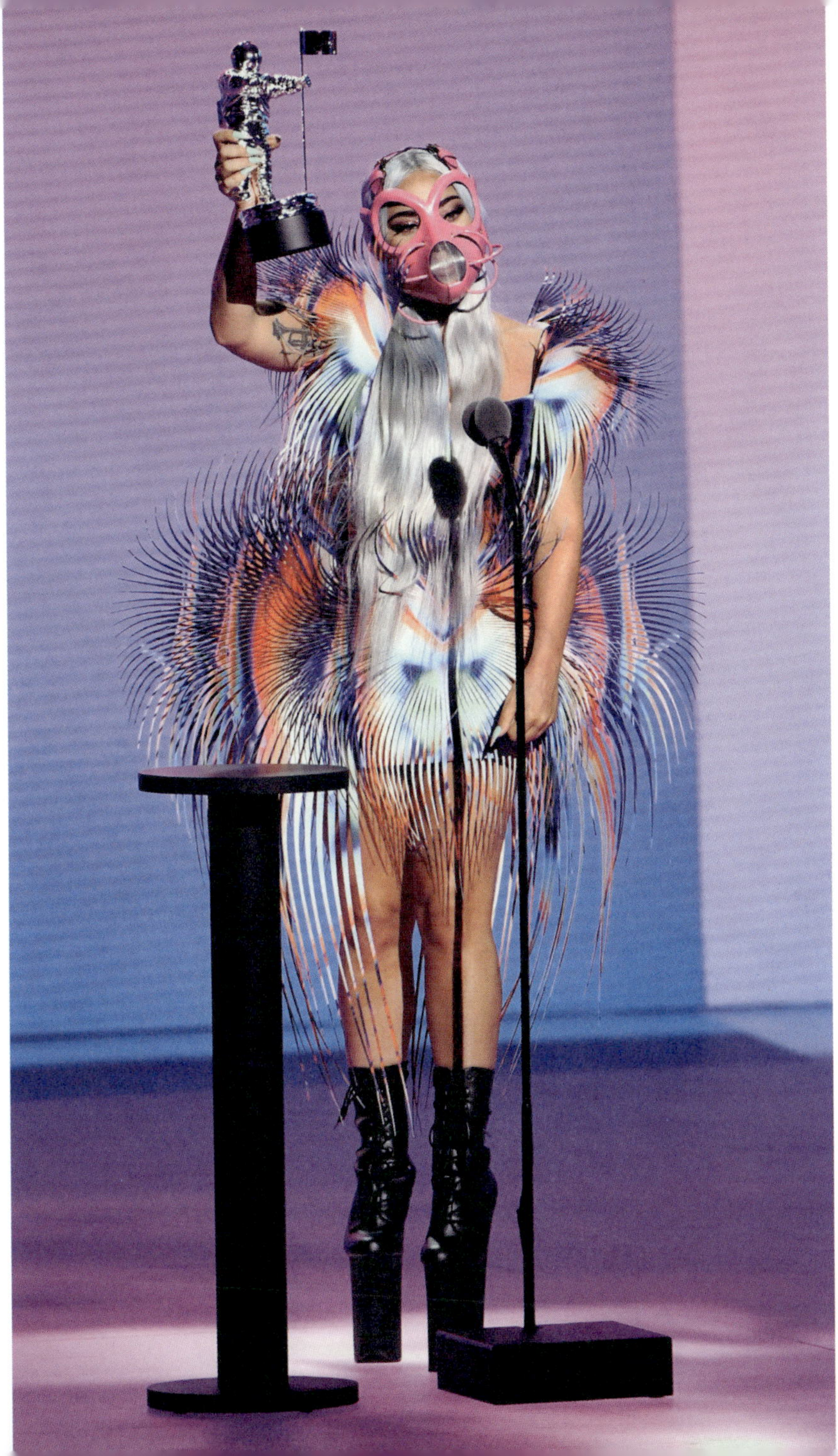

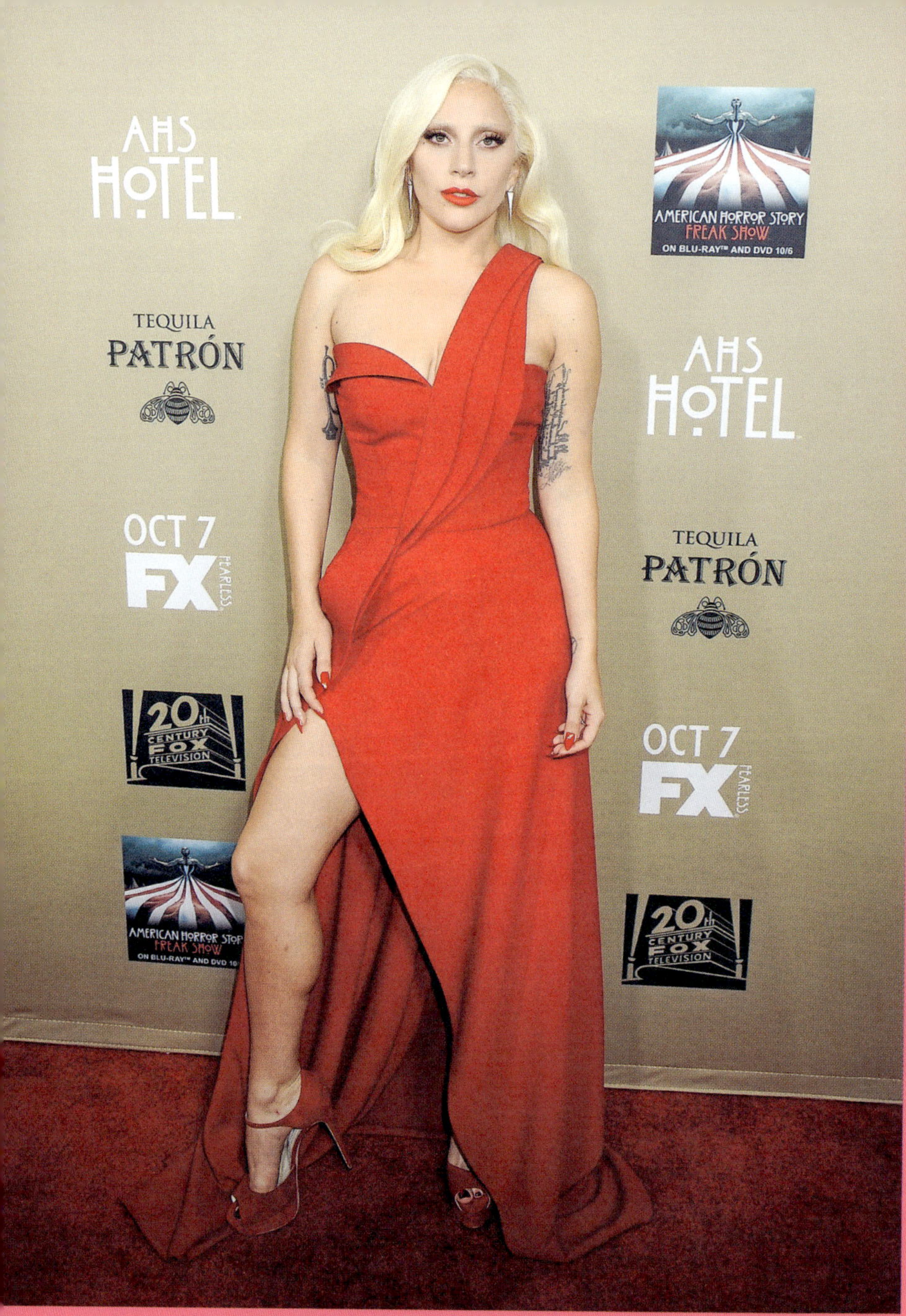
AHS HOTEL
TEQUILA PATRÓN
OCT 7 FX FEARLESS
20th CENTURY FOX TELEVISION
AMERICAN HORROR STORY FREAK SHOW
ON BLU-RAY™ AND DVD 10/6

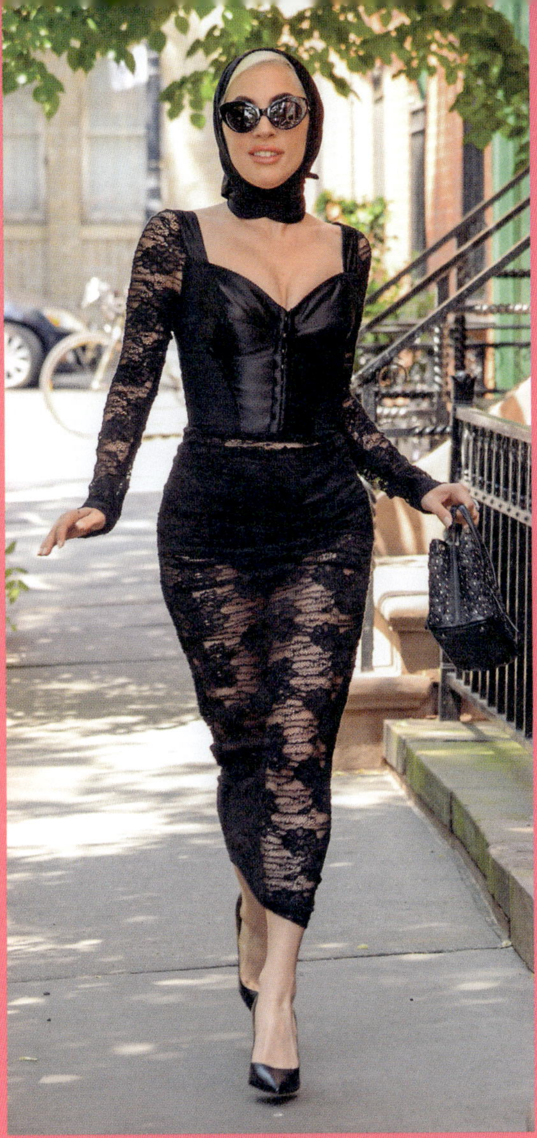

ABOVE An early look from Gaga, combining her love of Old Hollywood and edginess with a see-through lace skirt and bustier.

OPPOSITE Lady Gaga in one of her classic looks – a red gown, in her red carpet debut to promote the 2011 TV series *American Horror Story: Hotel.* She played self-styled Countess Elizabeth Johnson.

"We wanted to show the whole spectrum of Gaga because she's not just one thing, and that's what I love about who she is.

She can sing, dance, play the piano, be classic, avant-garde, or street, so we wanted to show all of that."

NICOLA FORMICHETTI

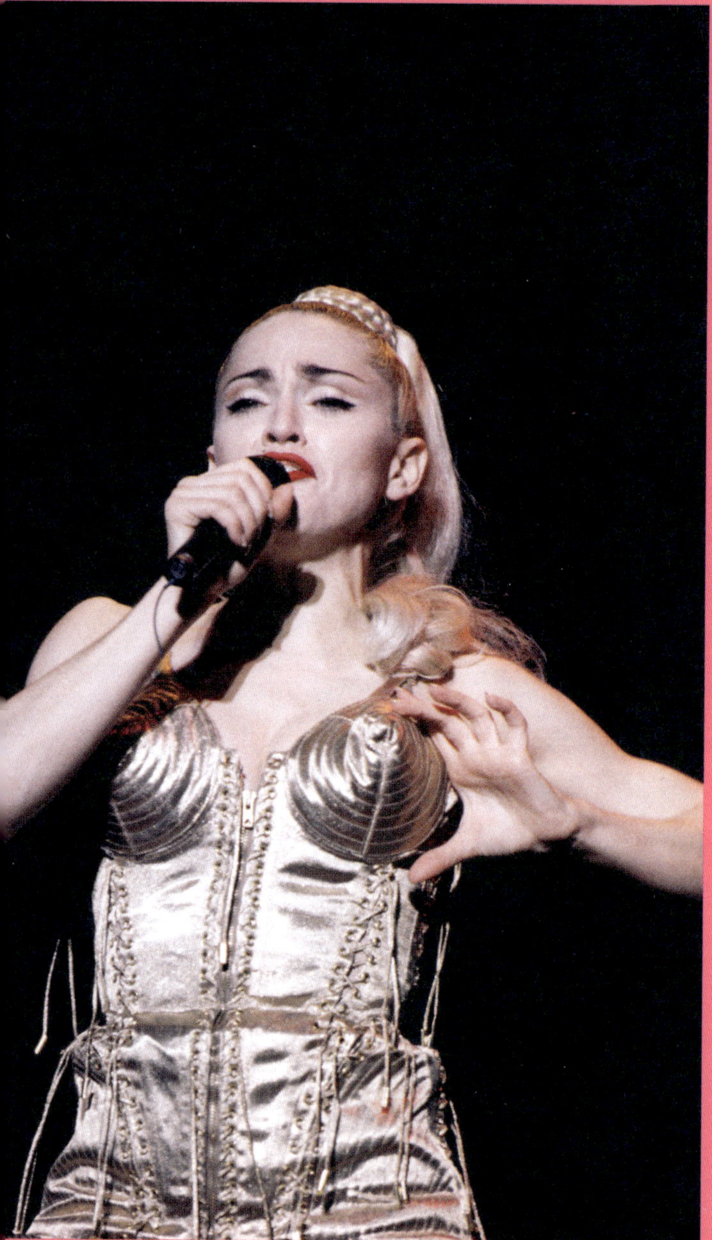

As for Lady Gaga's biggest wardrobe staple? It will always include underwear as outerwear. For her 2017 Super Bowl performance – a big deal by anyone's account – she wore a glittering leotard with shoulder pads and matching boots. True to herself, it looked like an elevated version of something she might have worn when she first started out, nearly 10 years earlier, in little clubs around New York City.

The underwear-as-outerwear look, or rather hotpants, was popular in the 1970s and 1980s. These super-short, underwear-like shorts could previously be seen on women in sports, such as cheerleaders, track runners and others. But musical artists and performers such as Cher and Grace Jones adopted leotards, briefs and super-short shorts during performances in the 1970s and 1980s. Madonna famously wore conical bras designed by the fashion legend Jean Paul Gaultier for her Blond Ambition world tour in the 1990s, which went down as one of the most memorable fashion moments in music of all time. Gaga, likewise, has always looked to Madonna as a source of inspiration. In her 2017 Netflix documentary, *Gaga: Five Foot Two*, she said, "I admired her always, and I still admire her, no matter what she might think of me."

OPPOSITE In the 1990s, Madonna made the trend of wearing underwear as outerwear mainstream. Gaga has often been compared to her where their style similarities overlap.

OVERLEAF Lady Gaga stunned for her 2017 Super Bowl performance, flying high while wearing an Atelier Versace leotard and matching boots.

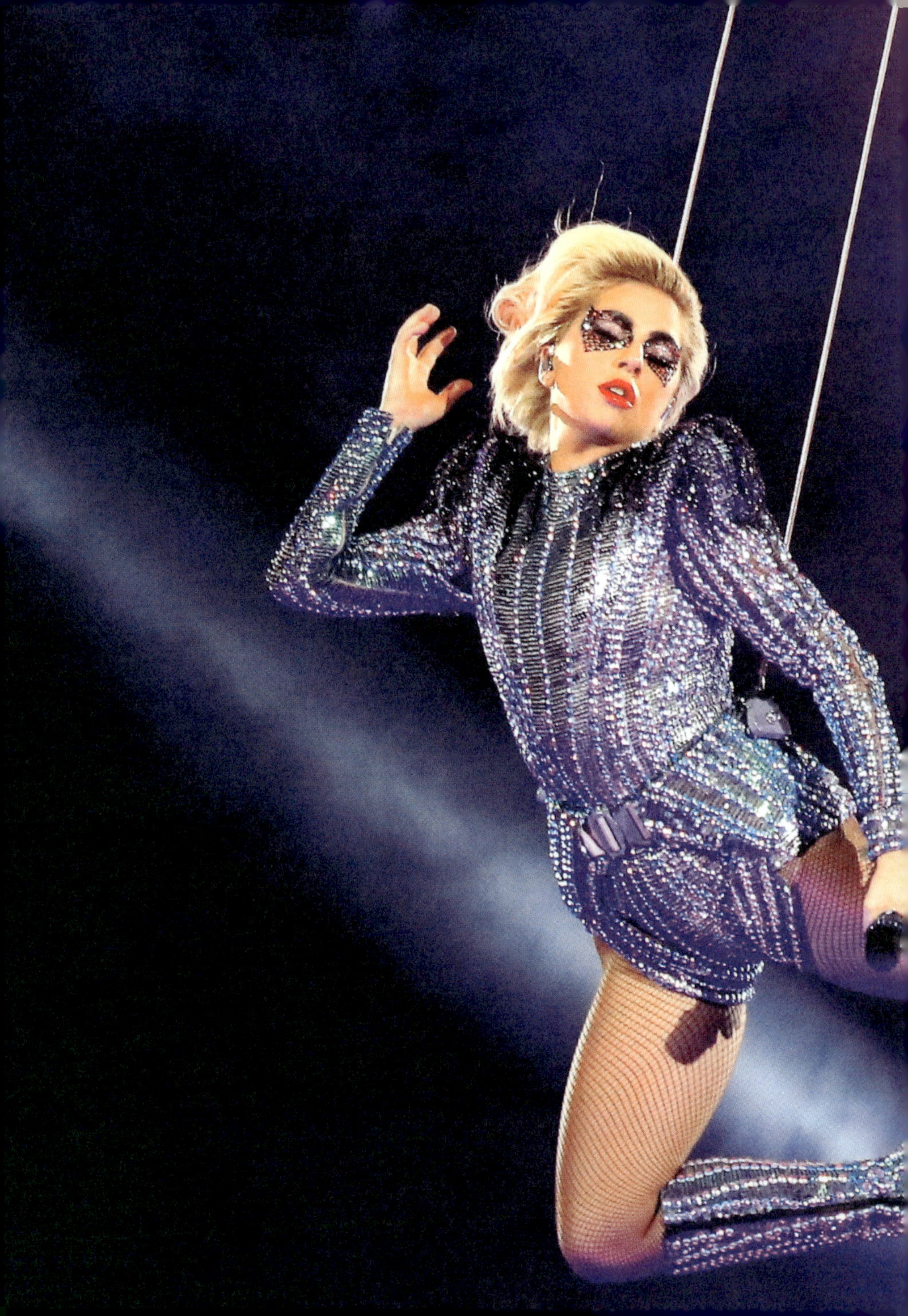

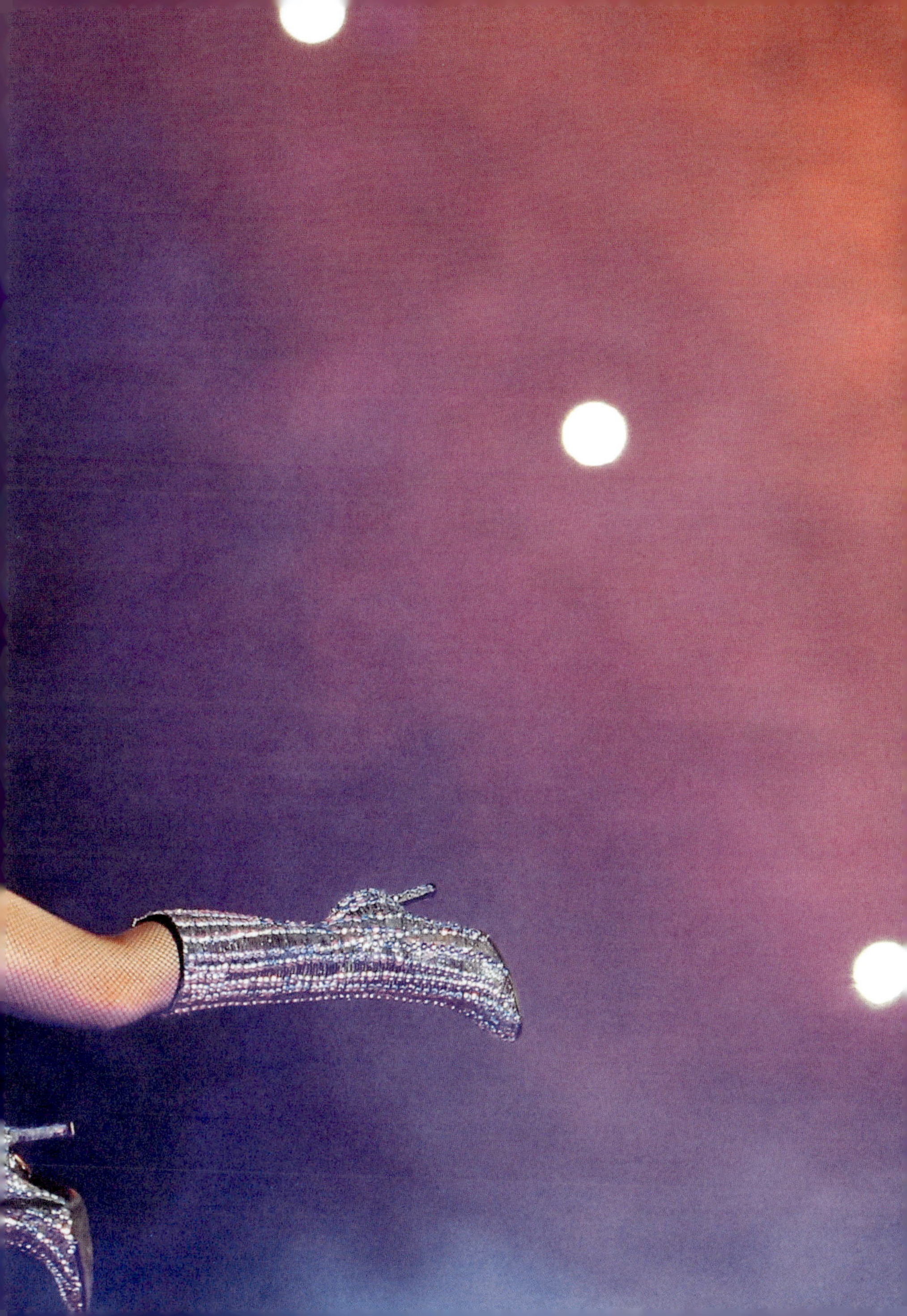

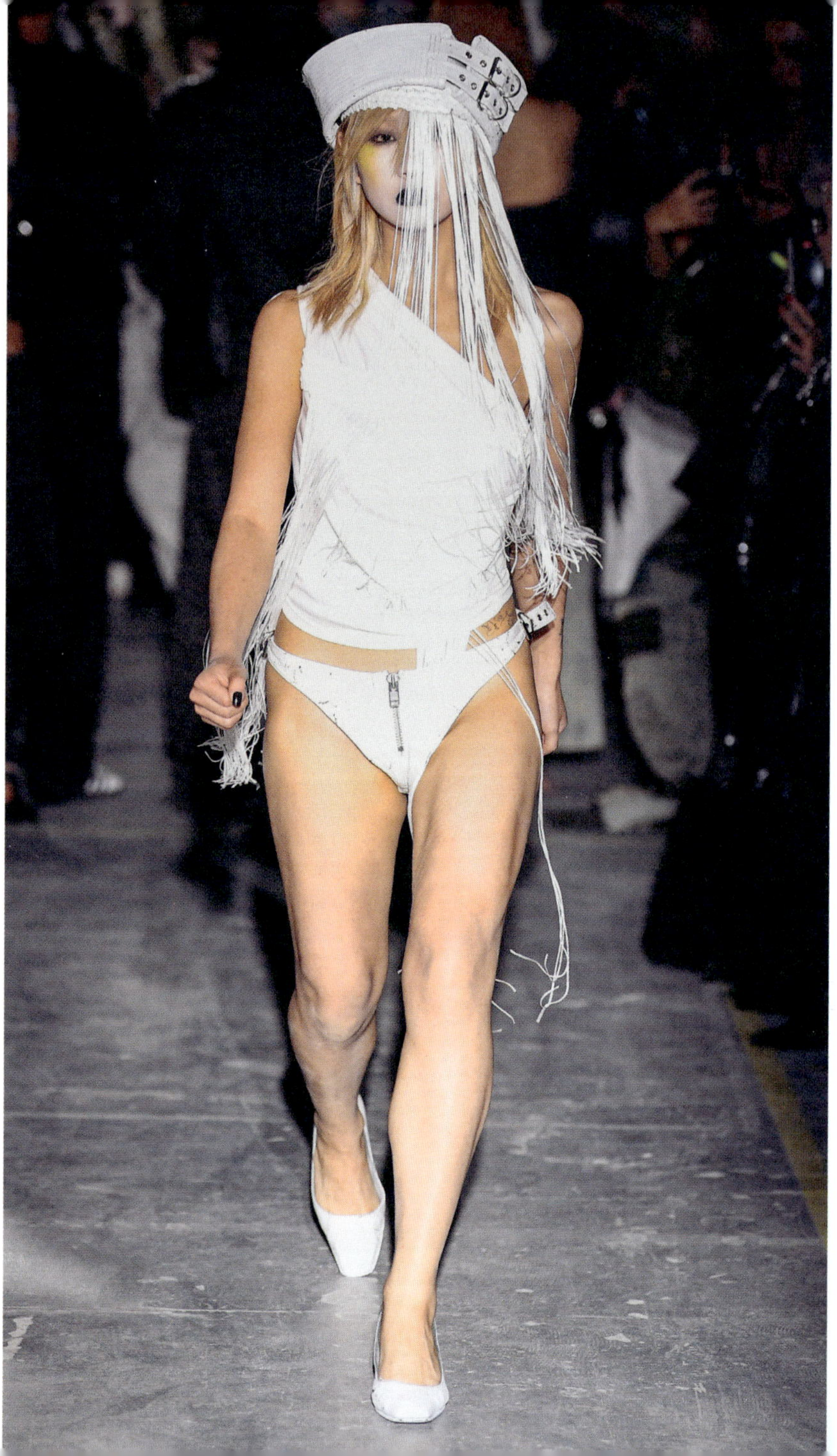

When Gaga started wearing little leotards and just her underwear and fishnets in the 2010s, it felt like a renaissance of sorts. She was clearly building her own distinct fashion DNA, later to be endlessly reblogged and appreciated by the online internet community on platforms like Tumblr and in real life by the fans who would wait with bated breath to see every last look that the star would don. Even in her most extreme eras, she incorporated underwear as outerwear as a base, using the concept as leotards or briefs that would be layered over with more extreme things. And during her *Joanne* reign, she kept the concept going by switching out the undies for extremely short denim cut-offs.

The origins of Gaga's underwear look go back to her very beginnings. "It was the first real Lady Gaga gig," she told *Rolling Stone* in 2009. "The bar was packed, and the crowd was full of fratty, drunk NYU students. They wouldn't shut up, and I couldn't play until everybody got quiet. So I took my clothes off down to my panties, fishnets and white pumps. Then everybody shut up."

For Gaga, a passionate lover of fashion, it makes total sense: the look shocks, surprises and captures the attention of everyone. Fashion itself has enjoyed a longtime obsession with the idea of underwear as outerwear anyway. Vivienne Westwood and Jean Paul Gaultier are examples, but now, popular contemporary fashion brands use the idea to build out iconic pieces, from brands like Vaquera who produce pieces with built-in underwear purposely showing to Simone Rocha's dainty tulle dresses and coats with subtle outlines of bra details.

As the aesthetic of the 2010s comes back into style, its influence as well as early Gaga can be seen on the runways, as with the brand Vaquera, pictured here.

"They wouldn't shut up, and I couldn't play until everybody got quiet. So I took my clothes off down to my panties, fishnets and white pumps. Then everybody shut up."

LADY GAGA

Another runway look by Vaquera, which would look perfectly at home on Lady Gaga in the early 2010s.

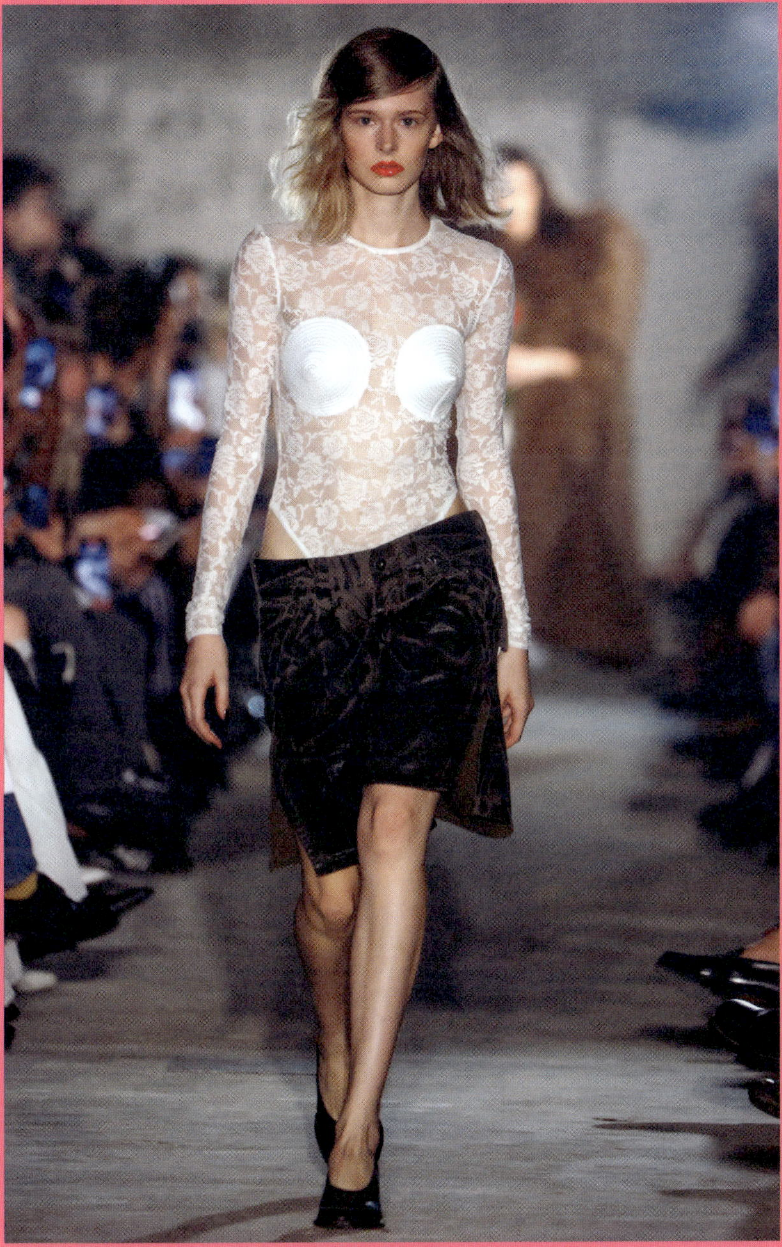

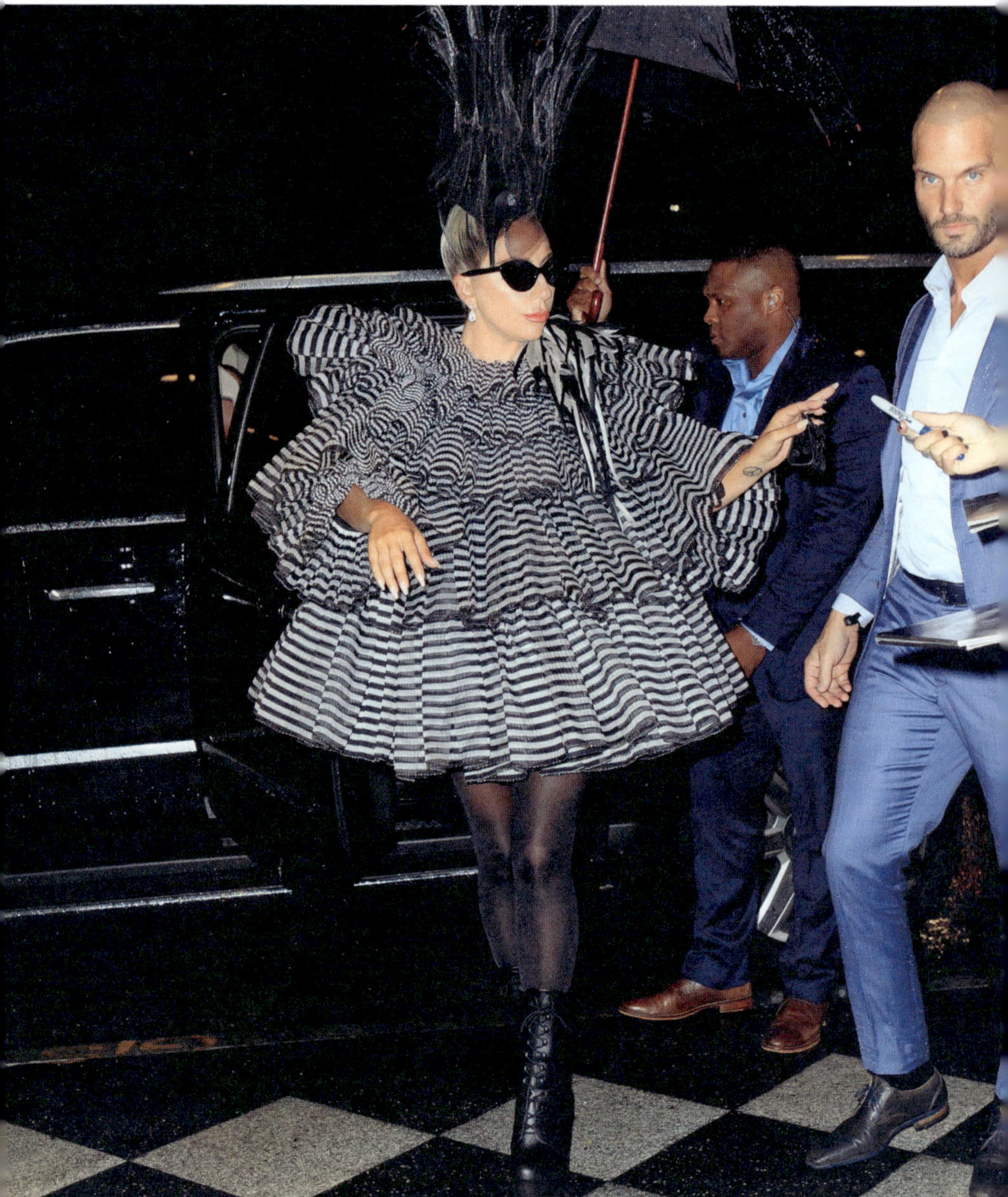

The accessories and shoes will always be at the heart of Lady Gaga's style too. No matter how extreme the rest of her look has been (or hasn't been), certain key accessories create a memorable, identifiable moment that makes a lasting impression. One example is the spades of pink hats she wore during her *Joanne* era. Against the backdrop of minimal T-shirts, denim shorts and soft neutral coats and sweaters, the hat was a defining marker that made her stand out against the noise.

Throughout her career, Gaga has used signature iconic accessories and shoes over and over again to create patterns. Take, for example, her Mickey Mouse sunglasses which had lens covers that flipped up to create a cartoon character-like appearance. Worn during her 'Paparazzi' music video and at various times when she was spotted out and about, the glasses were designed by Jeremy Scott in collaboration with Linda Farrow. They quickly became a hallmark of her style even years later and are highly collectible among fans and Little Monsters who dress up like her.

Much like the glasses, no matter what aesthetic she tries, some accessories and shoes stay for the long run. Perhaps the number one item would be her Pleaser stiletto boots, which are notoriously seven inches tall. Gaga has worn Pleaser's Adore-1020 heels with everything from jeans to gowns.

A big, impactful dress and towering heels: two important ingredients to Gaga style.

"I am a walking piece of art every day, with my dreams and my ambitions forward at all times in an effort to inspire my fans to lead their life in that way."

LADY GAGA

Dripping in diamonds, Lady Gaga wore a black structured gown by Versace to attend the 2023 Oscars.

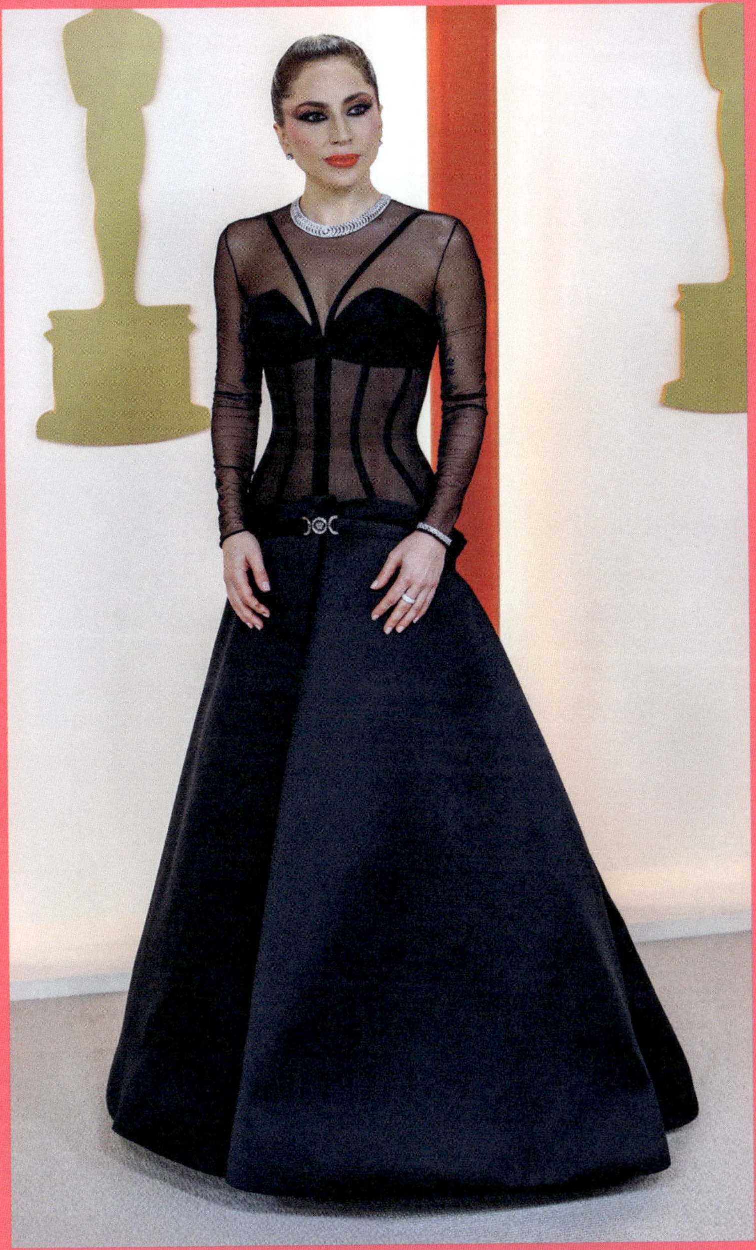

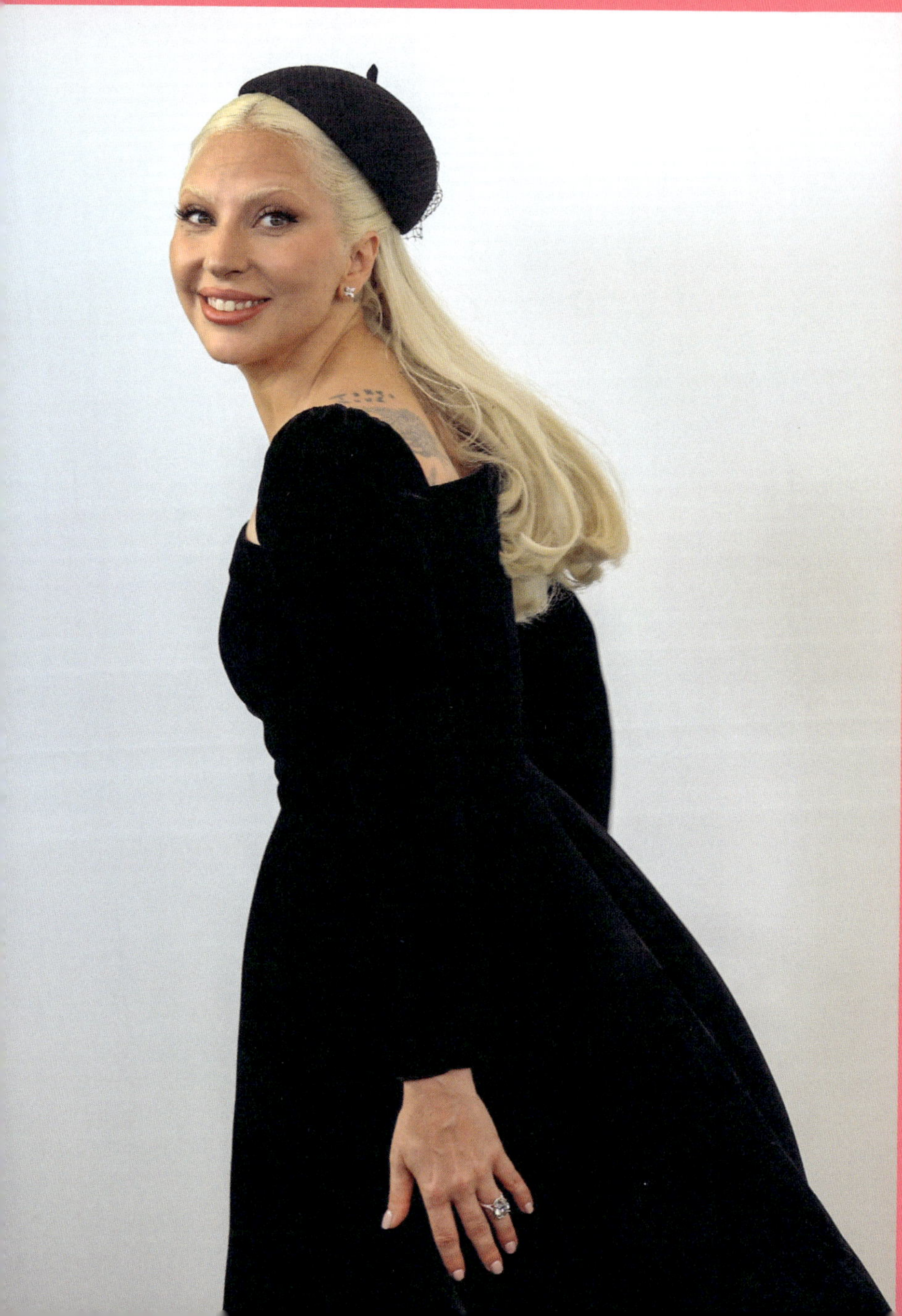

"I see myself as a real person who chooses to live my life in an open way – artistically," Gaga told *T Magazine*. "I am a walking piece of art every day, with my dreams and my ambitions forward at all times in an effort to inspire my fans to lead their life in that way." Guy Trebay reported in The *New York Time*s in 2009 that Lady Gaga "imagines the clothes she will wear to perform her songs in as she is writing them." And it shows. The influence of Gaga's style on fashion and music is undeniably prolific, from literal head (hats) to toe (seven-inch stiletto boots).

OPPOSITE Gaga always accessorizes, whether it's simple or over the top. Here, she wears a black beret to match her gown.

OVERLEAF At the Olympics Opening Ceremony of 2024 in Paris, Lady Gaga performed near the Pont de Sully with plenty of big pink feathers to match her all-black ensemble.

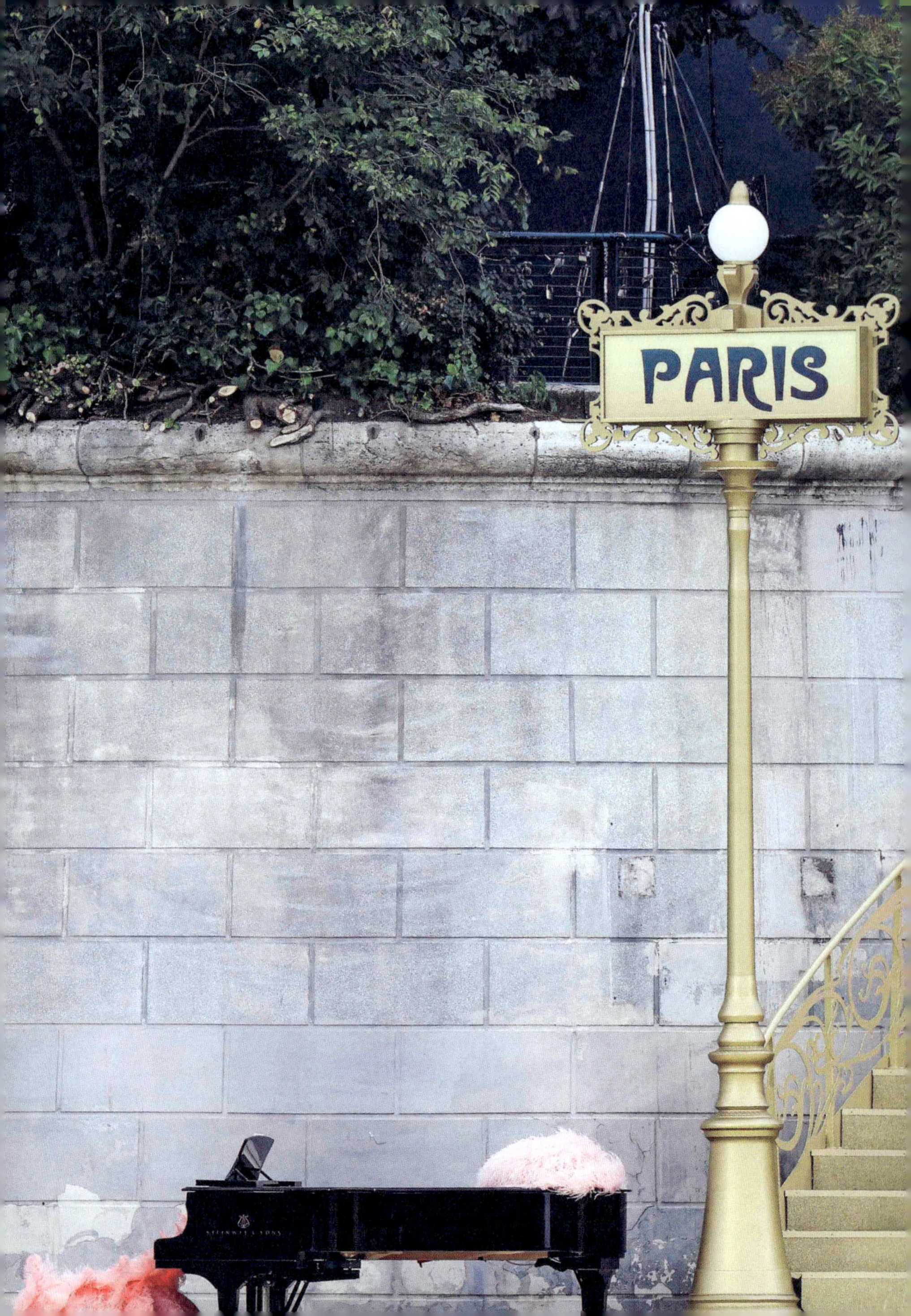
PARIS

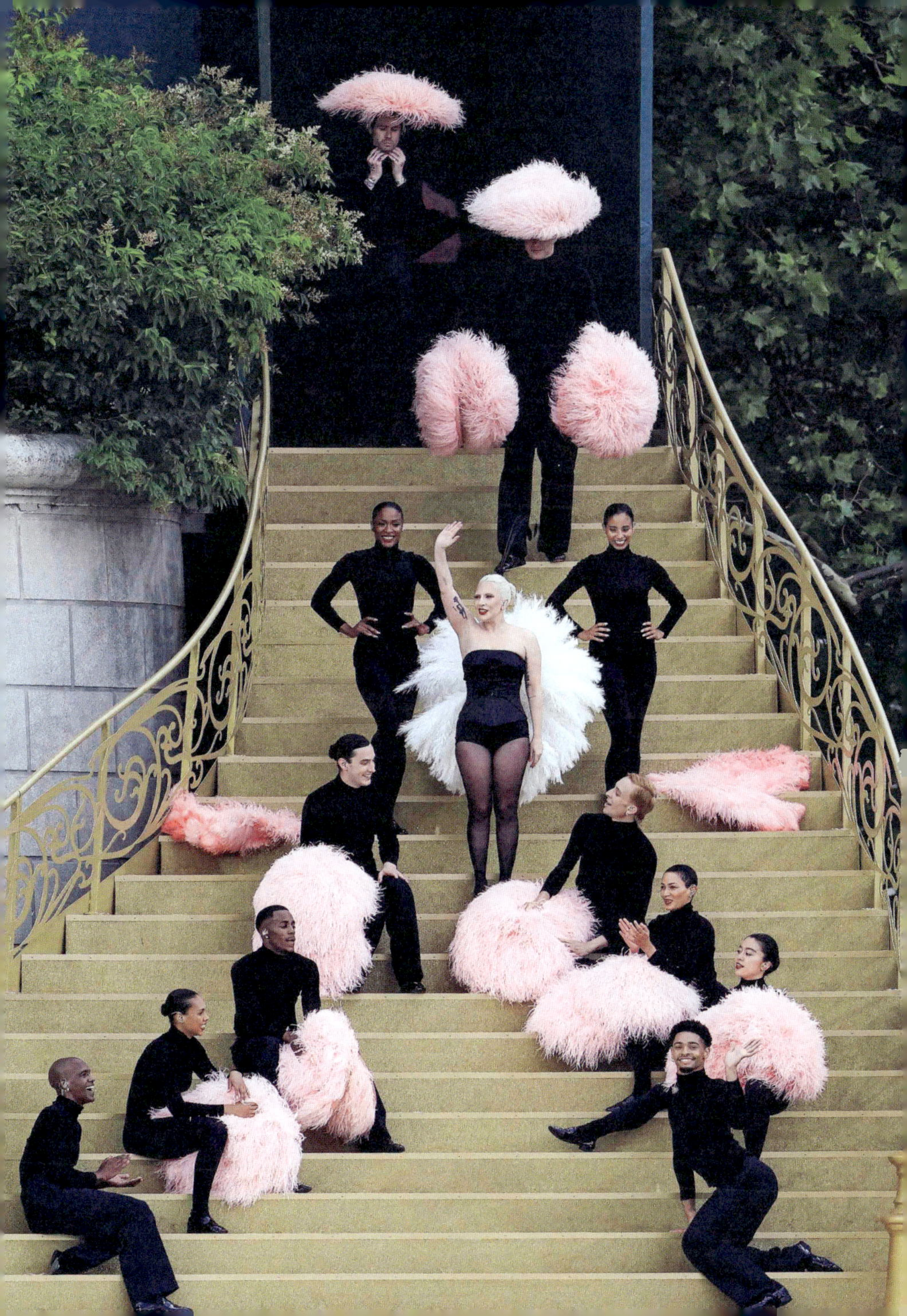

Index

Numbers in italics refer to pages with captions.

Credits

The publishers would like to thank the following sources for their kind permission to reproduce the pictures in this book.

Alamy: Archivio GBB 14; / WENN Rights Ltd 102-103

Getty Images: Tolga Akmen/AFP via Getty Images 160-161; /ANT/Bauer-Griffin/GC Images 99; /Elisabetta A. Villa 216; /Axelle/Bauer-Griffin/FilmMagic 122, 179; /Don Arnold/WireImage 10-11; /Bryan Bedder 24; /Dave Benett 188, 193; /David M. Benett/Getty Images for Moda Operandi 191; /Andreas Branch/Patrick McMullan via Getty Images 32, 40-41; /Larry Busacca 134; /Gareth Cattermole 169, 170; /Thierry Chesnot 211; /Gregg DeGuire/WireImage 200; /James Devaney/GC Images 128; /Dia Dipasupil/Getty Images for National Board of Review 153; /Fred Duval/FilmMagic 23; /FilmMagic 90; /C Flanigan/FilmMagic 28-29; /Jon Furniss/WireImage 81; /Giovanni Giannoni/WWD via Getty Images 208; /Gotham/GC Images 164; /Jesse Grant/Variety via Getty Images 167; /Steve Granitz 80; /Raymond Hall/GC Images 137, 201; /Maja Hitij 218-219; /Anwar Hussein 53; /Samir Hussein/Getty Images for Live Nation 181; /Veronica Ibarra/FilmMagic 17, 18, 20-21; /Dimitrios Kambouris/Getty Images for The Met Museum/Vogue 144-145; /Barry King 50; /Jon Kopaloff 175; /Jeff Kravitz 76; /Jeff Kravitz/FilmMagic 46; /Jackson Lee/GC Images 212; /Stephen Lovekin 60; /Kevin Mazur 79, 100, 121; /Kevin Mazur/AMA2013/WireImage 96-97; /Kevin Mazur/Getty Images for Citi 113; /Kevin Mazur/Getty Images for Live Nation 182-183, 186-187; /Kevin Mazur/WireImage 84, 106-107; /Kevin Mazur/WireImage for MAC Cosmetics 70; /Kevin Mazur/WireImage for MTV 91; /Jamie McCarthy/FilmMagic 131; /Jason Merritt 65, 72-73; /Michael Ochs Archives/Getty Images 123; /Lexie Moreland/WWD via Getty Images 215; /NCP/Star Max/GC Images 178; /Franco Origlia 151; /Neil P. Mockford/FilmMagic 95, 110, 163; /Arthur Mola/WireImage 42; /Tim Mosenfelder 94; /Marc Piasecki/GC Images 105;/George Pimentel/WireImage 36, 45; /Christopher Polk 49; /Brian Rasic 59; /Andreas Rentz 192; /Duncan Raban/Popperfoto via Getty Images 204; /Jewel Samad/AFP 69; /Jun Sato/WireImage 89; /Stephan Schraps 83; /Patrick Smith 206-207; /Jason Squires/WireImage 19; /Amy Sussman/WireImage 162; /Karwai Tang/WireImage 152; /Victor Virgile/Gamma-Rapho via Getty Images 118; /Theo Wargo/WireImage 30-31; /Will/GC Images 93; /Kevin Winter 66, 74-75; /Kevin Winter/MTV VMAs 2020/Getty Images for MTV 196, 199; /Sam Yeh/AFP via Getty Images 54

Shutterstock: Broadimage 125; /Henry Lamb/Photowire/BEI 27; /Benjamin Lozovsky/BFA.com 138-139; /MGM/Everett 155, 156-157, 158; /Netflix/Kobal 132-133; /Gregory Pace 142; /Erik Pendzich 37; /Warner Bros/Everett 147; /Warner Bros/Moviestore 148-149